SOURCE
The Prentice Hall
ENGINEERING SOURCE

Introduction to FORTRAN 90®

Larry Nyhoff

Calvin College

and

Sanford Leestma

Calvin College

Prentice Hall
Upper Saddle River, NJ 07458

Library of Congress Information Available

Editor-in-chief: **MARCIA HORTON**
Acquisitions editor: **ERIC SVENDSEN**
Director of production and manufacturing: **DAVID W. RICCARDI**
Managing editor: **EILEEN CLARK**
Editorial/production supervision: **ROSE KERNAN**
Cover director: **JAYNE CONTE**
Creative director: **AMY ROSEN**
Marketing manager: **DANNY HOYT**
Manufacturing buyer: **PAT BROWN**
Editorial assistant: **GRIFFIN CABLE**

The author and publisher of this book have used their best efforts in
preparing this book. These efforts include the development, research,
and testing of the theories and programs to determine their effective-
ness. The author and publisher shall not be liable in any event for inci-
dental or consequential damages in connection with, or arising out of,
the furnishing, performance, or use of these programs.

Printed in the United States of America

10 9 8 7 6 5 4 3

ISBN 0-13-013146-6

Prentice-Hall International (UK) Limited, *London*
Prentice-Hall of Australia Pty. Limited, *Sydney*
Prentice-Hall Canada, Inc., *Toronto*
Prentice-Hall Hispanoamericana, S.A., *Mexico*
Prentice-Hall of India Private Limited, *New Delhi*
Prentice-Hall of Japan, Inc., *Tokyo*
Prentice-Hall (Singapore) Pte., Ltd., *Singapore*
Editora Prentice-Hall do Brazil, Ltda., *Rio de Janeiro*

About ESource

The Challenge

Professors who teach the Introductory/First-Year Engineering course popular at most engineering schools have a unique challenge—teaching a course defined by a changing curriculum. The first-year engineering course is different from any other engineering course in that there is no real cannon that defines the course content. It is not like Engineering Mechanics or Circuit Theory where a consistent set of topics define the course. Instead, the introductory engineering course is most often defined by the creativity of professors and students, and the specific needs of a college or university each semester. Faculty involved in this course typically put extra effort into it, and it shows in the uniqueness of each course at each school.

Choosing a textbook can be a challenge for unique courses. Most freshmen require some sort of reference material to help them through their first semesters as a college student. But because faculty put such a strong mark on their course, they often have a difficult time finding the right mix of materials for their course and often have to go without a text, or with one that does not really fit. Conventional textbooks are far too static for the typical specialization of the first-year course. How do you find the perfect text for your course that will support your students educational needs, but give you the flexibility to maximize the potential of your course?

ESource—The Prentice Hall Engineering Source
http://emissary.prenhall.com/esource

Prentice Hall created ESource—The Prentice-Hall Engineering Source—to give professors the power to harness the full potential of their text and their freshman/first year engineering course. In today's technologically advanced world, why settle for a book that isn't perfect for your course? Why not have a book that has the exact blend of topics that you want to cover with your students?

More then just a collection of books, ESource is a unique publishing system revolving around the ESource website—http://emissary.prenhall.com/esource/. ESource enables you to put your stamp on your book just as you do your course. It lets you:

Control   You choose exactly what chapters or sections are in your book and in what order they appear. Of course, you can choose the entire book if you'd like and stay with the author's original order.

Optimize   Get the most from your book and your course. ESource lets you produce the optimal text for your student's needs.

Customize   You can add your own material anywhere in your text's presentation, and your final product will arrive at your bookstore as a professionally formatted text.

ESource Content

All the content in ESource was written by educators specifically for freshman/first-year students. Authors tried to strike a balanced level of presentation, one that was not either too formulaic and trivial, but not focusing heavily on advanced topics that most introductory students will not encounter until later classes. A developmental editor reviewed the books and made sure that every text was written at the appropriate level, and that the books featured a balanced presentation. Because many professors do not have extensive time to cover these topics in the classroom, authors prepared each text with the idea that many students would use it for self-instruction and independent study. Students should be able to use this content to learn the software tool or subject on their own.

While authors had the freedom to write texts in a style appropriate to their particular subject, all followed certain guidelines created to promote the consistency a text needs. Namely, every chapter opens with a clear set of objectives to lead students into the chapter. Each chapter also contains practice problems that tests a student's skill at performing the tasks they have just learned. Chapters close with extra practice questions and a list of key terms for reference. Authors tried to focus on motivating applications that demonstrate how engineers work in the real world, and included these applications throughout the text in various chapter openers, examples, and problem material. Specific Engineering and Science **Application Boxes** are also located throughout the texts, and focus on a specific application and demonstrating its solution.

Because students often have an adjustment from high school to college, each book contains several **Professional Success Boxes** specifically designed to provide advice on college study skills. Each author has worked to provide students with tips and techniques that help a student better understand the material, and avoid common pitfalls or problems first-year students often have. In addition, this series contains an entire book titled *Engineering Success* by Peter Schiavone of the University of Alberta intended to expose students quickly to what it takes to be an engineering student.

Creating Your Book

Using ESource is simple. You preview the content either on-line or through examination copies of the books you can request on-line, from your PH sales rep, or by calling(1-800-526-0485). Create an on-line outline of the content you want in the order you want using ESource's simple interface. Either type or cut and paste your own material and insert it into the text flow. You can preview the overall organization of the text you've created at anytime (please note, since this preview is immediate, it comes unformatted.), then press another button and receive an order number for your own custom book . If you are not ready to order, do nothing—ESource will save your work. You can come back at any time and change, re-arrange, or add more material to your creation. You are in control. Once you're finished and you have an ISBN, give it to your bookstore and your book will arrive on their shelves six weeks after the order. Your custom desk copies with their instructor supplements will arrive at your address at the same time.

To learn more about this new system for creating the perfect textbook, go to **http://emissary.prenhall.com/esource/**. You can either go through the on-line walkthrough of how to create a book, or experiment yourself.

Community

ESource has two other areas designed to promote the exchange of information among the introductory engineering community, the Faculty and the Student Centers. Created and maintained with the help of Dale Calkins, an Associate Professor at the University of Washington, these areas contain a wealth of useful information and tools. You can preview outlines created by other schools and can see how others organize their courses. Read a monthly article discussing important topics in the curriculum. You can post your own material and share it with others, as well as use what others have posted in your own documents. Communicate with our authors about their books and make suggestions for improvement. Comment about your course and ask for information from others professors. Create an on-line syllabus using our custom syllabus builder. Browse Prentice Hall's catalog and order titles from your sales rep. Tell us new features that we need to add to the site to make it more useful.

Supplements

Adopters of ESource receive an instructor's CD that includes solutions as well as professor and student code for all the books in the series. This CD also contains approximately **350 Powerpoint Transparencies** created by Jack Leifer—of University South Carolina—Aiken. Professors can either follow these transparencies as pre-prepared lectures or use them as the basis for their own custom presentations. In addition, look to the web site to find materials from other schools that you can download and use in your own course.

Titles in the ESource Series

Introduction to Unix
0-13-095135-8
David I. Schwartz

Introduction to Maple
0-13-095133-1
David I. Schwartz

Introduction to Word
0-13-254764-3
David C. Kuncicky

Introduction to Excel
0-13-254749-X
David C. Kuncicky

Introduction to MathCAD
0-13-937493-0
Ronald W. Larsen

Introduction to AutoCAD, R. 14
0-13-011001-9
Mark Dix and Paul Riley

Introduction to the Internet, 2/e
0-13-011037-X
Scott D. James

Design Concepts for Engineers
0-13-081369-9
Mark N. Horenstein

Engineering Design—A Day in the Life of Four Engineers
0-13-085089-6
Mark N. Horenstein

Engineering Ethics
0-13-784224-4
Charles B. Fleddermann

Engineering Success
0-13-080859-8
Peter Schiavone

Mathematics Review
0-13-011501-0
Peter Schiavone

Introduction to C
0-13-011854-0
Delores M. Etter

Introduction to C++
0-13-011855-9
Delores M. Etter

Introduction to MATLAB
0-13-013149-0
Delores M. Etter and David C. Kuncicky

Introduction to FORTRAN 90
0-13-013146-6
Larry Nyhoff and Sanford Leestma

About the Authors

No project could ever come to pass without a group of authors who have the vision and the courage to turn a stack of blank paper into a book. The authors in this series worked diligently to produce their books, provide the building blocks of the series.

Delores M. Etter is a Professor of Electrical and Computer Engineering at the University of Colorado. Dr. Etter was a faculty member at the University of New Mexico and also a Visiting Professor at Stanford University. Dr. Etter was responsible for the Freshman Engineering Program at the University of New Mexico and is active in the Integrated Teaching Laboratory at the University of Colorado. She was elected a Fellow of the Institute of Electrical and Electronic Engineers for her contributions to education and for her technical leadership in digital signal processing. IN addition to writing best-selling textbooks for engineering computing, Dr. Etter has also published research in the area of adaptive signal processing.

Sanford Leestma is a Professor of Mathematics and Computer Science at Calvin College, and received his Ph.D from New Mexico State University. He has been the long time co-author of successful textbooks on Fortran, Pascal, and data structures in Pascal. His current research interests are in the areas of algorithms and numerical computation.

Larry Nyhoff is a Professor of Mathematics and Computer Science at Calvin College. After doing bachelors work at Calvin, and Masters work at Michigan, he received a Ph.D. from Michigan State and also did graduate work in computer science at Western Michigan. Dr. Nyhoff has taught at Calvin for the past 34 years—mathematics at first and computer science for the past several years. He has co-authored several computer science textbooks since 1981 including titles on Fortran and C++, as well as a brand new title on Data Structures in C++.

Acknowledgments: We express our sincere appreciation to all who helped in the preparation of this module, especially our acquisitions editor Alan Apt, managing editor Laura Steele, development editor Sandra Chavez, and production editor Judy Winthrop. We also thank Larry Genalo for several examples and exercises and Erin Fulp for the Internet address application in Chapter 10. We appreciate the insightful review provided by Bart Childs. We thank our families—Shar, Jeff, Dawn, Rebecca, Megan, Sara, Greg, Julie, Joshua, Derek, Tom, Joan; Marge, Michelle, Sandy, Lori, Michael—for being patient and understanding. We thank God for allowing us to write this text.

Mark Dix began working with AutoCAD in 1985 as a programmer for CAD Support Associates, Inc. He helped design a system for creating estimates and bills of material directly from AutoCAD drawing databases for use in the automated conveyor industry. This system became the basis for systems still widely in use today. In 1986 he began collaborating with Paul Riley to create AutoCAD training materials, combining Riley's background in industrial design and training with Dix's background in writing, curriculum development, and programming. Dix and Riley have created tutorial and teaching methods for every AutoCAD release since Version 2.5. Mr. Dix has a Master of Arts in Teaching from Cornell University and a Masters of Education from the University of Massachusetts. He is currently the Director of Dearborn Academy High School in Arlington, Massachusetts.

Paul Riley is an author, instructor, and designer specializing in graphics and design for multimedia. He is a founding partner of CAD Support Associates, a contract service and professional training organization for computer-aided design. His 15 years of business experience and 20 years of teaching experience are supported by degrees in education and computer science. Paul has taught AutoCAD at the University of Massachusetts at Lowell and is presently teaching AutoCAD at Mt. Ida College in Newton, Massachusetts. He has developed a program, Computer-Aided Design for Professionals that is highly regarded by corporate clients and has been an ongoing success since 1982.

David I. Schwartz is a Lecturer at SUNY-Buffalo who teaches freshman and first-year engineering, and has a Ph.D from SUNY-Buffalo in Civil Engineering. Schwartz originally became interested in Civil engineering out of an interest in building grand structures, but has also pursued other academic interests including artificial intelligence and applied mathematics. He became interested in Unix and Maple through their application to his research, and eventually jumped at the chance to teach these subjects to students. He tries to teach his students to become incremental learners and encourages frequent practice to master a subject, and gain the maturity and confidence to tackle other subjects independently. In his spare time, Schwartz is an avid musician and plays drums in a variety of bands.

Acknowledgments: I would like to thank the entire School of Engineering and Applied Science at the State University of New York at Buffalo for the opportunity to teach not only my students, but myself as well; all my EAS140 students, without whom this book would not be possible—thanks for slugging through my lab packets; Andrea Au, Eric Svendsen, and Elizabeth Wood at Prentice Hall for advising and encouraging me as well as wading through my blizzard of e-mail; Linda and Tony for starting the whole thing in the first place; Rogil Camama, Linda Chattin, Stuart Chen, Jeffrey Chottiner, Roger Christian, Anthony Dalessio, Eugene DeMaitre, Dawn Halvorsen, Thomas Hill, Michael Lamanna, Nate "X" Patwardhan, Durvejai Sheobaran, "Able" Alan Somlo, Ben Stein, Craig Sutton, Barbara Umiker, and Chester "JC" Zeshonski for making this book a reality; Ewa Arrasjid, "Corky" Brunskill, Bob Meyer, and Dave Yearke at "the Department Formerly Known as ECS" for all their friendship, advice, and respect; Jeff, Tony, Forrest, and Mike for the interviews; and, Michael Ryan and Warren Thomas for believing in me.

Ronald W. Larsen is an Associate Professor in Chemical Engineering at Montana State University, and received his Ph.D from the Pennsylvania State University. Larsen was initially attracted to engineering because he felt it was a serving profession, and because engineers are often called on to eliminate dull and routine tasks. He also enjoys the fact that engineering rewards creativity and presents constant challenges. Larsen feels that teaching large sections of students is one of the most challenging tasks he has ever encountered because it enhances the importance of effective communication. He has drawn on a two year experince teaching courses in Mongolia through an interpreter to improve his skills in the classroom. Larsen sees software as one of the changes that has the potential to radically alter the way engineers work, and his book Introduction to Mathcad was written to help young engineers prepare to be productive in an ever-changing workplace.

Acknowledgments: To my students at Montana State University who have endured the rough drafts and typos, and who still allow me to experiment with their classes— my sincere thanks.

Peter Schiavone is a professor and student advisor in the Department of Mechanical Engineering at the University of Alberta. He received his Ph.D. from the University of Strathclyde, U.K. in 1988. He has authored several books in the area of study skills and academic success as well as numerous papers in scientific research journals.

Before starting his career in academia, Dr. Schiavone worked in the private sector for Smith's Industries (Aerospace and Defence Systems Company) and Marconi Instruments in several different areas of engineering including aerospace, systems and software engineering. During that time he developed an interest in engineering research and the applications of mathematics and the physical sciences to solving real-world engineering problems.

His love for teaching brought him to the academic world. He founded the first Mathematics Resource Center at the University of Alberta: a unit designed specifically to teach high school students the necessary survival skills in mathematics and the physical sciences required for first-year engineering. This led to the Students' Union Gold Key award for outstanding contributions to the University and to the community at large.

Dr. Schiavone lectures regularly to freshman engineering students, high school teachers, and new professors on all aspects of engineering success, in particular, maximizing students' academic performance. He wrote the book *Engineering Success* in order to share with you the *secrets of success in engineering study*: the most effective, tried and tested methods used by the most successful engineering students.

Acknowledgments: I'd like to acknowledge the contributions of: Eric Svendsen, for his encouragement and support; Richard Felder for being such an inspiration; the many students who shared their experiences of first-year engineering—both good and bad; and finally, my wife Linda for her continued support and for giving me Conan.

Scott D. James is a staff lecturer at Kettering University (formerly GMI Engineering & Management Institute) in Flint, Michigan. He is currently pursuing a Ph.D. in Systems Engineering with an emphasis on software engineering and computer-integrated manufacturing. Scott decided on writing textbooks after he found a void in the books that were available. "I really wanted a book that showed how to do things in good detail but in a clear and concise way. Many of the books on the market are full of fluff and force you to dig out the really important facts." Scott decided on teaching as a profession after several years in the computer industry. "I thought that it was really important to know what it was like outside of academia. I wanted to provide students with classes that were up to date and provide the information that is really used and needed."

Acknowledgments: Scott would like to acknowledge his family for the time to work on the text and his students and peers at Kettering who offered helpful critique of the materials that eventually became the book.

David C. Kuncicky is a native Floridian. He earned his Baccalaureate in psychology, Master's in computer science, and Ph.D. in computer science from Florida State University. Dr. Kuncicky is the Director of Computing and Multimedia Services for the FAMU-FSU College of Engineering. He also serves as a faculty member in the Department of Electrical Engineering. He has taught computer science and computer engineering courses for the past 15 years. He has published research in the areas of intelligent hybrid systems and neural networks. He is actively involved in the education of computer and network system administrators and is a leader in the area of technology-based curriculum delivery.

Acknowledgments: Thanks to Steffie and Helen for putting up with my late nights and long weekends at the computer. Thanks also to the helpful and insightful technical reviews by the following people: Jerry Ralya, Kathy Kitto of Western Washington University, Avi Singhal of Arizona State University, and Thomas Hill of the State University of New York at Buffalo. I appreciate the patience of Eric Svendsen and Rose Kernan of Prentice Hall for gently guiding me through this project. Finally, thanks to Dean C.J. Chen for providing continued tutelage and support.

Mark Horenstein is an Associate Professor in the Electrical and Computer Engineering Department at Boston University. He received his Bachelors in Electrical Engineering in 1973 from Massachusetts Institute of Technology, his Masters in Electrical Engineering in 1975

from University of California at Berkeley, and his Ph.D. in Electrical Engineering in 1978 from Massachusetts Institute of Technology. Professor Horenstein's research interests are in applied electrostatics and electromagnetics as well as microelectronics, including sensors, instrumentation, and measurement. His research deals with the simulation, test, and measurement of electromagnetic fields. Some topics include electrostatics in manufacturing processes, electrostatic instrumentation, EOS/ESD control, and electromagnetic wave propagation.

Professor Horenstein designed and developed a class at Boston University, which he now teaches entitled Senior Design Project (ENG SC 466). In this course, the student gets real engineering design experience by working for a virtual company, created by Professor Horenstein, that does real projects for outside companies—almost like an apprenticeship. Once in "the company" (Xebec Technologies), the student is assigned to an engineering team of 3-4 persons. A series of potential customers are recruited, from which the team must accept an engineering project. The team must develop a working prototype deliverable engineering system that serves the need of the customer. More than one team may be assigned to the same project, in which case there is competition for the customer's business.

Acknowledgements: Several individuals contributed to the ideas and concepts presented in Design Principles for Engineers. The concept of the Peak Performance design competition, which forms a cornerstone of the book, originated with Professor James Bethune of Boston University. Professor Bethune has been instrumental in conceiving of and running Peak Performance each year and has been the inspiration behind many of the design concepts associated with it. He also provided helpful information on dimensions and tolerance. Several of the ideas presented in the book, particularly the topics on brainstorming and teamwork, were gleaned from a workshop on engineering design help bi-annually by Professor Charles Lovas of Southern Methodist University. The principles of estimation were derived in part from a freshman engineering problem posed by Professor Thomas Kincaid of Boston University.

I would like to thank my family, Roxanne, Rachel, and Arielle, for giving me the time and space to think about and write this book. I also appreciate Roxanne's inspiration and help in identifying examples of human/machine interfaces.

Dedicated to Roxanne, Rachel, and Arielle

Charles B. Fleddermann is a professor in the Department of Electrical and Computer Engineering at the University of New Mexico in Albuquerque, New Mexico. He is a third generation engineer—his grandfather was a civil engineer and father an aeronautical engineer—so "engineering was in my genetic makeup." The genesis of a book on engineering ethics was in the ABET requirement to incorporate ethics topics into the undergraduate engineering curriculum. "Our department decided to have a one-hour seminar course on engineering ethics, but there was no book suitable for such a course." Other texts were tried the first few times the course was offered, but none of them presented ethical theory, analysis, and problem solving in a readily accessible way. "I wanted to have a text which would be concise, yet would give the student the tools required to solve the ethical problems that they might encounter in their professional lives."

Reviewers

ESource benefited from a wealth of reviewers who on the series from its initial idea stage to its completion. Reviewers read manuscripts and contributed insightful comments that helped the authors write great books. We would like to thank everyone who helped us with this project.

Concept Document
Naeem Abdurrahman- University of Texas, Austin
Grant Baker- University of Alaska, Anchorage
Betty Barr- University of Houston
William Beckwith- Clemson University
Ramzi Bualuan- University of Notre Dame
Dale Calkins- University of Washington
Arthur Clausing- University of Illinois at Urbana-Champaign
John Glover- University of Houston
A.S. Hodel- Auburn University
Denise Jackson- University of Tennessee, Knoxville
Kathleen Kitto- Western Washington University
Terry Kohutek- Texas A&M University
Larry Richards- University of Virginia
Avi Singhal- Arizona State University
Joseph Wujek- University of California, Berkeley
Mandochehr Zoghi- University of Dayton

Books
Stephen Allan- Utah State University
Naeem Abdurrahman - University of Texas Austin
Anil Bajaj- Purdue University
Grant Baker - University of Alaska - Anchorage
Betty Barr - University of Houston

William Beckwith - Clemson University
Haym Benaroya- Rutgers University
Tom Bledsaw- ITT Technical Institute
Tom Bryson- University of Missouri, Rolla
Ramzi Bualuan - University of Notre Dame
Dan Budny- Purdue University
Dale Calkins - University of Washington
Arthur Clausing - University of Illinois
James Devine- University of South Florida
Patrick Fitzhorn - Colorado State University
Dale Elifrits- University of Missouri, Rolla
Frank Gerlitz - Washtenaw College
John Glover - University of Houston
John Graham - University of North Carolina-Charlotte
Malcom Heimer - Florida International University
A.S. Hodel - Auburn University
Vern Johnson- University of Arizona
Kathleen Kitto - Western Washington University
Robert Montgomery- Purdue University
Mark Nagurka- Marquette University
Ramarathnam Narasimhan- University of Miami
Larry Richards - University of Virginia
Marc H. Richman - Brown University
Avi Singhal-Arizona State University
Tim Sykes- Houston Community College
Thomas Hill- SUNY at Buffalo
Michael S. Wells - Tennessee Tech University
Joseph Wujek - University of California - Berkeley
Edward Young- University of South Carolina
Mandochehr Zoghi - University of Dayton

Contents

8   ARRAYS   178

9   OTHER DATA TYPES   229

10   POINTERS AND LINKED STRUCTURES   247

1

Introduction to Computing

1.1 FORTRAN 90

The electronic computer is one of the most important attributes of the modern era. It is an essential tool in many areas, including business, industry, government, science, and education; indeed, it has touched nearly every aspect of our lives.

Early computers were very difficult to program. In fact, programming some of the earliest computers consisted of designing and building circuits to carry out the computations required to solve each new problem. Later, computer instructions could be coded in a language that the machine could understand. But these codes were very cryptic, and programming was therefore tedious and error-prone. Computers would not have gained widespread use if it had not been for the development of high-level programming languages such as Fortran. These languages made it possible to enter instructions using an English-like syntax.

Since its beginnings in the mid 1950s, Fortran has been refined and extended so that today it is one of the most widely used programming languages in engineering and science. Indeed, thousands of programs and routines in standard libraries such as IMSL (International Mathematics and Statistics Library) and NAG (Numerical Algorithms Group) used by scientists and engineers are written in Fortran.

Fortran 90 is the latest version of this programming language. It includes all of the major features of earlier versions, so that the large investment made in Fortran software is protected because these millions of lines of code will continue to execute properly in Fortran 90. Equally important, however, are the many new features added to the language to bring it up-to-date. These include the following:

SECTIONS

- 1.1 Fortran 90
- 1.2 Computer Hardware and Software
- 1.3 Programming and Problem Solving

OBJECTIVES

In this chapter, you will

- Learn the origins of Fortran 90.
- Read about the fundamentals of computer hardware and software.
- See how programming and problem solving can be applied to a radioactive-decay problem.

- Replacement of the old fixed format for programs (which dates back to the use of punched cards) with the free form allowed in Fortran 90
- Longer names for objects, making programs easier to read
- New control constructs for selective and repetitive execution (see Chapters 3 and 4)
- New kinds of subprograms to facilitate modular programming (see Chapters 6 and 7)
- Powerful new array-processing mechanisms (see Chapter 8)
- Programmer-defined data types (see Chapter 9)
- Dynamic memory allocation and pointers for constructing complex data structures (see Chapter 10)

All of these features combine with the continuing emphasis on efficient execution and ease of use to make Fortran 90 a powerful modern programming language for solving problems in science and engineering and to ensure that it will remain one of the dominant languages for scientific computing. It is this version of Fortran on which this text is based.

In this chapter we first provide some background by describing computing systems, their main components, and how information is stored in them. This is followed by a brief summary of how Fortran has been developed. We also begin our study of programming and problem solving by developing a Fortran 90 program to solve a simple problem.

1.2 COMPUTER HARDWARE AND SOFTWARE

The heart of any computing system is its **central processing unit**, or **CPU**. The CPU controls the operation of the entire system, performs the arithmetic and logic operations, and stores and retrieves instructions and data. The instructions and data are stored in a high-speed **memory unit**. The **control unit** fetches these instructions from memory, decodes them, and directs the system to execute the operations indicated by the instructions. Those operations that are arithmetical or logical in nature are carried out using the circuits of the **arithmetic-logic unit (ALU)** of the CPU.

The memory unit typically consists of several components. One of these components is used to store the instructions and data of the programs being executed and has many names, including **internal**, **main**, **primary**, and **random access memory (RAM)**. A second component is a set of special high-speed memory locations within the CPU, called **registers**. Values that are stored in registers can typically be accessed thousands of times faster than values stored in RAM.

One problem with both RAM and registers is that they are volatile memory components, that is, information stored in these components is lost if the power to the computing system is shut off (either intentionally or accidentally). **Read-only memory (ROM)** is nonvolatile memory used to store critical information, such as start-up instructions, which is too important to lose.

To provide long-term storage of programs and data, most computing systems also include memory components called **external** or **auxiliary** or **secondary memory**. Common forms of this type of memory are magnetic disks (such as hard disks and floppy disks) and magnetic tapes. These **peripheral devices** provide long-term storage for large collections of data, even if power is lost. However, the time required to access data stored on such devices can be thousands of times greater than the access time for data stored in RAM.

Other peripherals are used to transmit instructions, data, and computed results between the user and the CPU. These are the **input/output devices**, which have a

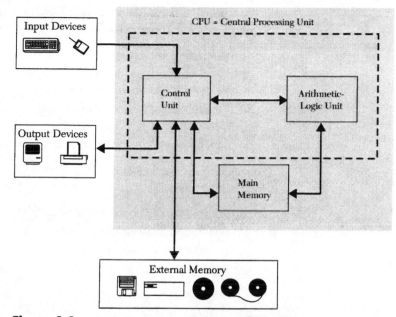

Figure 1.1. Major components of a computing system.

variety of forms, such as terminals, scanners, voice input devices, printers, and plotters. Their function is to convert information from an external form understandable to the user to a form that can be processed by the computer system, and vice versa.

Figure 1.1 shows the relationship between the components in a computer system. Collectively, the components are called computer **hardware**.

The devices that comprise the memory unit of a computer are two-state devices. If one of the states is interpreted as 0 and the other as 1, then it is natural to use a binary scheme, using only the two binary digits (**bits**) 0 and 1 to represent information in a computer. These two-state devices are organized into groups of eight called **bytes**. Memory is commonly measured in bytes, and a block of $2^{10} = 1024$ bytes is called **1 K (kilobyte)** of memory. Thus, one **megabyte** (= 1024 K) of memory consists of $1024 \times 2^{10} = 2^{10} \times 2^{10} = 2^{20} = 1,048,576$ bytes, or, equivalently, $2^{20} \times 2^3 = 2^{23} = 8,384,608$ bits.

Bytes are typically grouped together into **words**. The number of bits in a word is equal to the number of bits in a CPU register. The word size thus varies from one computer to another, but common word sizes are 16 bits (= 2 bytes) and 32 bits (= 4 bytes). Associated with each word or byte is an **address** that can be used to directly access that word or byte. This makes it possible for the control unit to store information in a specific memory location and then to retrieve it later.

Programs, or **software**, tell the computer hardware what to do. Program instructions for processing data must be stored in memory. They must be instructions that the machine can execute and they must be expressed in a form that the machine can understand, that is, they must be written in the **machine language** for that machine. These instructions consist of two parts: (1) a numeric **opcode**, which represents a basic machine operation such as load, multiply, add, and store; and (2) the address of the **operand**. Like all information stored in memory, these instructions must be represented in a binary form.

As an example, suppose that values have been stored in three memory locations with addresses 1024, 1025, and 1026 and that we want to multiply the first two values, add the third, and store the result in a fourth memory location 1027. To perform this computation, the following instructions must be executed:

1. Fetch the contents of memory location 1024 and move it into a register in the ALU.
2. Fetch the contents of memory location 1025 and compute the product of this value and the value in the register.
3. Fetch the contents of memory location 1026 and add this value to the value in the register.
4. Store the contents of the register in memory location 1027.

If the opcodes for move, store, add, and multiply are 16, 17, 35, and 36, respectively, these four instructions might be written in machine language as follows:

1. 00010000000000000000010000000000
2. 00100100000000000000010000000001
3. 00100011000000000000010000000010
4. 00010001000000000000010000000011

    $\underbrace{\hspace{2.2cm}}_{\text{opcode}}\underbrace{\hspace{3.5cm}}_{\text{operand}}$

These instructions can then be stored in four (consecutive) memory locations. When the program is executed, the control unit will fetch each of these instructions, decode it to determine the operation and the address of the operand, fetch the operand, and then perform the required operation, using the ALU if necessary.

Programs for early computers had to be written in such machine language, and later it became possible to write programs in **assembly language**, which uses mnemonics (names) in place of numeric opcodes and variable names in place of numeric addresses. For example, the preceding sequence of instructions might be written in assembly language as

1. MOV A, ACC
2. MUL B, ACC
3. ADD C, ACC
4. STO ACC, X

An **assembler**, which is part of the system software, translates such assembly-language instructions into machine language.

Today, most programs are written in a **high-level language** such as Fortran, and a compiler translates each statement in the program into a sequence of basic machine- (or assembly-) language instructions.

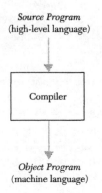

Source Program
(high-level language)

Compiler

Object Program
(machine language)

For example, for the preceding problem, the programmer could write the Fortran statement

$$X = A * B = C$$

which instructs the computer to multiply the values of A and B, add the value of C, and assign the value to X. The compiler then translates this statement into the sequence of four machine- (or assembly-) language instructions considered earlier.

FORTRAN (**FOR**mula **TRAN**slation) was one of the first high-level languages to gain widespread acceptance. It was developed for the IBM 704 computer by John Backus and a team of 13 other programmers at IBM over a 3-year period (1954 to 1957). The group's first report on the completed language included the following comments:

> The programmer attended a one-day course on FORTRAN and spent some more time referring to the manual. He then programmed the job in four hours, using 47 FORTRAN statements. These were compiled by the 704 in six minutes, producing about 1000 instructions. He ran the program and found the output incorrect. He studied the output and was able to localize his error in a FORTRAN statement he had written. He rewrote the offending statement, recompiled, and found that the resulting program was correct. He estimated that it might have taken three days to code the job by hand, plus an unknown time to debug it, and that no appreciable increase in speed of execution would have been achieved thereby.

In the years that followed, other computer manufacturers developed FORTRAN compilers for their machines. Several of these provided extensions and variations of FORTRAN that were specific to their particular computers. Consequently, programs written for one machine could not be used on a different machine without modification. Over time, users developed large collections of FORTRAN programs, and the cost of converting all these programs whenever a new computer was installed became prohibitive.

To remedy these problems, efforts were made to standardize FORTRAN so that programs were **portable**, which means they can be processed on several different machines with little or no alteration. One of the earliest standard versions appeared in 1966, and in 1977 another revision appeared, known as FORTRAN 77. While the changes introduced in FORTRAN 77 were significant, the new version did not solve all of the problems in earlier versions, nor did it include many of the new features that were appearing in newer programming languages. Consequently, work began almost immediately on a new standard version; in 1991, an extensive revision known as Fortran 90 appeared, and compilers to support this new version of Fortran have been developed.[1] The American National Standards Institute (ANSI), which establishes standards for programming languages, decided that during the transition period there should be two American standards for Fortran, FORTRAN 77 and Fortran 90, while International Standards Organization (ISO) groups decided that Fortran 90 will be the only international Fortran standard.

Fortran 90 has standardized earlier versions of Fortran and provides a base from which newer versions of the language will be developed. In fact, another ANSI committee is already at work preparing a new version that will make it possible to design Fortran programs that will execute efficiently on massively parallel computers and that incorporate modern programming techniques such as object-oriented programming.

---

[1] "FORTRAN" has traditionally been written in all upper case. The new ANSI standard, however, specifies "Fortran" as the official spelling for Fortran 90.

1.3 PROGRAMMING AND PROBLEM SOLVING

Programming and problem solving is an art in that it requires a good deal of imagination, ingenuity, and creativity. But it is also a science in that it uses certain techniques and methodologies. The term **software engineering** has come to be applied to the study and use of these techniques.

At least five steps can be identified in the program-development process:

1. Problem analysis and specification
2. Data organization and algorithm design
3. Program coding
4. Execution and testing
5. Program maintenance

In this section we illustrate these steps with a radioactive-decay problem. This example is very simple so that we can emphasize the main ideas at each stage without getting lost in a maze of details. It must be realized, however, that in more substantial problems, these stages will be considerably more complex.

APPLICATION: RADIOACTIVE DECAY

PROBLEM

Nick Nuke is a nuclear physicist at Dispatch University and is conducting research with the radioactive element polonium. The half-life of polonium is 140 days, which means that because of radioactive decay the amount of polonium that remains after 140 days is one-half of the original amount. Nick would like to know how much polonium will remain after running his experiment for 180 days if 10 milligrams are present initially.

STEP 1: PROBLEM ANALYSIS AND SPECIFICATION

The first stage in solving this problem is to analyze the problem and formulate a precise **specification** of it. This specification must include a description of the problem's **input**—what information is given and which items are important in solving the problem—and its **output**—what information must be produced to solve the problem. Input and output are two major parts of the problem's specification. Formulating the specification for this problem is easy:

INPUT	OUTPUT
Initial amount	Amount remaining
Half-life	
Time period	

The other items of information—the physicist's name, the name of the university, the name of the particular radioactive element—are not relevant (at least not to this problem) and can be ignored.

STEP 2: DATA ORGANIZATION AND ALGORITHM DESIGN

Now that we have a precise specification of the problem, we are ready to begin designing a plan for its solution. This plan has two parts:

1. Determine how to organize and store the data in the problem.
2. Develop procedures to process the data and produce the required output. These procedures are called algorithms.

Data Organization

As we noted, the input for this problem consists of the initial amount of some radioactive element, its half-life, and a time period. The output to be produced is the amount of the substance that remains at the end of the specified time period. We will use the variables *InitialAmount*, *HalfLife*, *Time*, and *AmountRemaining* to represent these quantities.

Algorithm Design

The first step in an algorithm for solving this problem is to obtain the values for the input items—initial amount, half-life, and time period. Next we must determine how to use this information to calculate the amount of the substance remaining after the given time period. Finally, the amount remaining must be displayed. Thus, our initial description of an algorithm for solving the problem is

1. Get values for *InitialAmount*, *HalfLife*, and *Time*.
2. Compute the value of *AmountRemaining* for the given *Time*.
3. Display *AmountRemaining*.

Algorithm Refinement

The next step in developing an algorithm to solve the problem is the refinement of any steps in the algorithm that require additional details. For example, in step 2 of the preceding algorithm, a formula is needed to compute the amount of polonium that remains after a given time period. The half-life of polonium is 140 days, and if we assume that the initial amount of polonium is 10 mg, then after 140 days, or one half-life,

$$10 \times 0.5$$

milligrams remain. At the end of 280 days, or two half-lives, the amount of polonium remaining is one half of this amount,

$$(10 \times 0.5) \times 0.5$$

which can also be written as

$$10 \times (0.5)^2$$

Similarly, the amount of polonium at the end of 420 days, or three half-lives, is

$$10 \times (0.5)^3$$

The general formula for the amount of the substance remaining is

$$\text{amount remaining} = \text{initial amount} \times (0.5)^{\text{time/half-life}}$$

Thus, the second step in our algorithm is to perform this calculation for the data entered in step 1.

This rather lengthy description of the algorithm can be expressed more concisely using **pseudocode** as follows.

Algorithm for Radioactive-Decay Problem

This algorithm calculates the amount of a radioactive substance that remains after a specified time for a given initial amount and a given half-life.

Input: An *InitialAmount* of a radioactive substance, its *HalfLife*, and a *Time* period in days
Output: The *AmountRemaining*

1. Enter *InitialAmount*, *HalfLife*, and *Time*.
2. Calculate

$$AmountRemaining =$$
$$InitialAmount \ ^\circ \ (0.5) \ ^{\circ\circ} \ (Time \ /HalfLife)$$

3. Display *AmountRemaining*.

Unlike the definitions of high-level programming languages such as Fortran, there is no set of rules that precisely define pseudocode. It varies from one programmer to another. Pseudocode is a mixture of natural language and symbols, terms, and other features commonly used in high-level programming languages. Typically, one finds the following features in various pseudocodes:

1. The usual computer symbols are used for arithmetic operations: + for addition, − for subtraction, * for multiplication, / for division, and °° for exponentiation.
2. Symbolic names (variables) are used to represent the quantities being processed by the algorithm.
3. Certain key words that are common in high-level languages may be used: for example, *Read* or *Enter* to indicate input operations, and *Display*, *Print*, or *Write* for output operations.
4. Indentation is used to indicate key blocks of instructions.

Some programmers use graphical representations of algorithms in addition to or in place of pseudocode descriptions. A number of such representations have been developed over the years, but probably the most common one is the **flowchart**, a diagram that uses symbols like those shown in the following figure, which graphically displays the steps in this algorithm:

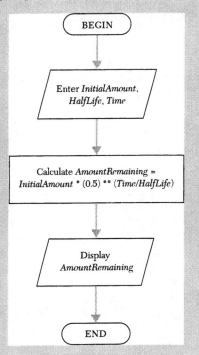

Each step of the algorithm is placed in a box of the appropriate shape, and the order in which these steps are to be carried out is indicated by connecting them with arrows called *flow lines*. Here, parallelograms are used to indicate input/output operations, and rectangles represent assignments of values to variables.

Once we have finished the algorithm, we are ready to proceed to the coding stage.

STEP 3: PROGRAM CODING

The first two steps of the program-development process are extremely important, because the remaining phases will be much more difficult if the first two steps are skipped or are not done carefully. On the other hand, if the problem has been carefully analyzed and specified and if an effective plan has been designed, the program-coding step is usually straightforward.

Coding is the process of implementing data objects and algorithms in some programming language. In the second step of the problem-solving process, algorithms may be described in a natural language or pseudocode, but a program that implements an algorithm must be written in the vocabulary of a programming language and must conform to the syntax, or grammatical rules, of that language. Figure 1.2 shows a Fortran 90 program for this example.

Figure 1.2. Radioactive Decay.

```fortran
PROGRAM Radioactive_Decay
!----------------------------------------------------------------
! This program calculates the amount of a radioactive substance that
! Remains after a specified time, given an initial amount and its
! half-life. Variables used are:
!    InitialAmount   : initial amount of substance (mg)
!    HalfLife        : half-life of substance (days)
!    Time            : time at which the amount remaining is
!                      calculated (days)
!    AmountRemaining : amount of substance remaining (mg)
!
! Input : InitialAmount, HalfLife, Time
! Output : AmountRemaining
!----------------------------------------------------------------

IMPLICIT NONE
REAL :: InitialAmount, HalfLife, Time, AmountRemaining

! Gel values for InitialAmount, HalfLife, and Time

PRINT *, "Enter initial amount (mg) of substance, its half-life (days)<"
PRINT *, "and time (days) at which to find amount remaining:"
READ *, InitialAmount, HalfLife, Time
```

```
        ! Compute the amount remaining at the specified time
        AmountRemaining = InitialAmount * 0.5 ** (Time / HalfLife)

        ! Display AmountRemaining
        PRINT *, "Amount remaining =", AmountRemaining, "mg"

    END PROGRAM Radioactive_Decay
```

The program begins with the PROGRAM statement

```
PROGRAM Radioactive_Decay
```

which marks the beginning of the program and associates the name Radioactive_Decay with it.

The PROGRAM statement is followed by **opening documentation** in the form of comments that describe the program. These comments summarize the purpose of the program and give the specification of the problem the program is to solve. An exclamation mark (!) indicates the beginning of a comment.

The statement

```
IMPLICIT NONE
```

that follows the opening documentation specifies that all variables to be used in this program must be declared explicitly. Thus, the next statement

```
REAL :: InitialAmount, HalfLife, Time, AmountRemaining
```

declares that variables InitialAmount, HalfLife, Time, and AmountRemaining will be used in the program and that their values will be real numbers.

The first step in the algorithm is an input instruction to enter values for the variables *InitialAmount*, *HalfLife*, and *Time:*

1. Enter *InitialAmount, HalfLife,* and *Time.*

This is translated into three statements in the program:

```
PRINT *, "Enter initial amount (mg) of substance, its half-life (days),"
PRINT *, "and time (days) at which to find amount remaining:"
READ *, InitialAmount, HalfLife, Time
```

The PRINT statements are used to prompt the user that the input values are to be entered. The READ statement actually assigns the three values entered by the user to the three variables InitialAmount, HalfLife, and Time. Thus, if the user enters

```
2, 140, 180
```

the value 2 will be assigned to InitialAmount, 140 to HalfLife, and 180 to Time.

The next step in the algorithm

2. Calculate

$$AmountRemaining = InitialAmount \circ (0.5)^{\circ\circ}(Time / HalfLife)$$

translates into the Fortran assignment statement

```
AmountRemaining = InitialAmount * 0.5 ** (Time / HalfLife)
```

The output instruction

3. Display AmountRemaining.

is translated into the Fortran statement

```
PRINT *, "Amount remaining =", AmountRemaining, "mg"
```

The end of the program is indicated by the Fortran statement

```
END PROGRAM Radioactive_Decay
```

This statement terminates execution of the program.

STEP 4: EXECUTION AND TESTING

Once an algorithm has been coded, the fourth step in the development process is to check that the algorithm and program are *correct*. One way to do this is to execute the program with input values for which the correct output values are already known (or are easily calculated). The procedure for submitting a program to a computer and executing it varies from one system to another; the details regarding your particular system can be obtained from your instructor, computer center personnel, or user manuals supplied by the manufacturer.

First you must gain access to the computer system. In the case of a personal computer, this may only mean turning on the machine and inserting the appropriate disk into the disk drive. For a larger system, some **login** procedure may be required to establish contact between a remote terminal and the computer. When you have gained access, you must enter the program, often by using an editor provided as part of the system software.

Once the Fortran source program has been entered, it must be compiled to produce an object file by giving appropriate system commands.[2] The resulting object file can then be executed with test data to check its correctness. For example, the program in Figure 1.2 might be compiled on a UNIX system with the command

```
f90 fig1-8.f90 -o fig1-8
```

Giving the command

```
fig1-8
```

then causes the program to execute:

```
Enter initial amount (mg) of substance, its half-life (days),
and time (days) at which to find amount remaining:
2, 140, 140
Amount remaining = 1.0000000 mg
```

The program displays a message prompting the user for three input values, and after these values (highlighted in color) are entered, the desired output value is calculated and displayed.

Here we have entered the values 2, 140, and 140 since it is easy to check that the correct answer for these inputs is 1.0. Similarly, the correct results for simple input values like 4, 140, 280 and 4, 140, 420 are easily calculated and can be used as a quick check of the answers produced by the program.

Once we are confident that the program its correct, we can use it to solve the original problem of finding the amount of polonium remaining after 180 days if there are 10 mg present initially:

```
Enter initial amount (mg) of substance, its half-life (days),
and time (days) at which to find amount remaining:
10, 140, 180
Amount remaining = 4.1016769 mg
```

In this example, the program was entered, compiled, and executed without error. Usually, however, a programmer will make some errors when designing the program or when attempting to enter and execute it. Errors may be detected at various stages of program processing and may cause the processing to be terminated. For example, an incorrect system command will be detected early in the processing and will usually prevent compilation and

[2] On some systems it may also be necessary to link the object file with certain system files.

execution of the program. Errors in the program's syntax, such as incorrect punctuation or misspelled key words, will be detected during compilation. (On some systems, syntax errors may be detected while the program is being entered.) Such errors are called **syntax errors** or **compile-time errors** and usually make it impossible to complete the compilation and execution of the program. For example, if the output statement that displays the residual amount of radioactive substance were mistakenly written as

```
PRINT *, "Amount remaining =, Amount Remaining, "mg"
```

without a quotation mark after the equal sign, an attempt to compile and execute the program might result in a message like the following, signaling a "fatal" error:

```
Error: Unterminated character literal at line 27
Error: syntax error at line 27
***Malformed statement
[f90 terminated - errors found by pass 1]
```

Less severe errors may generate "warning" messages, but the compilation will continue.

Other errors, such as an attempt to divide by zero in an arithmetic expression, may not be detected until execution of the program has begun. Such errors are called **run-time errors.** Explanations of the error messages displayed by your particular system can be found in the user manuals supplied by the manufacturer. In any case, the errors must be corrected by replacing the erroneous statements with correct ones, and the modified program must be recompiled and reexecuted.

Errors that are detected by the computer system are relatively easy to identify and correct. There are, however, other errors that are more subtle and difficult to identify. These are **logic errors** that arise in the design of the algorithm or in the coding of the program that implements the algorithm. For example, if the statement

```
AmountRemaining = InitialAmount * 0.5 ** (Time / HalfLife)
```

in the program of Figure 1.2 were mistakenly entered as

```
AmountRemaining = InitialAmount * 0.5 * (Time / HalfLife)
```

with the exponentiation symbol (**) replaced by the symbol for multiplication (*), the program would still be syntactically correct. No error would occur during the compilation or execution of the program. But the results produced by the program would be incorrect because an incorrect formula would have been used to calculate the residual amount of the substance. If the values 2, 140, and 140 were entered for the variables `InitialAmount`, `HalfLife`, and `Time`, respectively, the output produced by the program would be

```
Amount remaining = 1.0000000 mg
```

which is correct, even though the formula is not. However, for the test data 4, 140, 280, the output is

```
Amount remaining = 4.0000000 mg
```

which is obviously incorrect (since the initial and remaining amounts cannot be the same).

As this example demonstrates, *it is important to execute a program with several different sets of input data for which the correct results are known in advance.* This process of **program testing** is ex-tremely important, as *a program cannot be considered to be correct until it has been checked with several sets of test data.* The test data should be carefully selected so that each part of the program is tested.

Thorough testing of a program will increase one's confidence in its correctness, but it must be realized that it is almost never possible to test a program with every possible set of test data. No matter how much testing has been done, more can always be done. Testing is never finished; it is only stopped. Consequently, there is no guarantee that all the errors in a program have been found and corrected. Testing can only show the presence of errors, not their absence. It cannot prove that the program is correct; it can only show that it is incorrect.

STEP 5: MAINTENANCE

The life cycle of a program written by a student programmer normally ends with the fourth step; that is, once the program has been written, executed, and tested, the assignment is complete. Programs in real-world applications, however, are often used for several years and are likely to require some modification. Software systems, especially large ones developed for complex projects, may have obscure bugs that were not detected during testing and that surface after the software has been placed in use. One important aspect of software maintenance is fixing such flaws in the software. It may also be necessary to modify software to improve its performance, to add new features, and so on. Other modifications may be required because of changes in the computer hardware and/or the system software such as the operating system. External factors may also force program modification; for example, changes in building codes may mean revising part of a construction-cost program. It is easier to make such changes in a well-structured program than in one that is poorly designed.

PRACTICE!

1. Name the five steps in the program-development process.
2. What are two important parts of a problem's specification?
3. (True or false) Pseudocode is a high-level programming language.
4. A _____ is a graphical display of an algorithm.
5. The grammatical rules of a language are called its _____.
6. What are the three types of errors that can occur in developing a program?

For each of the problems described in Exercises 7–9, identify both the information that must be produced to solve the problem and the given information that will be useful in obtaining the solution. Then design an algorithm to solve the problem.

7. Convert a temperature of C degrees on the Celsius scale to the corresponding Fahrenheit temperature $(F = \frac{9}{5}C + 32)$.
8. Calculate and display the radius, circumference, and area of a circle with a given diameter.
9. Three resistors are arranged in parallel in the following circuit:

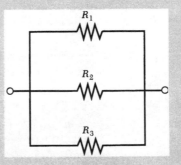

Calculate and display the combined resistance

$$\frac{1}{\frac{1}{R_1} + \frac{1}{R_2} + \frac{1}{R_3}}$$

for given values of R_1, R_2, and R_3.

10. Enter and execute the following Fortran 90 program on your computer system, but with the name, course name, and date replaced with your name and course name and the current date.

```
PROGRAM Arithmetic
!-----------------------------------------------------------
! John Doe              CPSC 141C          MonthName dd, yyyy
!                     ASSIGNMENT #1
!
! Program to add two real numbers. Variables used are:
!   X, Y :  the two real numbers
!   Sum  :  the sum of X and Y
!
! Output: X, Y, and Sum
!-----------------------------------------------------------

   IMPLICIT NONE
   REAL :: X, Y, Sum

   X = 1.234
   Y = 5.5
   Sum = X + Y
   PRINT *, "Sum of", X, " and", Y, " is", Sum

END PROGRAM Arithmetic
```

11. For the program in Exercise 10, make the following changes and execute the modified program:

(a) Change 1.234 to 17.2375 in the statement that assigns a value to X.

(b) Change the variable names X and Y to Alpha and Beta throughout.

(c) Insert the comment

```
! Calculate the sum
```

(d) before the statement that assigns a value to Sum. **(d)** Insert the following comment and statement before the PRINT statement:

```
! Now calculate the difference
Difference = Alpha - Beta
```

add the variable Difference to the list of variables in the REAL statement, and add another PRINT statement to display the value of Difference. Also, change the comments in the opening documentation appropriately.

12. Using the program in Figure 1.2 as a guide, write a Fortran program for the temperature problem in Exercise 7.

13. Proceed as in Exercise 12, but for the circle problem in Exercise 8.

14. Proceed as in Exercise 12, but for the resistance problem in Exercise 9.

KEY TERMS

Address	Bit	Editor
Algorithm	Byte	External (auxiliary,
Arithmetic-logic unit	Central processing	secondary) memory
(ALU)	unit (CPU)	Flowchart
Assembler	Coding	FORTRAN
Assembly language	Control unit	Hardware

High-level language
Input
Input/output device
Internal (main, primary)
  memory
K (kilobyte)
Logic error
Login
Machine language
Megabyte
Memory unit

Opcode
Opening documentation
Operand
Output
Peripheral device
Portable
Program testing
Pseudocode
Random access memory
  (RAM)

Read-only memory
  (ROM)
Register
Run-time error
Software
Software engineering
Specification
Syntax (compile-time)
  error
Word

2

Basic Fortran

2.1 DATA TYPES, CONSTANTS, AND VARIABLES

We have seen in the preceding chapter that organizing a problem's data is an important part of developing a program to solve that problem. This may be numeric data representing times or temperatures, or character data representing names, or logical data used in designing a circuit, and so on. Consequently, a program for solving a problem must be written in a language that can store and process various types of data.

Fortran provides five basic data types:

```
INTEGER
REAL
COMPLEX
CHARACTER
LOGICAL
```

The first three are numeric types used to store and process various kinds of numbers; the character type is used to store and process strings of characters; and the logical type is used to store and process logical data values (.FALSE. and .TRUE.). In this section we describe the most commonly used forms of the Fortran integer, real, and character data types and tell how to declare constants and variables of these types.

Integers

An **integer** is a whole number (positive, negative, or zero) and may be represented in Fortran by a string of digits *that does not contain commas or a decimal point;* negative

OBJECTIVES

In this chapter, you will

- Learn how Fortran 90 handles different types of data.
- Study the arithmetic operations and functions and how they are used to process data.
- See how to use the assignment statement.
- Learn the fundamentals of input and output.
- See what the general form of a Fortran program is.
- Apply the concepts learned to a temperature-conversion overflow.

integer constants must be preceded by a minus sign, but a plus sign is optional for non-negative integers. Thus

```
     0
   137
 -2516
 17745
```

are valid integer constants, whereas the following are invalid for the reasons indicated:

```
9,999   (Commas are not allowed in numeric constants.)
16.0    (Integer constants may not contain decimal points.)
--5     (Only one algebraic sign is allowed.)
7--     (The algebraic sign must precede the string of digits.)
```

Real Data Type

Another numeric data type is the **real** type. Constants of this type may be represented as ordinary decimal numbers or in exponential notation. *In the decimal representation of real constants, a decimal point must be present, but no commas are allowed.* Negative real constants must be preceded by a minus sign, but the plus sign is optional for nonnegative reals. Thus

```
   1.234
 -0.01536
 +56473.
```

are valid real constants, whereas the following are invalid for the reasons indicated:

```
12,345   (Commas are not allowed in numeric constants.)
63       (Real constants must contain a decimal point.)
```

The exponential representation of a real constant consists of an integer or decimal number, representing the mantissa or fractional part, followed by an exponent written as the letter E *with an integer constant following.* For example, the real constant 337.456 may also be written as

```
3.37456E2
```

which means 3.37456×10^2, or it may be written in a variety of other forms, such as

```
0.337456E3
337.456E0
33745.6E-2
337456E-3
```

Character Strings

Character constants, also called **strings**, are sequences of symbols from the Fortran character set. The ANSI standard character set for Fortran is given in Table 2.1.

The sequence of characters that comprise a character constant must be enclosed between double quotes or between apostrophes (single quotes), as long as the same character is used at the beginning and the end. The number of such characters is the *length* of the constant. For example,

```
"PDQ123-A"
```

is a character constant of length 8;

```
"John Q. Doe"
```

TABLE 2-1 Fortran Character Set

CHARACTER	MEANING	CHARACTER	MEANING
0,...,9	digits	:	colon
A,...,Z	uppercase letters	=	equal sign
a,...,z	lowercase letters	!	exclamation mark
'	apostrophe (single quote)	&	ampersand
"	double quote	$	dollar sign
(	left parenthesis	;	semicolon
)	right parenthesis	<	less than
*	asterisk		greater than
+	plus sign	%	percent symbol
-	minus sign	?	question mark
/	slash	,	comman
blank	blank or space	.	period

is a character constant of length 11, because blanks are characters and are included in the character count. If an apostrophe is to be one of the characters in a constant, double quotes should be used to enclose the string; for example,

```
"Don't"
```

Identifiers

Identifiers are names used to identify programs, constants, variables, and other entities in a program. In standard Fortran, *identifiers must begin with a letter, which may be followed by up to 30 letters, digits, or underscores.* Thus

```
Mass
Rate
Velocity
Speed_of_Light
```

are valid Fortran identifiers, but the following are invalid for the reasons indicated:

```
R2-D2   (Only letters, digits, and underscores are allowed in identifiers.)
6Feet   (Identifiers must begin with a letter.)
```

One should always use meaningful identifiers that suggest what they represent.

Fortran 90 makes no distinction between upper case and lower case (except in character constants). For example, `Velocity` is a valid identifier and will not be distinguished from `VELOCITY` or `vELocITy`, even if one form is used in one place in the program and another is used somewhere else. A common practice—and one that we use in the sample programs in this text—is to write all Fortran key words (e.g., `READ` and `PRINT`) in upper case and all programmer-defined identifiers in lower case, usually capitalizing the first letter. If an identifier is made up of several words, we usually capitalize the first letter of each and sometimes separate the words by underscores.

Variables

When a variable is used in a Fortran program, the compiler associates it with a memory location. The value of a variable at any time is the value stored in the associated memory location at that time. Variable names are identifiers and thus must follow the rules for forming valid identifiers.

The type of a Fortran variable determines the type of value that may be assigned to that variable. It is therefore necessary to declare the type of each variable in a Fortran program. This can be done using **type statements**. Basic forms of the type statements used to declare integer variables and real variables are

```
INTEGER :: list

REAL :: list
```

The names in the list must be separated by commas. For example, the statements

```
INTEGER :: NumValues, Factorial, Sum
REAL :: Mass, Velocity
```

declare `NumValues`, `Factorial`, and `Sum` to be integer variables and `Mass` and `Velocity` to be real variables.

One form of the type statement used to declare character variables is

```
CHARACTER(LEN = n) :: list
```

or simply

```
CHARACTER (n) :: list
```

where n is an integer constant specifying the length of character constants to be assigned to the variables in the list. The length specifier may be omitted, in which case the length of the values for the variables in the list is 1. For example, the type statement

```
CHARACTER(LEN = 15) :: FirstName, LastName
```

or

```
CHARACTER(15) :: FirstName, LastName
```

declares `FirstName` and `LastName` to be character variables and specifies that the length of any character value assigned to one of these variables is 15. The statement

```
CHARACTER :: Initial
```

declares `Initial` to be a character variable with values of length 1.

A length specifier of the form *n may also be attached to any of the individual variables in the list of a `CHARACTER` statement. In this case, this length specification for that variable overrides the length specification given for the list. The statement

```
CHARACTER(15) :: FirstName, LastName*20, Initial*1, Street,
                 City
```

declares that `FirstName`, `LastName`, `Initial`, `Street`, and `City` are character variables and that the length of values for `FirstName`, `Street`, and `City` is 15, the length of values for `LastName` is 20, and the length of values for `Initial` is 1.

Variables of a given type must be used in a manner that is appropriate to that data type, since the program may fail to execute correctly otherwise. *It is therefore important to specify the correct type of each variable used in a program.* One must think carefully about each variable, what it represents, what type of values it will have, what operations will be performed on it, and so on. This will avoid (or at least lessen) the mixed-mode errors caused by combining values of different types or assigning a value of one type to a variable of a different type.

The IMPLICIT NONE Statement

In Fortran, any variable whose type is not *explicitly* declared in a type statement will be assigned a type according to an **implicit naming convention:** any undeclared identifier whose name begins with I, J, K, L, M, or N or their lowercase equivalents will be typed as integer, and all others will be typed as real.

An unfortunate consequence of this naming convention is that failing to declare the type of a variable is not an error because these variables will be implicitly typed. Fortran 90 provides the

```
IMPLICIT NONE
```

statement to cancel this naming convention. *It should be used in every program (and module)* to guard against errors caused by implicit typing of a variable to have a type different than what was intended. Placing IMPLICIT NONE at the beginning of the specification part requires that the types of all named constants and variables (and functions) *must be* specified explicitly in type statements. Using any named constant or variable (or function) without declaring it explicitly in a type statement will be treated as an error by the compiler.

Variable Initialization

It is important to note that in Fortran, *all variables are initially undefined*. Initial values can be assigned to variables (at compile time) in their declarations. For example, to initialize the values of variables W, X, Y, and Z to 1.0, 2.5, 7.73, and −2.956, respectively, we could use the statement

```
REAL :: W = 1.0, X = 2.5, Y = 7.73, Z = -2.956
```

Named Constants: The PARAMETER Attribute

Certain constants occur so often that they are given names. For example, the name "pi" is commonly given to the constant 3.14159... and the name "*e*" to the base 2.71828... of natural logarithms. Fortran allows the programmer to specify that an identifier names a constant by including a PARAMETER **attribute** in the declaration of that identifier:

```
type-specifier, PARAMETER :: list
```

For example, the declarations

```
INTEGER, PARAMETER :: Limit = 50
REAL, PARAMETER :: Pi = 3.141593, TwoPi = 2.0 * Pi
CHARACTER(2), PARAMETER :: Units = "cm"
```

associate the name Limit with the integer 50: the names Pi and TwoPi with the real constants 3.141593 and 6.283186, respectively; and the name Units with the character string "cm". The last declaration can also be written

```
CHARACTER(*), PARAMETER :: Units = "cm"
```

Here the asterisk (*) is an **assumed length specifier** indicating that the length of the named constant (Units) being declared is to be the length (2) of the string constant ("cm") with which it is being associated.

The names `Limit`, `Pi`, `TwoPi`, and `Units` can be used anywhere in the program that the corresponding constant value can be used (except as noted later in the text). For example, a statement such as

```
XCoordinate = Rate * COS(TwoPi * Time)
```

is equivalent to

```
XCoordinate = Rate * COS(6.283186 * Time)
```

but the first form is preferable because it is more readable and does not require modification if a different value with more or fewer significant digits is required for `Pi`.

PRACTICE!

1. Name the five basic Fortran data types.
2. Character constants must be enclosed in _____ or _____.
3. Identifiers must begin with _____.
4. The maximum number of characters in a Fortran identifier is _____.

For Exercises 5–14, tell whether the string of characters forms a legal identifier. If it is not legal, indicate the reason.

5. X Axis
6. X-Axis
7. XAxis
8. X_A_X_I_S
9. Carbon14
10. PS.175
11. N/4
12. 3M
13. M$
14. A+

For Exercises 15–30, tell whether the string of characters forms an integer constant, a real constant, or a character constant. If it is none of these, indicate the reason.

15. 5,280
16. 5280
17. "5280"
18. 528.0
19. 5280E0
20. -5280
21. 0.528E+04
22. E5280
23. $52.80
24. '$52.80'
25. fifty
26. 'Ohm's law'
27. +5280
28. 52+80
29. "isn't"
30. "$5,280.00"

31. Write type statements to declare `Temperature`, `Pressure`, and `Volume` to be real variables.
32. Write type statements to declare `Code` and `Count` to be integer variables, `XCoordinate` and `YCoordinate` to be real variables.
33. Write type statements to declare `Name1` and `Name2` to be character variables with values of length 20 and `Name3` a character variable with values of length 10.

For Exercises 34–37, write declarations to name the constants with the specified names.

34. 1.25 with `Rate`
35. 100 with `Celsius_Boiling_Point` and 212 with `Fahrenheit_Boiling_Point`
36. 1.2E12 with `Mars` and 1.5E10 with `Earth`
37. 'FE2O3' with `Formula`, 'Ferric Oxide' with `Name`, and .182 with `SpecificHeat`

For Exercises 38–40, write initialization declarations for each variable.

38. `Rate1` and `Rate2` to be real variables with initial values 1.25 and 2.33, respectively

39. `Department` to be a character variable with initial value `"ENGR"` and `Course1`, `Course2` to be integer variables with initial values 141 and 142, respectively

40. `Units_1`, `Units_2`, and `Units_3` to be character variables with initial values `"feet"`, `"inches"`, and `"centimeters"`, respectively; `Num_1`, `Num_2`, and `Num_3` to be integer variables with initial values 0, 0, and 1, respectively; and `Rate_1` and `Rate_2` to be real variables with initial values 0.25 and 1.5, respectively

2.2 OPERATIONS AND FUNCTIONS

In the preceding section we considered variables and constants of various types. These variables and constants can be processed by using operations and functions appropriate to their types. In this section we discuss the arithmetic operations and functions that are used with numeric data and character operations.

Numeric Operations

In Fortran, addition and subtraction are denoted by the usual plus (+) and minus (−) signs, multiplication by an asterisk (*), division by a slash (/), and exponentiation by a pair of asterisks (**). For example, the quantity $B^2 - 4AC$ is written as

```
B ** 2 - 4 * A * C
```

in a Fortran program.

When two constants or variables of the same type are combined using one of the four basic arithmetic operations (+, −, *, /), the result has the same type as the operands. For example, the sum of the integers 3 and 4 is the integer 7, whereas the sum of the real numbers 3.0 and 4.0 is the real number 7.0. This distinction may seem unimportant until one considers the division operation. Division of the real constant 9.0 by the real constant 4.0,

```
9.0 / 4.0
```

produces the real quotient 2.25, whereas dividing the integer 9 by the integer 4,

```
9 / 4
```

produces the integer quotient 2, which is the integer part of the real quotient 2.25. Similarly, if the integer variable N has the value 2 and the real variable X has the value 2.0, the real division

```
1.0 / X
```

yields 0.5, whereas the integer division

```
1 / N
```

yields 0.

Mixed-Mode Expressions.   It is possible to combine integer and real quantities using arithmetic operations. Expressions involving different types of numeric operands are called **mixed-mode expressions**. When an integer quantity is combined with a real one, the integer quantity is converted to its real equivalent, and the result is of real type.

The following examples illustrate the evaluation of some mixed-mode expressions; note that type conversion does not take place until necessary:

```
1.0 / 4 → 1.0 / 4.0 → 0.25
3.0 + 8 / 5 → 3.0 + 1 → 3.0 + 1.0 → 4.0
3 + 8.0 / 5 → 3 + 8.0 / 5.0 → 3 + 1.6 → 3.0 + 1.6 → 4.6
```

The last two examples show why *using mixed-mode expressions is usually considered poor programming practice.* The two expressions 3.0 + 8 / 5 and 3 + 8.0 / 5 are algebraically equal but are in fact not equal because of the differences in real and integer arithmetic.

The only expressions in which operands of different types should be used are those in which a real value is raised to an integer power. For such expressions, exponentiation is carried out using repeated multiplication, as the following examples illustrate:

```
  2.0 ** 3 → 2.0 * 2.0 * 2.0 → 8.0
(-4.0) ** 2 → (-4.0) * (-4.0) → 16.0
```

If, however, the exponent is a real quantity, exponentiation is performed using logarithms. For example,

```
2.0 ** 3.0
```

is evaluated as

$$e^{3.0 \ln(2.0)}$$

which will not be exactly 8.0 because of roundoff errors that arise in storing real numbers and because the exponentiation and logarithm functions produce only approximate values. Another consequence of this method of performing exponentiation is that a negative quantity raised to a real power is undefined because the logarithms of negative values are not defined. Consequently, (-4.0) ** 2.0 is undefined, even though (-4.0) ** 2 is evaluated as (-4.0) * (-4.0) = 16.0. These examples show why *a real exponent should never be used in place of an integer exponent.*

There are, however, computations in which real exponents are appropriate. For example, in mathematics, $7^{1/2}$ denotes $\sqrt{7}$, the square root of 7. In Fortran, this operation of extracting roots can be performed using exponentiation with real exponents. Thus, to compute the square root of 7.0, we could write 7.0 ** 0.5 or 7.0 ** (1.0 / 2.0). (Note, however, that 7.0 ** (1 / 2) yields 7.0 ** 0 = 1.0.) Similarly, the cube root of a real variable X can be computed using X ** (1.0 / 3.0).

Priority Rules.   Arithmetic expressions are evaluated in accordance with the following **priority rules**:

1. *All exponentiations are performed first; consecutive exponentiations are performed from right to left.*
2. *All multiplications and divisions are performed next, in the order in which they appear from left to right.*
3. *The additions and subtractions are performed last, in the order in which they appear from left to right.*

The following examples illustrate this order of evaluation:

```
2 ** 3 ** 2 = 2 ** 9 = 512
10 - 8 - 2 = 2 - 2 = 0
10 / 5 * 2 = 2 * 2 = 4
2 + 4 / 2 = 2 + 2 = 4
2 + 4 ** 2 / 2 = 2 + 16 / 2 = 2 + 8 = 10
```

The standard order of evaluation can be modified by using parentheses to enclose subexpressions within an expression. For example, consider the expression

```
(5 * (11 - 5) ** 2) * 4 + 9
```

The subexpression 11 - 5 is evaluated first, producing

```
(5 * 6 ** 2) * 4 + 9
```

Next, the subexpression 5 * 6 ** 2 is evaluated in the standard order, giving

```
180 * 4 + 9
```

Now the multiplication is performed, giving

```
720 + 9
```

and the addition produces the final result:

```
729
```

The symbols + and − can also be used as **unary operators**; for example, +X and − (A + B) are allowed. But unary operators must be used carefully, because Fortran *does not allow two operators to follow in succession*. (Note that ** is interpreted as a single operator rather than two operators in succession.) For example, the expression N * −2 is not allowed; rather, it must be written as N * (−2). The unary operations have the same low priority as the corresponding binary operations.

Numeric Functions

Fortran provides functions for many of the common mathematical operations and functions. For example, many computations involve the square root of a quantity. Consequently, Fortran provides a special **function** to implement this operation. This function is denoted by SQRT and is used by writing

```
SQRT(argument)
```

where argument is a *real-valued* constant, variable, or expression. For example, to calculate the square root of 7, we would write

```
SQRT(7.0)
```

but not SQRT(7). If B ** 2 - 4.0 * A * C is a nonnegative, real-valued expression, its square root can be calculated by writing

```
SQRT(B ** 2 - 4.0 * A * C)
```

If the value of the expression B ** 2 - 4.0 * A * C is negative, an error will result because the square root of a negative number is not defined. To calculate the square root of an integer variable Number, it is necessary to convert its value to a real value using the type conversion function REAL before using SQRT:

```
SQRT(REAL(Number))
```

The Nth root of a real variable X can be computed by using

    X ** (1.0 / REAL(N))

and the Nth root of an integer variable NUM by using

    REAL(NUM) ** (1.0 / REAL(N))

Many other functions are provided in Fortran; some of the more commonly used functions are listed in Table 2.2. Other functions, including the inverse trigonometric functions (ACOS, ASIN, ATAN, ATAN2) and the hyperbolic functions (COSH, SINH, TANH), are described in Appendix A. To use any of these functions, we simply give the function name followed by the argument(s) enclosed in parentheses. In each case, the argument(s) must be of the type specified for that function in the table.

Character Operations

The **concatenation** operation // is used to combine two character values. For example,

    "centi" // "meters"

produces the string

    "centimeters"

and if SquareUnit is a character variable whose value is

    "square "

then

    SquareUnit // "centi" // "meters"

yields the string

    "square centimeters"

TABLE 2-2 Some Fortran Functions

FUNCTION	DESCRIPTION	TYPE OF ARGUMENT(S)*	TYPE OF VALUE
ABS(x)	Absolute value of x	Integer or real	Same as argument
COS(x)	Cosine of x radians	Real	Real
EXP(x)	Exponential function	Real	Real
INT(x)	Integer part of x	Real	Integer
FLOOR(x)	Greatest integer $\leq x$	Real	Integer
FRACTION(x)	Fractional part (mantissa) of x	Real	Real
LOG(x)	Natural logarithm of x	Real	Real
MAX($x_1, \ldots, x_n$)	Maximum of $x_1, \ldots, x_n$	Integer or real	Same as arguments
MIN($x_1, \ldots, x_n$)	Minimum of $x_1, \ldots, x_n$	Integer or real	Same as arguments
MOD(x, y)	x (mod y); x - INT (x/y) * y	Integer or real	Same as arguments
INT(x)	x rounded to nearest integer	Real	Integer
REAL(x)	Conversion of x to real type	Integer	Real
SIN(x)	Sine of x radians	Real	Real
SQRT(x)	Square root of x	Real	Real
TAN(x)	Tangent of x radians	Real	Real

*In several cases, the arguments (and values) may be of extended-precision or complex types. See Chapter 9.

Another operation commonly performed on character strings is accessing a **substring** of a given string. For example, the substring consisting of the fourth through seventh characters of the character constant `"centimeters"` is the string `"time"`.

In Fortran, a substring can be extracted from the value of a character variable or character constant by specifying the variable or constant followed by the positions of the first and last characters of the substring, separated by a colon (:) and enclosed in parentheses. For example, if the character variable `Units` has the value

```
"centimeters"
```

then

```
Units (4:7)
```

has the value

```
"time"
```

The initial and final positions of the substring may be specified by integer constants, variables, or expressions. If the initial position is not specified, it is assumed to be 1. If the final position is not specified, it is assumed to be the last position in the value of the character variable. To illustrate, consider the following statements:

```
CHARACTER(15) :: Course
Course = "Engineering"
```

Then

```
Course(:6)
```

has the value

```
"Engine"
```

and the value of

```
Course(8:)
```

is

```
"ringƂƂƂƂ"
```

where Ƃ denotes a blank. The first position specified for a substring must be positive, and the last position is greater than or equal to the first position but not greater than the length of the given string.

Fortran 90 also provides several functions for processing characters. These are described in Appendix A.

PRACTICE!

Find the value of each of the expressions in Exercises 1–19.

1. `9 - 5 - 3`   **2.** `2.0 + 3.0 / 5.0`

3. `2 + 3 / 5`   **4.** `5 / 2 + 3`

5. `2 + 3 ** 2`   **6.** `(2 + 3) ** 2`

7. `25.0 ** 1 / 2`   **8.** `12.0 / 1.0 * 3.0`

9. `(2 + 3 * 4) / (8 - 2 + 1)`   **10.** `((2 + 3) ** 2) / (8 - (2 + 1))`

11. `(2 + 3 ** 2) / (8 - 2 + 1)`   **12.** `(2.0 + 3 ** 2) / (8 - 2 + 1)`

13. `-3.0 ** 2`   **14.** `SQRT(6.0 + 3.0)`

15. `ABS(1 - 2 - 3)`   **16.** `EXP(3.0 - 2.0 - 1.0)`

17. `INT(5.0 + 4.0 / 3.0)`   **18.** `"one" // "two"`

19. `"abc" // "deed"(:2)`

Given that `Two` = 2.0, `Three` = 3.0, `Four` = 4.0, `IntEight` = 8, and `IntFive` = 5, `Str_1` = `"For"`, `Str_2` = `"tran"`, `Label_1` = `"foot"`, and `Label_2` = `"lbs"`, find the value of each of the expressions in Exercises 20–30.

20. `Two + Three * Three + 3`   **21.** `IntFive / 3`

22. `(Three + Two / four) ** 2`   **23.** `IntEight / IntFive * 5.1`

24. `Four ** 2 / Two ** 2`   **25.** `IntFive ** 2 / Two ** 2`

26. `SQRT(Two + Three + Four)`   **27.** `Str_1 // Str_2 // "-90"`

28. `Label_1 // "-" // Label_2`   **29.** `Str_1 // Str_2(:1)`

30. `Str_2(2:3) // "ndom"`

31. Write a Fortran expression equivalent to $10 + 5B - 4AC$.

32. Write a Fortran expression equivalent to the square root of $A + 3B^2$.

33. Write a Fortran expression equivalent to $A^2 + B^2 - 2AB \cos T$.

2.3 THE ASSIGNMENT STATEMENT

The **assignment statement** is used to assign values to variables and has the form

```
variable = expression
```

For example, suppose that `XCoordinate` and `YCoordinate` are real variables and `Number` and `Term` are integer variables, as declared by the following statements:

```
REAL :: XCoordinate, YCoordinate
INTEGER :: Number, Term
```

Now consider the following assignment statements:

```
XCoordinate = 5.23
YCoordinate = SQRT(25.0)
Number = 17
Term = Number / 3 + 2
XCoordinate = 2.0 * XCoordinate
```

The first assignment statement assigns the real constant 5.23 to the real variable `XCoordinate`, and the second assigns the real constant 5.0 to the real variable `YCoordinate`. The next assignment statement assigns the integer constant 17 to the integer variable `Number`. These values will be substituted for the variable names in any subsequent expression containing these variables. Thus, in the fourth assignment statement, the value 17 is substituted for the variable `Number`; the expression `Number / 3 + 2` is evaluated, yielding 7; and this value is then assigned to the integer variable `Term`; the value of `Number` is unchanged.

In the last assignment statement, the variable `XCoordinate` appears on both sides of the assignment operator (=). In this case, the current value 5.23 for `XCoordinate` is used in evaluating the expression `2.0 * XCoordinate`, yielding the value

10.46; this value is then assigned to XCoordinate. The old value 5.23 is lost because it has been replaced with the new value, 10.46.

If an integer-valued expression is assigned to a real variable, the integer value is converted to a real constant and then assigned to the variable. Thus, if the integer variable N has the value 9, and Alpha and Beta are real variables, the statements

```
Alpha = 3
Beta = (N + 3) / 5
```

assign the real value 3.0 to Alpha and the real value 2.0 to Beta.

In the case of a real-valued expression assigned to an integer variable, the fractional part of the real value is truncated, and the integer part is assigned to the variable. For example, if the real variable X has the value 5.75, and I, Kappa, and Mu are integer variables, the statements

```
I = 3.14159
Kappa = X / 2.0
Mu = 1.0 / X
```

assign the integer values 3, 2, and 0 to the variables I, Kappa, and Mu, respectively. As this example shows, *using mixed-mode assignments is dangerous and should usually be avoided.* If it is necessary to truncate the fractional part of a real-valued expression and assign only the integer part, it would be better to indicate this explicitly by writing, for example,

```
Kappa = INT(X / 2.0)
```

An assignment statement may also be used to assign a value to a character variable or to modify a string. To illustrate, suppose that the character variables String, Truncated, and Padded are declared by the type statement

```
CHARACTER(5) :: String, Truncated, Padded*10
```

The assignment statement

```
String = "alpha"
```

assigns the value "alpha" to String. In this example, the declared length of the variable is equal to the length of the value assigned to this variable. *If, however, the lengths do not match, the values are padded with blanks or truncated as necessary.* If the declared length of the variable is greater than the length of the value being assigned, trailing blanks are added to the value; thus the statement

```
Padded = "particle"
```

assigns the value "particleƀƀ" to the variable Padded (where ƀ denotes a blank character). If the declared length of the variable is less than the length of the value being assigned, the value is truncated to the size of the variable, and the leftmost characters are assigned; thus the statement

```
Truncated = "temperature"
```

assigns the value "tempe" to the variable Truncated.

An assignment statement may also be used to modify part of a string by using a substring reference. Only the character positions specified in the substring name are assigned values; the other positions are not changed. For example,

```
String(3:5) = "ter"
```

or

```
String(3:) = "ter"
```

changes the value of String to

```
"alter"
```

Positions to which new values are being assigned may not be referenced, however, in the character expression on the right side of such assignment statements. Thus

```
String(2:3) = String(4:5)
```

is valid, but

```
String(2:4) = String(3:5)
```

is not, because the substring being modified overlaps the substring being referenced.

PRACTICE!

Exercises 1–8 assume the following declarations have been made:

```
INTEGER :: M, N
REAL :: Pi, Alpha
```

Tell whether each is a valid Fortran assignment statement. If it is not valid, explain why not.

1. `Pi = 3.141593`	**2.** `3 = N`
3. `N = N+ 1`	**4.** `N+1 = N`
5. `Alpha = 1`	**6.** `Alpha = "1"`
7. `Alpha = Alpha`	**8.** `M = N = 1`

For Exercises 9–16, assume the following declarations have been made:

```
INTEGER :: IntEight = 8, IntFive = 5, JobId
REAL :: Two = 2.0, Three = 3.0, Four = 4.0, XValue
```

Find the value assigned to the given variable, or indicate why the statement is not valid.

9. `XValue = (Three + Two / Four) ** 2`

10. `XValue = IntEight / IntFive + 5.1`

11. `JobId = IntEight / IntFive + 5.1`

12. `IntEight = IntEight + 2`

13. `XValue = SQRT(Three ** 2 + Four ** 2)`

14. `IntEight = ABS(Three - 4.5)`

15. `XValue = SQRT(ABS(Two - Three))`

16. `JobId = MAX(INT(Four / 3), 1.5)`

For each of Exercises 17–23, write a Fortran assignment statement that calculates the given expression and assigns the result to the specified variable.

17. *Rate* times *Time* to *Distance*

18. $\sqrt{A^2 + B^2}$ to *C*

19. Increments *Count* by 1

20. $\dfrac{1}{\dfrac{1}{R1} + \dfrac{1}{R2} + \dfrac{1}{R3}}$ to *Resistance*

21. $\dfrac{2V^2 \sin A \cos A}{G}$ to *Range*

22. *P* times $(1 + R)^N$ to *Accumulated_Value*

23. Area of triangle (one-half base times height) of base *B* and height *H* to *Area*

For Exercises 24–40, assume that the declarations

```
CHARACTER(10) :: Alpha, Beta*5, Gamma*1, &
                 Label_1*4,Label_2*3, Str_1*3, Str_2*4
```

have been made and that `Str_1 = "For"`, `Str_2 = "tran"`, `Label_1 = "foot"`, `Label_2 = "lbs"`. Find the value assigned to the given variable, or indicate why the statement is not valid.

24. `Gamma = 123`

25. `Gamma = "123"`

26. `Alpha = "one" // "two"`

27. `Alpha = "1" // "2"`

28. `Beta = "antidisestablishmentarianism"`

29. `Beta = "1,000,000,000"`

30. `Beta = "one" // 23`

31. `Alpha = Str_1 // Str_2 // "-90"`

32. `Beta = Str_1 // Str_2 // "-90"`

33. `Alpha = Label_1 // Label_2`

34. `Gamma = Label_1`

35. `Alpha = Label_1 // "-" // Label_2`

36. `Beta = Str_1 // Str_2(:1)`

37. `Alpha = Str_2(2:3) // "ndom"`

38. `Str_2(2:3) = "ur"`

39. `Str_2(:2) = Str_2(3:)`

40. `Str_1(:2) = Str_1(2:)`

2.4 INPUT/OUTPUT

Fortran provides two types of input/output statements: **list-directed** and **formatted**. In this section we consider list-directed input/output, which is the simpler of the two.

The simplest list-directed output statement has the following form:

```
    PRINT *, output-list
```

or

```
    WRITE (*, *) output-list
```

For example, the PRINT statements

```
    PRINT *, "At time", Time, "seconds"
    PRINT *, "the vertical velocity is", Velocity, "m/sec"
    PRINT *, "and the height is", Height, "meters"
```

could be used to display values of `Time`, `Height`, and `Velocity`. Execution of these statements will produce output similar to the following:

```
At time 4.5000000 seconds
the vertical velocity is 45.8700752 m/sec
and the height is 4.0570767E+02 meters
```

Note that each `PRINT` statement produces a new line of output. The exact format and spacing used to display these values are compiler-dependent, however. In some systems, for example, real values might be displayed in exponential notation, and the number of spaces in an output line might be different from that shown.

The `PRINT` and `WRITE` statements may also be used with no output list:

```
PRINT *
```

or

```
WRITE (*, *)
```

Execution of these statements produces a blank line of output.

The simplest form of the list-directed input statement is

```
READ *, input-list
```

or

```
READ (*, *) input-list
```

Values will be obtained (normally from the keyboard) and assigned to the variables in the input list. The following rules apply:

1. A new line of data is processed each time a `READ` statement is executed.
2. If there are fewer entries in a line of input data than there are variables in the input list, successive lines of input are processed until values for all variables in the list have been obtained.
3. If there are more entries in a line of input data than there are variables in the input list, the first data values are used, and all remaining values are ignored.
4. The entries in each line of input data must be constants and of the same type as the variables to which they are assigned. (However, an integer value may be assigned to a real variable, with automatic conversion taking place.)
5. Consecutive entries in a line of input data must be separated by a comma or by one or more spaces.

For example, if the following line of input data

```
100.0, 90.0, 4.5
```

is entered in response to the statement

```
READ *, InitialHeight, InitialVelocity, Time
```

the values 100.0, 90.0, and 4.5 will be assigned to the variables `InitialHeight`, `InitialVelocity`, and `Time`, respectively. Spaces could be used as separators in place of the commas,

```
100.0 90.0 4.5
```

or more than one line of data could be used:

```
100.0 90.0
4.5
```

Character values can also be read using list-directed input, but they must be enclosed in single or double quotes if any of the following is true:

1. The character value extends over more than one line.
2. The character value contains blanks, commas, or slashes.
3. The character value begins with an apostrophe, a double quote, or a string of digits followed by an asterisk.

Truncation or blank padding is done when necessary, as described earlier for assignment statements. For example, if `Units_1` and `Units_2` have been declared by

```
CHARACTER(8) :: Units_1, Units_2
```

then entering the values

```
meter, centimeter
```

in response to the statement

```
READ *, Units_1, Units_2
```

assigns the value "meter♭♭♭" to `Units_1` (where ♭ denotes a blank) and the value "centimet" to `Units_2`.

In an interactive mode of operation, the values assigned to variables in an input list are entered during program execution. In this case, when a `READ` statement is encountered, program execution is suspended while the user enters values for all the variables in the input list. Program execution then automatically resumes. Because execution is interrupted by a `READ` statement, and because the correct number and types of values must be entered before execution can resume, *it is good practice to provide some message to prompt the user when it is necessary to enter data values.* This is done by preceding each `READ` statement with a `PRINT` or `WRITE` statement that displays the appropriate prompts. The program in Figure 2.1 illustrates this by prompting the user when values for `InitialHeight`, `InitialVelocity`, and `Time` are to be entered.

Figure 2.1.   Projectile problem

```
PROGRAM Projectile
!-----------------------------------------------------------------
! This program calculates the velocity and height of a projectile
! given its initial height, initial velocity, and constant
! acceleration. Identifiers used are:
!
!   InitialHeight   : initial height of projectile (meters)
!   Height          : height at any time (meters)
!   InitialVelocity : initial vertical velocity (m/sec)
!   Velocity        : vertical velocity at any time (m/sec)
!   Acceleration    : vertical acceleration (m/sec/sec)
!   Time            : time since launch (seconds)
! Input:  InitialHeight, InitialVelocity, Time
! Output: Velocity, Height
!-----------------------------------------------------------------
```

```
IMPLICIT NONE
REAL :: InitialHeight, Height, InitialVelocity, Velocity, &
        Acceleration = -9.80665, Time

! Obtain values for InitialHeight, InitialVelocity, and Time
PRINT *, "Enter the initial height (m) and velocity (m/sec):"
READ *, InitialHeight, InitialVelocity
PRINT*, "Enter time in seconds at which to calculate height and
         velocity:"
READ*, Time

! Calculate the height and velocity
Height = 0.5 * Acceleration * Time ** 2 &
         + InitialVelocity * Time + InitialHeight
Velocity = Acceleration * Time + InitialVelocity

! Display Velocity and Height
PRINT*, "At time", Time, "seconds"
PRINT*, "the vertical velocity is", Velocity, "m/sec"
PRINT*, "and the height is", Height, "meters"

END PROGRAM Projectile
```

Sample runs:

```
Enter the initial height (m) and velocity (m/sec):
100.0 90.0
Enter time in seconds at which to calculate height and velocity:
4.5
At time 4.5000000 seconds
the vertical velocity is 45.8700752 m/sec
and the height is 4.0570767E+02 meters
Enter the initial height (m) and velocity (m/sec):
150.0 100.0
Enter time in seconds at which to calculate height and velocity:
5.0
At time 5.0000000 seconds
the vertical velocity is 50.9667511 m/sec
and the height is 5.2741687E+02 meters

Enter the initial height (m) and velocity (m/sec):
150.0 100.0
Enter time in seconds at which to calculate height and velocity:
0
At time 0.0000000E+00 seconds
the vertical velocity is 1.0000000E+02 m/sec
and the height is 1.5000000E+02 meters

Enter the initial height (m) and velocity (m/sec):
150.0 100.0
Enter time in seconds at which to calculate height and velocity:
21.75
At time 21.7500000 seconds
the vertical velocity is -1.1329465E+02 m/sec
and the height is 5.4208984 meters
```

Figure 2.1 (cont.)

2.5 PROGRAM COMPOSITION AND FORMAT

The general form of a Fortran program is

heading
specification part
execution part
subprogram part
END PROGRAM statement

The **program heading** has the form

```
PROGRAM name
```

where name is a legal Fortran identifier. This statement marks the beginning of the program and gives it a name.

Following the PROGRAM statement, there should be **opening documentation** like that in Figure 2.1 that explains the purpose of the program, clarifies the choice of variable names, and provides other pertinent information about the program. This documentation consists of comments, which are preceded by an exclamation mark (!) and run to the end of the line. Comments can be used to clarify the purpose and structure of key parts of the program.

The **specification part** of a program must appear next. The first statement in this part should be

```
IMPLICIT NONE
```

to cancel the naming convention and ensure that all variables and constants are explicitly declared. These declarations are type statements such as

```
REAL :: InitialHeight, Height, InitialVelocity, Velocity, &
        Acceleration = -9.80665, Time
```

whose purpose is to specify the type of each of the variables used in the program. They also are placed in the specification part. The type statements we have considered thus far have the form

```
REAL :: list
```

for declaring real variables,

```
INTEGER :: list
```

for declaring integer variables, and

```
CHARACTER(LEN = n)::list
```

or

```
CHARACTER(n)::list
```

for declaring character variables.

Declarations of the form

```
type-specifier :: var₁ = const₁, . . . , varₙ = constₙ
```

may be included to initialize the values of variables at compile time. A declaration may also contain the PARAMETER attribute to associate names with constants to be used in the program. These declarations have the form

```
type-specifier, PARAMETER :: name₁ = const₁,..., nameₙ = constₙ
```

Fortran statements are classified as either executable or nonexecutable. **Non-executable statements** provide information that is used during compilation of a program, but they do not cause any specific action to be performed during execution. For example, the PROGRAM statement and type statements are nonexecutable statements.

Statements that specify actions to be performed during execution of the program such as assignment statements and input/output statements are placed in the **execution part** of a program. These may be followed by a **subprogram section** that contains internal subprograms, as described in Chapter 6.

The last statement in every program must be the END PROGRAM **statement**. This statement indicates to the compiler the end of the program; it also halts execution of the program.

Execution can also be terminated with a STOP **statement** of the form

```
STOP
```

or

```
STOP constant
```

where constant is an integer constant or a character constant. The constant will be displayed when execution is terminated by a STOP statement of the second form, but the precise form of the termination message depends on the compiler.[1]

Program Format

Although earlier versions of Fortran had rather strict rules about where statements and comments were placed, Fortran 90 allows considerably more flexibility in the program format. The main rules that must be followed are

- A line may have a maximum of 132 characters.

- A line may contain more than one statement, provided the statements are separated by semicolons. It is good practice, however, to put at most one statement per line.

- An ampersand (&) must be placed at the end of each line that is to be continued to the next line. At most 39 continuation lines are permitted.

- If a character string must be continued from one line to the next, an ampersand must be placed at the end of the line containing the first part of the string, and another ampersand must be placed before the first character of the continuation of the string; for example,

  ```
  PRINT *, "Enter the initial height (m) and &
           &the initial velocity (m/sec):"
  ```

- Any characters following an exclamation mark (!)—except within a string constant—and running to the end of the line form a comment. For example,

  ```
  ! This program displays a table of conversion formulas
  ```

- is a comment line. Comments may also be attached to statements; for example,

  ```
  INTEGER :: Number ! Number of data values read
  ```

- If a statement requires a **statement label**, this label must precede the statement and must be separated from it by at least one blank. Statement labels must be integers in the range 1 through 99999.

---

[1] Some compilers require that a STOP statement be placed before the END statement to stop program execution.

PRACTICE!

1. Name the parts of a Fortran program.
2. How are comments indicated?
3. (True or false)   Each execution of a PRINT statement produces output on a new line.
4. (True or false)   Data values for a READ statement must be entered on the same line.
5. (True or false)   Entries in a line of input data must be separated by commas.
6. (True or false)   Every program must have a heading.
7. (True or false)   Execution of an END PROGRAM statement halts program execution.
8. What output does the statement PRINT * produce?
9. What output (if any) will the following program produce?

```
PROGRAM Demonstration

  IMPLICIT NONE
  INTEGER :: I, J
  REAL :: X, Y
  X = 37
  I = INT(X / 5)
  PRINT *, X, I
  READ *, X, I
  PRINT *, "X = ", X, " I = ", I
  READ *, Y
  READ *, J
  PRINT *, Y
  PRINT *, J

END PROGRAM Demonstration
```

Assume that the data values are entered as follows:

```
1.74 29
4.23 10
15
```

As you gain programming experience, you will no doubt notice that there is more than one method available to solve most computer problems. For example, sorting can be accomplished using the selection or quick sort algorithms described in the text, or other methods such as the bubble, heap, and straight insertion sorts. What frequently dictates algorithm choice is space (memory) and computation requirements. Often, algorithms require extra space for the storage of intermediate results so that they may be retained for alter reuse. These auxiliary space require-

ments will differ among algorithms. For instance, when using the secant method to calculate the roots of an equation, two previously calculated values must be retained, while the Newton-Raphson method requires saving only the most recent intermediate result. The Newton-Raphson method is therefore more space efficient than the secant method. Computation requirements refer to the number of *operations*, or basic tasks, the computer must perform to complete a job. The straight inserion method of sorting, for example, requires on the order of N^2 swaps (number of swaps required is CN^2, where C is a

*All Professional Success boxed material was contributed by Jack Leifer, University of South Carolina—Aiken.

constant) to arrange an array of N values in ascending or descending order; the quick sort method generally requires on the order of $N\log_2 N$ operations to order the same array. The quick sort algorithm is therefore more efficient. Space and computation efficiency must always be considered when designing software, however, these issues are most crucial in applications where complex code interacts with large databases.

APPLICATION: TEMPERATURE CONVERSION

PROBLEM

A program is needed that will convert a Celsius temperature to the corresponding Fahrenheit temperature.

Solution

Specification.   It is clear that the input for this problem is a temperature on the Celsius scale and the output is a temperature on the Fahrenheit scale:

Input: A Celsius temperature

Output: A Fahrenheit temperature

Design.   An initial description of an algorithm for solving this problem is straightforward:

1.   Obtain the Celsius temperature.
2.   Calculate the corresponding Fahrenheit temperature.
3.   Display the Fahrenheit temperature.

Here, steps 1 and 3 are easy to implement using input and output statements. Step 2, however, requires some refinement, because we need a formula for converting a Celsius temperature into the equivalent Fahrenheit temperature. This well-known formula is

$$F = \frac{9}{5}C + 32$$

In a program to solve this problem, variables must be used to store two temperatures. We will use the following self-documenting names:

VARIABLES FOR TEMPERATURE PROBLEM

Celsius   Temperature on the Celsius scale

Fahrenheit   Temperature on the Fahrenheit scale

A final version of the algorithm in pseudocode can now be given:

ALGORITHM FOR TEMPERATURE PROBLEM

This algorithm converts a temperature of *Celsius* degrees on the Celsius scale to the corresponding *Fahrenheit* degrees on the Fahrenheit scale.

Input: A temperature in degrees Celsius

Output: A temperature in degrees Fahrenheit

1.   Enter *Celsius*.
2.   Calculate the Fahrenheit temperature:

$$Fahrenheit = \frac{9}{5}Celcius + 32$$

3.   Display *Fahrenheit*.

Program Coding.   The program in Figure 2.2 is a first attempt to implement this algorithm. Note that the opening documentation contains a brief description of the program, a variable directory that explains what each variable represents, and the input/output specifications. Such documentation is important because it provides a brief summary of what the program does and makes it easier to read and understand the program itself.

```fortran
PROGRAM Temperature_Conversion_1
!------------------------------------------------------------------
! Program to convert a temperature on the Celsius scale to the
! corresponding temperature on the Fahrenheit scale.
! Variables used are:
!    Celsius     : temperature on the Celsius scale
!    Fahrenheit : temperature on the Fahrenheit scale
!
! Input: Celsius
! Output: Fahrenheit
!------------------------------------------------------------------

   IMPLICIT NONE
   REAL :: Celsius, Fahrenheit

   ! Obtain Celsius temperature
   PRINT *, "Enter temperature in degrees Celsius:"
   READ *, Celsius

   ! Calculate corresponding Fahrenheit temperature
   Fahrenheit = (9/5) * Celsius + 32.0

   ! Display temperatures
   PRINT *, Celsius, "degrees Celsius =", &
            Fahrenheit, "degrees Fahrenheit"

END PROGRAM Temperature_Conversion_1
```

Figure 2.2.   Temperature conversion—a first attempt

Execution and Testing.   Beginning programmers are sometimes tempted to skip the testing phase of program development. Once a program has compiled without errors, they are content simply to execute the program using the input data given in the assignment and then hand in the output. For example, if the program is to be used to convert the three Celsius temperatures 11.193, −17.728, and 49.1 into Fahrenheit temperatures, a student might simply execute the program three times and hand in the output produced:

```
Enter temperature in degrees Celsius:
11.193
 11.1929998 degrees Celsius = 43.1930008 degrees Fahrenheit

Enter temperature in degrees Celsius:
-17.728
-17.7280006 degrees Celsius = 14.2719994 degrees Fahrenheit

Enter temperature in degrees Celsius:
49.1
 49.0999985 degrees Celsius = 81.0999985 degrees Fahrenheit
```

The fact that the program compiled without errors is no guarantee that it is correct, however, because it may contain logical errors. As we noted in Chapter 1, program testing is extremely important. Programs should be executed with test data for which the output produced can be verified by hand. For this program, we might first use an input value of 0 since it is easy to check that 0° C corresponds to 32° F.

Test Run #1:
```
Enter temperature in degrees Celsius:
0
    0.0000000E+00 degrees Celsius =  32.0000000 degrees Fahrenheit
```

We see that the program has indeed produced the correct answer. However, we cannot be confident that a program is correct simply because it executes correctly for one set of test data.

Another natural test value to use for the temperature-conversion program is 100° C, which corresponds to 212° F.

Figure 2.3. Temperature conversion—final version

```
PROGRAM Temperature_Conversion_2
!-------------------------------------------------------------
!Program to convert a temperature on the Celsius scale to the
!corresponding temperature on the Fahrenheit scale.
!Variables used are:
!  Celsius     : temperature on the Celsius scale
!  Fahrenheit : temperature on the Fahrenheit scale
!
!Input:  Celsius
!Output: Fahrenheit
!-------------------------------------------------------------

  IMPLICIT NONE
  REAL :: Celsius, Fahrenheit

  ! Obtain Celsius temperature
  PRINT *, "Enter temperature in degrees Celsius:"
  READ *, Celsius

  ! Calculate corresponding Fahrenheit temperature
  Fahrenheit = 1.8 * Celsius + 32.0

  ! Display temperatures
  PRINT *, Celsius, "degrees Celsius =', &
           Fahrenheit, "degrees Fahrenheit"

END PROGRAM Temperature_Conversion_2
```

Test Run #2:
```
Enter temperature in degrees Celsius:
100
    1.0000000E+02 degrees Celsius =   1.3200000E+02 degrees Fahrenheit
```

From this test run we see that the program is not correct. In fact, additional test runs will show that each output value is simply 32 plus the input value.

A review of the algorithm indicates that it is correct; thus, the error apparently did not occur in the design stage. The error must therefore have occurred in the coding step. The statement that is suspect is the one that carries out the conversion:

```
Fahrenheit = (9/5) * Celsius + 32
```

The fact that each output value is simply 32 plus the input value suggests that the Celsius temperature `Celsius` is being multiplied by 1 instead of by 1.8 (5 9/5). This is indeed the case since the integer division 9/5 in this expression produces the value 1.

Making this correction gives the program in Figure 2.3. (A version that uses repetition to process several temperatures is given in Section 4.3.)

The following test runs suggest that the program is correct:

Test Run #1:

```
Enter temperature in degrees Celsius:
0
  0.0000000E+00 degrees Celsius =  32.0000000 degrees Fahrenheit
```

Test Run #2:

```
Enter temperature in degrees Celsius:
100
  1.0000000E+02 degrees Celsius =   2.1200000E+02 degrees Fahrenheit
```

After several more successful test runs have been made, so that we are confident the program is correct, we can execute the program with the given input values and be quite sure that the output values are correct:

```
Enter temperature in degrees Celsius:
11.193
  11.1929998 degrees Celsius =  52.1473999 degrees Fahrenheit

Enter temperature in degrees Celsius:
-17.728
-17.7280006 degrees Celsius =   8.9599609E-02 degrees Fahrenheit

Enter temperature in degrees Celsius:
49.1
  49.0999985 degrees Celsius =   1.2038000E+02 degrees Fahrenheit
```

KEY TERMS

Assignment statement	INTEGER statement	Real data
Assumed length specifier	List-directed input	REAL statement
Character constant (string)	List-directed output	Specification part
Concatenation	Mixed-mode expression	Statement label
END PROGRAM statement	Named constant	STOP statement
Executable statement	Nonexecutable statement	Subprogram section
Execution part	Opening documentation	Substring
Function	PARAMETER attribute	Type statement
Identifier	PRINT statement	Unary operator
Implicit naming convention	Priority rule	Variable
IMPLICIT NONE statement	Program heading	
Integer	READ statement	

PROGRAMMING POINTERS

In this section we consider some aspects of program design and suggest guidelines for good programming style. We also point out some errors that may occur when writing Fortran programs.

Program Style and Design.   Programs must be *correct, readable, and understandable*. There are several basic principles for developing such programs.

1. *Programs cannot be considered correct until they have been validated using test data.* Test all programs with data for which the results are known or can be checked by hand calculation.

2. *Programs should be well structured.* Two helpful guidelines in this regard are as follows:

    *   *Use a top-down approach when developing a program for a complex problem.* Divide the problem into simpler and simpler subproblems until the solution of these subproblems is clear.

    *   *Strive for simplicity and clarity.* Avoid clever programming tricks intended only to demonstrate the programmer's ingenuity or to produce code that executes only slightly faster.

3. *Each program unit should be documented.* In particular:

    *   *Include opening documentation* to explain what the program does, how it works, special algorithms it uses, a specification of the problem, assumptions, the name of the programmer, when the program was written and/or last modified, references to books and manuals that give additional information about the program, explanations of the variables being used in the program, and so on.

    *   *Use comments to explain key program segments and/or segments whose purpose or design is not obvious.*

    *   *Use meaningful identifiers.* For example, the statement

            Distance = Rate * Time

        is more meaningful than

            D = R * T

        or

            X7 = R * Zeke

        Don't use "skimpy" abbreviations just to save a few keystrokes. Also, avoid "cute" identifiers, as in

            HowFar = GoGo * Squeal

    *   *Label all output produced by a program.* For example,

            PRINT *, 'Rate =', 'Rate, ' Time =', Time

        produces more informative output than

            PRINT *, 'Rate, Time

4. *A program should be formatted in a style that enhances its readability.* Some guidelines for good program style are as follows:

    *   *Use spaces between the items in a statement to make it more readable,* for example, before and after each operator (+, −, =, etc.).

    *   *Insert a blank line between sections of a program and wherever appropriate in a sequence of statements to set off blocks of statements.*

    *   *Adhere rigorously to alignment and indentation guidelines to emphasize the relationship between various parts of the program.*

    *   *Break up long expressions into simpler subexpressions.*

5. *Programs should be readable and understandable.*
   - *Do not use "magic numbers" that suddenly appear without explanation,* as in the statement

     ```
     Output = 0.1237 * Amount + 1.34E-5
     ```

     If these numbers must be changed, someone must search through the program to determine what they represent and which ones should be changed and to locate all their occurrences. Thus, it is better to associate them with named constants, as in

     ```
     REAL, PARAMETER :: Rate = 0.1758, Error = 1.34E-5
     ```

     or assign them to variables, as in

     ```
     REAL :: Rate = 0.1758, Error = 1.34E-5
     ```

   - *Use comments to describe the purpose of a program, the meaning of variables, and the purpose of key program segments.* However, do not clutter the program with needless comments; for example, the comment in

     ```
     ! Add 1 to Count
       Count = Count + 1
     ```

     is not helpful in explaining the statement that follows it and so should be omitted.
   - *Label all output produced by a program.* For example,

     ```
     PRINT *, "Rate =", Rate, " Time =", Time
     ```

     produces more informative output than does

     ```
     PRINT *, Rate, Time
     ```

6. *Programs should be general and flexible.* They should solve a class of problems rather than one specific problem. It should be relatively easy to modify a program to solve a related problem without changing much of the program. Avoiding the use of magic numbers, as described in 5, is important in this regard.

Potential Problems

1. *Do not confuse* I *or* l *(lowercase "ell") and* 1 *or* 0 *(zero) and* O *(the letter "oh").*
2. *String constants must be enclosed between double quotes or between apostrophes.* If the beginning quote and the ending quote are different or if either is missing, an error will result.
3. *If a string constant must be broken at the end of a line, an ampersand (&) must be placed after the last character on that line and another ampersand before the first character on the next line.*
4. *All multiplications must be indicated by* *. For example, 2 * N is valid, but 2N is not.
5. *Division of integers produces an integer.* For example, 1 / 2 has the value 0. Similarly, if N is an integer variable greater than 1, 1/N will have the value 0.
6. *Parentheses in expressions must be paired.* For each left parenthesis there must be a matching right parenthesis that appears later in the expression.
7. *The values of named constants may not be changed.* Any attempt to do so produces a compile-time error.

8. *All variables are initially undefined.* For example, the statement `Y = X + 1` usually produces a "garbage" value for `Y` if `X` has not previously been assigned a value.

9. *Initializations in declarations are done only once, during compilation, before execution of the program begins.* (See also Potential Problem 3 in the Programming Pointers of Chapter 4.)

10. *A value assigned to a variable must be of a type that is appropriate to the type of the variable.*

11. *Mixed-mode assignment must be used with care.*

12. *In assignment statements and in list-directed input, if a character value being assigned or read has a length greater than that specified for the character variable, the rightmost characters are truncated.* If the value has a length less than that specified for the variable, blanks are added at the right.

13. *Use* `IMPLICIT NONE` *to prevent a variable from being implicitly typed by the Fortran naming convention.* Types of all variables should be declared in type statements.

14. *A comma must precede the input/output list in input/output statements of the form*

```
READ *, input-list
PRINT *, output-list
```

Programming Problems

1. Write a program to read values for the three sides a, b, and c of a triangle and then calculate its perimeter and its area. These should be displayed together with the values of a, b, and c using appropriate labels. (For the area, you might use Hero's formula for the area of a triangle:

$$\text{area} = \sqrt{s(s-a)(s-b)(s-c)}$$

where s is one-half the perimeter.)

2. The current in an alternating current circuit that contains resistance, capacitance, and inductance in series is given by

$$I = \frac{E}{\sqrt{R^2 + (2\pi fL - 1/(2\pi fC))^2}}$$

where I = current (amperes), E = voltage (volts), R = resistance (ohms), L = inductance (henrys), C = capacitance (farads), and f = frequency (hertz). Write a program that reads values for the voltage, resistance, capacitance, and frequency and then calculates and displays the current.

3. At t seconds after firing, the horizontal displacement x and the vertical displacement y (in feet) of a rocket are given by

$$x = v_0 t \cos \theta$$

$$y = v_0 t \sin \theta - 16t_2$$

where v_0 is the initial velocity (ft/sec) and θ is the angle at which the rocket is fired. Write a program that reads values for v_0, θ, and t, calculates x and y using these formulas, and displays these values.

4. The equation of the curve formed by a hanging cable weighing w pounds per foot of length can be described by

$$y = a \cosh \frac{x}{a}$$

where $a = H/w$, with H representing the horizontal tension pulling on the cable at its low point, and cosh is the hyperbolic cosine function. Write a program that reads values of w, H, and x and calculates and displays the corresponding value of y.

5. The period of a pendulum is given by the formula

$$P = 2\pi \sqrt{\frac{L}{g}\left(1 + \frac{1}{4}\sin^2\left(\frac{\alpha}{2}\right)\right)}$$

where

g = 980 cm/sec²
L = pendulum length (cm)
α = angle of displacement

Write a program to read values for L and a and then calculate and display the period of a pendulum having this length and angle of displacement. Run your program with the following input:

L (CM)	α (DEGREES)
120	15
90	20
60	5
74.6	10
83.6	12

6. A containing tank is to be constructed that will hold 500 cubic meters of oil when filled. The shape of the tank is to be a cylinder (including a base) surmounted by a cone, whose height is equal to its radius. The material and labor costs to construct the cylindrical portion of the tank are $300 per square meter, and the costs for the conical top are $400 per square meter. Write a program that calculates and displays the heights of the cylinder and the cone for a given radius that is input and that also calculates and displays the total cost of constructing the tank. Starting with a radius of 4.0 meters and incrementing by various (small) step sizes, run your program several times to determine the dimensions of the tank that will cost the least.

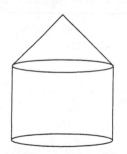

7. The castings produced at Dispatch Die-Casting must be shipped in special containers that are available in four sizes—huge, large, medium, and small—that can hold 50, 20, 5, and 1 castings, respectively. Write a program that reads the number of castings to be shipped and displays the number of containers needed to send the shipment most efficiently. The output for input value 598 should be similar to the following:

```
CONTAINER    NUMBER
===================
  HUGE          11
  LARGE          2
  MEDIUM         1
  SMALL          3
```

3

Selective Execution

3.1 LOGICAL EXPRESSIONS

Several of the Fortran statements used to implement selection and repetition structures involve logical expressions. Consequently, before we can describe these control structures, we must examine logical expressions in more detail.

Simple Logical Expressions

Logical expressions may be either **simple** or **compound**. Simple logical expressions are logical constants (`.TRUE.` and `.FALSE.`) or logical variables (see Section 3.7) or **relational expressions** of the form

> `expression relational-operator expression`

where both `expression₁` and `expression₂` are numeric or character (or logical) expressions, and the `relational-operator` may be any of the following:

SYMBOL	MEANING
`<` or `.LT.`	Is less than
`>` or `.GT.`	Is greater than
`==` or `.EQ.`	Is equal to
`<=` or `.LE.`	Is less than or equal to
`>=` or `.GE.`	Is greater than or equal to
`/=` or `.NE.`	Is not equal to

Note that there are two forms for each of the relational operators: a symbolic form and an abbreviated form of the operator's name. Since it promotes program readability, we will use only the symbolic forms in this text. *Note the double*

OBJECTIVES

In this chapter, you will

- Study how to construct logical expressions.
- Learn how to implement selection structures using an IF construct.
- Apply IF constructs to classify pollution indexes.
- See how IF-ELSE IF constructs can implement selection structures.
- Study the use of CASE constructs to implement selection structures.
- Learn about the LOGICAL data type.
- Apply the LOGICAL type to model a binary half-adder.

equal (==) used for equality; remember that a single equal (=) is the assignment opera-
tor.

The following are examples of simple logical expressions:

```
.TRUE.
X < 5.2
Number == -999
```

If X has the value 4.5, the logical expression X < 5.2 is true. If Number has the value 400, the logical expression Number == -999 is false. In logical expressions such as

```
B ** 2 >= 4.0 * A * C
```

which contain both arithmetic operators and relational operators, the arithmetic operations are performed first; that is, this logical expression is equivalent to

```
(B ** 2) >= (4.0 * A * C)
```

Thus, if A, B, and C have the values 2.0, 1.0, and 3.0, respectively, this logical expression is evaluated as

```
1.0 >= 24.0
```

which is clearly false.

For character data, numeric codes are used to establish an ordering for the character set. One of the most common standard coding schemes is ASCII, which uses codes in the range 0 through 255; for example, the codes for A, B, . . . , Z are 65, 66, 90, respectively, and the codes for a, b, . . . , z are 97, 98, . . . , 122, respectively.[1] Thus

```
"A" < "F"
"6" > "4"
```

are true logical expressions. Two strings are compared character by character using these numeric codes. For example,

```
"cat" < "dog"
```

is true, since c is less than d. If the first characters of the strings are the same, the second characters are compared; if they are the same, the third characters are compared, and so on. Thus,

```
"cat" < "cow"
```

is true, since a is less than o. Similarly,

```
"June" > "July"
```

is true, since n is greater than l. Two strings with different lengths are compared as though blanks are appended to the shorter string, resulting in two strings of equal length to be compared. For example, the logical expression

```
"cat" < "cattle"
```

is evaluated as

```
"catɃɃɃ" < "cattle"
```

(where Ƀ denotes a blank), which is true because a blank character precedes all letters.

---

[1] For a complete table of ASCII and EBCDIC codes, see Appendix A of our more comprehensive text, Larry Nyhoff and Sanford Leestma, *Fortran 90 for Engineers and Scientists* (Upper Saddle River, NJ: Prentice-Hall, 1996).

Compound Logical Expressions

Compound logical expressions are formed by combining logical expressions by using the **logical operators**

.NOT.	*(negation)*
.AND.	*(conjunction)*
.OR.	*(disjunction)*
.EQV.	*(equivalence)*
.NEQV.	*(nonequivalence)*

These operators are defined by the following **truth tables**, which display all possible values for the logical expressions p and q and the corresponding values of the compound logical expression:

p	.NOT. p
.TRUE.	.FALSE.
.FALSE.	.TRUE.

p	q	p .AND. q	p .OR. q	p .EQV. q	p .NEQV. q
.TRUE.	.TRUE.	.TRUE.	.TRUE.	.FALSE.	.TRUE.
.TRUE.	.FALSE.	.FALSE.	.TRUE.	.FALSE.	.TRUE.
.FALSE.	.TRUE.	.FALSE.	.TRUE.	.FALSE.	.TRUE.
.FALSE.	.FALSE.	.FALSE.	.FALSE.	.TRUE.	.FALSE.

If a logical expression contains arithmetic operators, relational operators, and logical operators, the operations are performed in the following order:

1. Arithmetic operations (and functions)
2. Relational operations
3. Logical operations in the order .NOT., .AND., .OR., .EQV. (or .NEQV.)

For example, if the integer variable N has the value 4, the logical expression

```
N**2 + 1 > 10 .AND. .NOT. N < 3
```

or with parentheses inserted to improve readability,

```
(N**2 + 1 > 10) .AND. .NOT. (N < 3)
```

is true. The logical expression

```
N == 3 .OR. N == 4
```

is valid and is true, whereas

```
N == 1 .OR. 2
```

is not, since this would be evaluated as

```
(N == 1) .OR. 2
```

and 2 is not a logical expression to which .OR. can be applied.

PRACTICE!

1. The two logical constants are _____ and _____ .
2. List the six relational operators.
3. List the five logical operators.

For Exercises 4–13, assume that M and N are integer variables with the values –5 and 8, respectively, and that X, Y, and Z are real variables with the values –3.56, 0.0, and 44.7, respectively. Find the value of the logical expression.

4. M <= N
5. 2 * ABS(M) <= 8
6. X * X < SQRT(Z)
7. NINT(Z) == (6 * N - 3)
8. (X <= Y) .AND. (Y <= Z)
9. .NOT. (X < Y)
10. .NOT. ((M <= N) .AND. (X + Z > Y))
11. .NOT. (M <= N) .OR..NOT. (X + Z > Y)
12. .NOT. ((M > N) .OR. (X < Z)) .EQV. &
     ((M <= N) .AND. (X >= Z))
13. .NOT. ((M > N) .AND. (X < Z)) .NEQV. &
     ((M <= N) .AND. (X >= Z))

For Exercises 14-22, write a logical expression to express the given condition.

14. X is greater than 3.
15. Y is strictly between 2 and 5.
16. R is negative and Z is positive.
17. Alpha and Beta are both positive.
18. Alpha and Beta have the same sign (both are negative or both are positive).
19. –5 < X < 5.
20. A is less than 6 or is greater than 10.
21. P = Q = R.
22. X is less than 3, or Y is less than 3, but not both.

For Exercises 23–25, assume that A, B, and C are logical expressions.

23. Write a logical expression that is true if and only if A and B are true and C is false.
24. Write a logical expression that is true if and only if A is true and at least one of B or C is true.
25. Write a logical expression that is true if and only if exactly one of A and B is true.

3.2 IF CONSTRUCTS

A **selection structure** selects one of several alternative sets of statements for execution. This selection is based on the value of a logical expression.

Simple IF Construct

In the simplest selection structure, a sequence of statements (also called a **block** of statements) is executed or bypassed depending on whether a given logical expression is true or false. This is pictured in the following diagram:

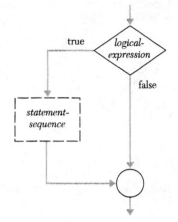

This selection structure is implemented in Fortran by using an IF **construct** (also called a **block** IF **construct**) of the form

```
IF (logical-expression) THEN
    statement-sequence
END IF
```

If the logical expression is true, the specified sequence of statements is executed; otherwise it is bypassed. In either case, execution continues with the statement in the program following the END IF. For example, in the IF construct

```
IF (X >= 0) THEN
    Y = X * X
    Z = SQRT(X)
END IF
```

the logical expression X >= 0 is evaluated, and if it is true, Y is set equal to the square of X and Z is set equal to the square root of X; otherwise, these assignment statements are not executed.

Fortran also provides a still simpler IF construct that can be used if the statement sequence consists of a single statement. This short form is called a **logical** IF **statement** and has the following form:

```
IF (logical-expression) statement
```

If the logical expression is true, the specified statement is executed; otherwise it is bypassed. In either case, execution continues with the next statement in the program. For example, in the logical IF statement

```
IF (1.5 <= X .AND. X <= 2.5) PRINT *, X
```

if $1.5 \le X \le 2.5$, the value of X is displayed; otherwise, the PRINT statement is bypassed. In either case, execution continues with the next statement in the program.

General Form of the IF Construct

In the preceding selection structure, the selection is made between (1) executing a given sequence of statements and (2) bypassing these statements. In the two-way selection pictured in the following diagram, the selection is made between (1) executing one sequence (block) of statements and (2) executing a different sequence (block) of statements.

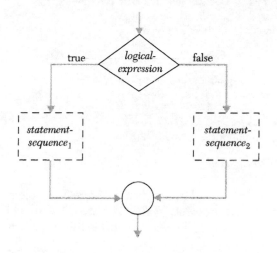

This selection structure is implemented in Fortran by an IF construct of the form

```
IF (logical-expression) THEN
    statement-sequence₁
ELSE
    statement-sequence₂
END IF
```

If the logical expression is true, `statement-sequence₁` is executed and `statement-sequence₂` is bypassed. If the logical expression is false, `statement-sequence₁` is bypassed; if there is an `ELSE` part, `statement-sequence₂` is executed; otherwise, execution will simply continue with the next statement following the `END IF` statement that terminates the IF construct. In either case, execution continues with the next statement in the program (unless, of course, execution is terminated or control is transferred elsewhere).

Example: Quadratic Equations

As an illustration of using an IF construct to implement a two-alternative selection structure, consider the problem of solving the quadratic equation

$$Ax^2 + Bx + C = 0$$

by using the quadratic formula to obtain the roots

$$\frac{-B \pm \sqrt{B^2 - 4AC}}{2A}$$

In this problem, the input values are the coefficients A, B, and C of the quadratic equation, and the output is the pair of real roots or a message indicating that there are no real roots (in case $B^2 - 4AC$ is negative). An algorithm for solving a quadratic equation is as follows:

ALGORITHM FOR SOLVING QUADRATIC EQUATIONS

This algorithm solves a quadratic equation $Ax^2 + Bx + C = 0$ using the quadratic formula. If the discriminant $Discriminant = B^2 - 4AC$ is nonnegative, the pair of real roots $Root\_1$ and $Root\_2$ is calculated; otherwise, a message is displayed indicating that there are no real roots.

Input: The coefficients A, B, and C

Output: The roots of the equation or the (negative) discriminant and a no-real-roots message

1. Enter A, B, and C.
2. Calculate $Discriminant = B ** 2 - 4 * A * C$.

3. If $Discriminant \geq 0$ then do the following:
   a. Calculate $Discriminant = \sqrt{Discriminant}$.
   b. Calculate $Root\_1 = (-B + Discriminant) / (2 * A)$.
   c. Calculate $Root\_2 = (-B - Discriminant) / (2 * A)$.
   d. Display $Root\_1$ and $Root\_2$.
   Else do the following:
   a. Display $Discriminant$.
   b. Display a message that there are no real roots.

The program in Figure 3.1 implements this algorithm. Note the indentation of the statements in the IF construct. Although not required, it is good programming style to set off these statements in this manner to emphasize that they constitute a single block.

Figure 3.1. Quadratic equations

```
PROGRAM QuadraticEquations_1
!------------------------------------------------------------------
! Program to solve a quadratic equation using the quadratic formula.
! Variables used are:
!    A, B, C          : the coefficients of the quadratic equation
!    Discriminant   : the discriminant, B**2 - 4.0*A*C
!    Root_1, Root_2 : the two roots of the equation
!
! Input:  The coefficients A, B, and C
! Output: The two roots of the equation or the (negative) discriminant
!         and a message indicating that there are no real roots
!------------------------------------------------------------------

  IMPLICIT NONE
  REAL :: A, B, C, Discriminant, Root_1, Root_2

  ! Get the coefficients
  PRINT *, "Enter the coefficients of the quadratic equation:"
  READ *, A, B, C

  ! Calculate the discriminant
  Discriminant = B**2 - 4.0*A*C

  ! Check if discriminant is nonnegative. If it is, calculate and
  ! display the roots. Otherwise, display the value of the discriminant
  ! and a no-real-roots message.
  IF (Discriminant >= 0) THEN
     Discriminant = SQRT(Discriminant)
     Root_1 = (-B + Discriminant) / (2.0 * A)
     Root_2 = (-B - Discriminant) / (2.0 * A)
     PRINT *, "The roots are", Root_1, Root_2
```

```
    ELSE
       PRINT *, "Discriminant is", Discriminant
       PRINT *, "There are no real roots"
    END IF

END PROGRAM QuadraticEquations_1
```

Sample runs:

```
Enter the coefficients of the quadratic equation:
1, -5, 6
The roots are    3.0000000    2.0000000

Enter the coefficients of the quadratic equation:
1, 0, -4
The roots are    2.0000000   -2.0000000

Enter the coefficients of the quadratic equation:
1, 0, 4
Discriminant is -16.0000000
There are no real roots

Enter the coefficients of the quadratic equation:
3.7, 16.5, 1.7
The roots are  -0.1055275   -4.3539319
```

Figure 3.1   (cont.)

PROFESSIONAL SUCCESS: ALGORITHMS*

Algorithms, namely the step-by-step procedures required to solve a problem, encompass the heart of all computer programs. Every computer program in this book may be regarded as a collection of interconnected algorithms which have been translated from pseudocode (or English) into the appropriate Fortran 90 commands. Testing an algorithm before translating it into a program is vital, as it is unreasonable to expect that a program will function properly if the underlying algorithm is incorrect. One means of accomplishing this is to "run" the algorithm by hand, using pencil and paper to perform the calculations. For each step of the algorithm, the input and output data flow, as well as all the calculations, must be monitored to ensure that the error-free results are produced.

Where do algorithms come from? Often, they are constructed by simply breaking a complex problem into small steps, each of which can be performed in sequence by a computer. Many times, however, the sequential steps necessary to solve a problem will not be obvious. One such case is the problem of finding the roots of a polynomial. For problems such as that, specialized procedures (such as the well-known Newton-Raphson method for the polynomial example) have been developed, and may be obtained from any numerical methods reference. These procedures generally require repeated operations that, once expressed in step-by-step algorithmic form, can easily be translated into pseudocode, and then Fortran 90.

*All Professional Success boxed material was contributed by Jack Leifer, University of South Carolina—Aiken.

APPLICATION: POLLUTION INDEX

PROBLEM

The level of air pollution in the city of Dogpatch is measured by a pollution index. Readings are made at 12:00 P.M. at three locations: at the Abner Coal Plant; downtown at the corner of Daisy Avenue and 5th Street; and at a randomly selected location in a residential area.

The integer average of these three readings is the pollution index, and a value of 50 parts per million or greater for this index indicates a hazardous condition, whereas values lower than 50 parts per million indicate a safe condition. Because this index must be calculated daily, the Dogpatch environmental statistician would like a program that calculates the pollution index and then determines the appropriate condition, safe or hazardous.

Solution

Specification. The relevant given information consists of three pollution readings and the cutoff value used to distinguish between safe and hazardous conditions. A solution to the problem consists of the pollution index and a message indicating the condition. Generalizing so that any cutoff value, not just 50, can be used, we can specify the problem as follows:

Input:	Three pollution readings
Constant:	Cutoff value to distinguish between safe and hazardous conditions
Output:	Pollution index = integer average of the pollution readings Condition: safe or hazardous

Design. The first step in an algorithm to solve this problem is to obtain values for the input items-the three pollution readings. The next step is to calculate the pollution index by averaging the three readings. An appropriate air-quality message must then be displayed. Thus, an initial description of an algorithm is

1. Obtain the three pollution readings.
2. Calculate the pollution index.
3. Display an appropriate air-quality message.

Coding step 1 is straightforward, but steps 2 and 3 require some refinement. For step 2, once the three pollution readings have been entered, we need only add them and divide the sum by 3 to obtain their average. We will use the following identifiers to store the input values, the cutoff value, and the pollution index:

IDENTIFIERS FOR POLLUTION-INDEX PROBLEM

Level_1, Level_2, Level_3	Three pollution readings
Cutoff	Cutoff value
Index	Pollution index

In step 3, one of two possible actions must be selected. Either a message indicating a safe condition

Smog over Los Angeles, California. (Photo courtesy of Uniphoto Picture Agency)

or a message indicating a hazardous condition must be displayed. The appropriate action is selected by comparing the pollution index with the cutoff value. A refined version of step 3 might thus be written in pseudocode as

If *Index* ≤ *Cutoff* then
>   Display "Safe condition"

Else
>   Display "Hazardous condition"

A final version of the algorithm can now be given:

ALGORITHM FOR POLLUTION-INDEX PROBLEM

This algorithm reads three pollution levels and then calculates a pollution index, which is the integer average of these three readings. If this index is less than a specified cutoff value, a message indicating a safe condition is displayed; otherwise, a message indicating a hazardous condition is displayed.

Input: *Level_1, Level_2, Level_3*
Constant: *Cutoff*
Output: The pollution *Index* and a message indicating the air quality

1. Enter *Level_1, Level_2,* and *Level_3*.

2. Calculate
$$Index = \frac{Level\_1 + Level\_2 + Level\_3}{3}.$$

3. If *Index* ≤ *Cutoff* then
>   Display "Safe condition"

   Else
>   Display "Hazardous condition"

Coding.   The Fortran program in Figure 3.2 implements the preceding algorithm. The cutoff point is stored as a named constant `Cutoff` so that it can be easily modified later if necessary. The selection structure

If *Index* ≤ *Cutoff* then
>   Display "Safe condition"

Else
>   Display "Hazardous condition"

in the algorithm is implemented in the Fortran program by the following `IF` construct:

```
IF (Index < Cutoff) THEN
    PRINT *, "Safe condition"
ELSE
    PRINT *, "Hazardous condition"
END IF
```

Figure 3.2.   Pollution index

```
PROGRAM Pollution
!-------------------------------------------------------------------
! Program that reads 3 pollution levels, calculates a pollution
! index as their integer average, and then displays an appropriate
! air-quality message. Identifiers used are:
!   Level_1, Level_2, Level_3 : the three pollution levels
!   Cutoff : a cutoff value that distinguishes between hazardous
!               and safe conditions (constant)
!   Index  : the integer average of the pollution levels
!
! Input:    The three pollution levels
! Constant: The cutoff value (parts per million)
! Output:   The pollution index and a "safe condition" message if
!           this index is less than the cutoff value, otherwise a
!           "hazardous condition" message
!-------------------------------------------------------------------

  IMPLICIT NONE
  INTEGER :: Level_1, Level_2, Level_3, Index
  INTEGER, PARAMETER :: Cutoff = 50
```

```
            ! Get the 3 pollution readings
            PRINT *, "Enter 3 pollution readings (parts per million):"
            READ *, Level_1, Level_2, Level_3

            ! Calculate the pollution index
            Index = (Level_1 + Level_2 + Level_3) / 3

            ! Check if the pollution index is less than the cutoff and
            ! display an appropriate air-quality message
            IF (Index < Cutoff) THEN
                PRINT *, "Safe condition"
            ELSE
                PRINT *, "Hazardous condition"
            END IF

    END PROGRAM Pollution
```

Figure 3.2 (cont.)

Execution and Testing. Test runs with input data like the following indicate that the program is correct:

```
Enter 3 pollution readings (parts per million):
1, 2, 3
Safe condition

Enter 3 pollution readings (parts per million):
50, 60, 70
Hazardous condition
```

It can then be used to calculate pollution indices and conditions for other inputs such as

```
Enter 3 pollution readings (parts per million):
55, 39, 48
Safe condition

Enter 3 pollution readings (parts per million):
68, 49, 57
Hazardous condition
```

3.3 `IF-ELSE IF` CONSTRUCTS

The selection structures considered thus far have involved selecting one of two alternatives. It is also possible to use the `IF` construct to design selection structures that contain more than two alternatives. For example, a three-alternative selection structure can be implemented using an `IF` construct of the form

```
IF (logical-expression1) THEN
    statement-sequence₁
ELSE
    IF (logical-expression₂) THEN
        statement-sequence₂
    ELSE
        statement-sequence₃
    END IF
END IF
```

However, compound `IF` constructs that implement selection structures with many alternatives can become quite complex, and the correspondence among the `IF`s, `ELSE`s, and `END` `IF`s may not be clear, especially if the statements are not indented properly. A better format that clarifies the correspondence between `IF`s and `ELSE`s and also emphasizes that the statement implements a **multialternative selection structure** is an `IF-ELSE IF` **construct**:

```
If (logical-expression₁) THEN
    statement-sequence₁
ELSE IF statement-sequence₂) THEN
    statement-sequence₂
ELSE IF (logical-expression₃) THEN
    statement-sequence₃
        ⋮
ELSE
    statement-sequenceₙ
END IF
```

When an `IF-ELSE IF` construct is executed, the logical expressions are evaluated to determine the first expression that is true; the associated sequence of statements is executed, and execution then continues with the next statement following the construct (unless one of these statements transfers control elsewhere or terminates execution). If none of the logical expressions is true, the statement sequence associated with the `ELSE` statement is executed, and execution then continues with the statement following the construct (unless it is terminated or transferred to some other point by a statement in this block). This `IF` construct thus implements an n-way selection structure in which exactly one of `statement-sequence₁`, `statement-sequence₂`,…,`statement-sequenceₙ` is executed.

Example: Modified Pollution-Index Problem

As an example of an `IF-ELSE IF` construct, suppose that in the pollution-index problem of the preceding section, three air-quality conditions—good, fair, and poor—are to be used instead of two—safe and hazardous. Two cutoff values will be used, *LowCutoff* and *HighCutoff*, both in parts per million. A pollution index less than *LowCutoff* indicates a good condition; an index between *LowCutoff* and *HighCutoff* a fair condition; and an index greater than *HighCutoff* a poor condition. The following algorithm solves this problem.

ALGORITHM FOR MODIFIED POLLUTION-INDEX PROBLEM

This algorithm reads three pollution levels and then calculates a pollution index, which is the integer average of these three readings. If this index is less than a specified cutoff value, a message indicating a good condition is displayed; if it is between this cutoff value and a larger one, a message indicating a fair condition is displayed; and if the index is greater than the larger cutoff value, a message indicating a poor condition is displayed.

Input: *Level_1, Level_2, Level_3*
Constants: *LowCutoff* and *HighCutoff*
Output: The pollution *Index* and a message indicating the air quality

1. Enter *Level_1, Level_2,* and *Level_3*.

2. Calculate *Index* = $\dfrac{Level\_1 + Level\_2 + Level\_3}{3}$.

3. If *Index* ≤ *LowCutoff* then
        Display "Good condition"
   Else if *Index* ≤ *HighCutoff* then
        Display "Fair condition"
   Else
        Display "Poor condition"

The program in Figure 3.3 implements this algorithm. Note the `IF-ELSE  IF` construct used to implement this three-way selection structure in step 3.

Figure 3.3.　Pollution index—version 2

```
PROGRAM Pollution_2
!------------------------------------------------------------------
! Program that reads 3 pollution levels, calculates a pollution
! index as their integer average, and then displays an appropriate
! air-quality message. Identifiers used are:
!    Level_1, Level_2, Level_3 : the three pollution levels
!    LowCutoff, HighCutoff     : cutoff values that distinguish
!                                between good/fair, and fair/poor
!                                conditions, respectively
!    Index : the integer average of the pollution levels
!
! Input:     The three pollution levels
! Constants: The two cutoff values
! Output:    The pollution index and a "good condition" message if
!            this index is less than LowCutoff, a "fair condition"
!            message if it is between LowCutoff and HighCutoff,
!            and a "poor condition" message otherwise
!------------------------------------------------------------------

   IMPLICIT NONE
   INTEGER :: Level_1, Level_2, Level_3, Index
   INTEGER, PARAMETER :: LowCutoff = 25, HighCutoff = 50


   ! Get the 3 pollution readings
   PRINT *, "Enter 3 pollution readings (parts per million):"
   READ *, Level_1, Level_2, Level_3


   ! Calculate the pollution index
   Index = (Level_1 + Level_2 + Level_3) / 3


   ! Classify the pollution index and display an appropriate
   ! air-quality message
   IF (Index < LowCutoff) THEN
      PRINT *, "Good condition"
   ELSE IF (Index < HighCutoff) THEN
      PRINT *, "Fair condition"
   ELSE
      PRINT *, "Poor condition"
   END IF

END PROGRAM Pollution_2
```

Sample runs:

```
Enter 3 pollution readings (parts per million):
30, 40, 50
Fair condition
```

```
Enter 3 pollution readings (parts per million):
50, 60, 70
Poor condition

Enter 3 pollution readings (parts per million):
20, 21, 24
Good condition
```

Figure 3.3 (cont.)

Named Constructs

In Fortran 90, `IF` and `IF-ELSE IF` constructs may be named by attaching a label at the beginning and end of the construct so that it has the form

```
name: IF (logical-expression) THEN
         ⋮
END IF name
```

for example,

```
Update: IF (X > Largest) THEN
   Largest = X
   Position = N
END IF Update
```

The purpose of this naming feature is to clarify lengthy or complex constructs such as nested `IF`s in which there are several `END IF`s and it may not be clear which `END IF` corresponds to which `IF`. In this case it may be helpful to label corresponding `IF`s and `END IF`s; for example,

```
EmpType: IF (EmployeeType == "S") THEN  ! salaried employee
   PRINT *, "Enter employee's annual salary:"
   READ *, Salary
   Pay = Salary / 52
ELSE                                     ! hourly employee
   PRINT *, "Enter hours worked and hourly rate:"
   READ *, HoursWorked, HourlyRate
   Overtime: IF (HoursWorked > 40.0) THEN
      Pay = 40.0 * HourlyRate &
         + Multiplier * HourlyRate * (HoursWorked - 40.0)
   ELSE
      Pay = HoursWorked * HourlyRate
   END IF Overtime
END IF EmpType
```

The name used in an `IF` or `IF-ELSE IF` construct may also be attached following the keyword THEN in any `ELSE IF` part of the construct and following the keyword `ELSE` in an `ELSE` part; for example,

```
EmpType: IF (EmployeeType == "S") THEN   ! salaried employee
   PRINT *, "Enter employee's annual salary:"
   READ *, Salary
   Pay = Salary / 52
```

```
   ELSE EmpType                              ! hourly employee
      PRINT *, "Enter hours worked and hourly rate:"
      READ *, HoursWorked, HourlyRate
      Overtime: IF (HoursWorked > 40.0) THEN
         Pay = 40.0 * HourlyRate &
             + Multiplier * HourlyRate * (HoursWorked - 40.0)
      ELSE Overtime
         Pay = HoursWorked * HourlyRate
      END IF Overtime
   END IF EmpType
```

PRACTICE!

For Exercises 1–6, determine if each is a legal IF statement.

1. `IF (A > B) PRINT *, A`   **2.** `IF B < C N = N+1`

3. `IF (X <= Y) STOP`   **4.** `IF (A = X) READ *, Y`

5. `IF (1 <= N <= 10) N = 10`   **6.** `IF (N > 1) PRINT*, "*"`

Exercises 7–9 refer to the following IF construct:

```
   IF (X >= Y) THEN
      PRINT *, X
   ELSE
      PRINT *, Y
   END IF
```

7. Describe the output produced if X = 5 and Y = 6.

8. Describe the output produced if X = 5 and Y = 5.

9. Describe the output produced if X = 6 and Y = 5.

Exercises 10–12 refer to the following IF construct:

```
   IF (X >= 0) THEN
      IF (Y >= 0) THEN
         PRINT *, X + Y
      ELSE
         PRINT *, X - Y
      END IF
   ELSE
      PRINT *, Y - X
   END IF
```

10. Describe the output produced if X = 5 and Y = 5.

11. Describe the output produced if X = 5 and Y = –5.

12. Describe the output produced if X = –5 and Y = 5.

Exercises 13–17 refer to the following IF construct:

```
   IF (N >= 90) THEN
      PRINT *, "Excellent"
   ELSE IF (N >= 80)
      PRINT *, "Good"
   ELSE IF (N >= 70)
      PRINT *, "Fair"
   ELSE
      PRINT *, "Bad"
   END IF
```

13. Describe the output produced if N = 100.

14. Describe the output produced if N = 90.

15. Describe the output produced if N = 89.

16. Describe the output produced if N = 70.

17. Describe the output produced if N = 0.

18. Write a statement that displays "Out of range" if Number is negative or greater than 100.

19. Write an efficient IF statement to assign N the value 1 if X ≤ 1.5, 2 if 1.5 < X < 2.5, and 3 otherwise.

20. Display the message "Leap year" if the integer variable Year is the number of a leap year. (A leap year is a multiple of 4; and if it is a multiple of 100, it must also be a multiple of 400.)

21. Assign a value to Cost corresponding to the value of Distance given in the following table:

22.

DISTANCE	COST
0 through 100	5.00
More than 100 but not more than 500	8.00
More than 500 but less than 1000	10.00
1000 or more	12.00

3.4 THE CASE CONSTRUCT

In the preceding sections we saw that an IF-ELSE IF construct can be used to implement a selection structure in which exactly one of several alternative actions is selected and performed. In this section we describe the CASE construct, which, although it is not as general as the IF-ELSE IF construct, is useful for implementing some selection structures.

A CASE construct has the following form:

```
SELECT CASE (selector)
   CASE (label-list₁)
      statement-sequence₁
   CASE (label-list₂)
      statement-sequence₂
         ⋮
   CASE (label-listₙ)
      statement-sequenceₙ)
END SELECT
```

where the selector is an integer, character, or logical expression; each of the (label-list$_i$) is a list of one or more possible values of the selector, enclosed in parentheses, or is the word DEFAULT; the values in this list may have any of the forms

```
value
value₁ : value₂
value₁ :
: value₂
```

to denote a single value, the range of values from $value_1$ through $value_2$, the set of all values greater than or equal to $value_1$, or the set of all values less than or equal to $value_2$, respectively. Note that the values of the selector may not be real numbers.

When a CASE construct is executed, the selector is evaluated; if this value is in label-list$_i$, statement-sequence$_i$ is executed, and execution continues with the statement following the END SELECT statement. If the value is not in any of the lists of values, the sequence of statements associated with DEFAULT is executed, if there is such a statement sequence, and continues with the statement following the CASE construct otherwise.

Named CASE Constructs

Like IF and IF-ELSE IF constructs, a name may be attached to a CASE construct:

```
name: SELECT CASE (selector)
          :
      END SELECT name
```

For example,

```
Class: SELECT CASE (ClassCode)
   CASE (1)
      PRINT *, "Freshman"
   CASE (2)
      PRINT *, "Sophomore"
   CASE (3)
      PRINT *, "Junior"
   CASE (4)
      PRINT *, "Senior"
   CASE (5)
      PRINT *, "Graduate"
   CASE DEFAULT
      PRINT *, "Illegal class code", Class code
END SELECT Class
```

Example: Pollution Indices Revisited

In Section 3.3 we considered the problem of classifying a pollution index, computed as the integer average of three pollution readings. The program in Figure 3.2 used an IF-ELSE IF construct to select the appropriate pollution condition (good, fair, poor) determined by the pollution Index. A CASE construct can also be used to carry out this classification, as shown in the program in Figure 3.4. This program is a modification of that in Figure 3.2 that results from replacing the preceding IF-ELSE IF construct by a CASE construct.

Figure 3.4. Pollution indices—version 3

```
PROGRAM Pollution_3
!--------------------------------------------------------------------
! Program that reads 3 pollution levels, calculates a pollution
! index as their integer average, and then displays an appropriate
! air-quality message.   Identifiers used are:
!   Level_1, Level_2, Level_3 : the three pollution levels
!   LowCutoff, HighCutoff     : cutoff values that distinguish
!                               between good/fair, and fair/poor
!                               conditions, respectively
```

```
!    Index : the integer average of the pollution levels
!
! Input:      The three pollution levels
! Constants: The two cutoff values
! Output:     The pollution index and a "good condition" message if
!             this index is less than LowCutoff, a "fair condition"
!             message if it is between LowCutoff and HighCutoff,
!             and a "poor condition" message otherwise
!-------------------------------------------------------------------

  IMPLICIT NONE
  INTEGER :: Level_1, Level_2, Level_3, Index
  INTEGER, PARAMETER :: LowCutoff = 25, HighCutoff = 50

  ! Get the 3 pollution readings
  PRINT *, "Enter 3 pollution readings (parts per million):"
  READ *, Level_1, Level_2, Level_3

  ! Calculate the pollution index
  Index = (Level_1 + Level_2 + Level_3) / 3

  ! Classify the pollution index and display an appropriate
  ! air-quality message
  SELECT CASE (Index )
     CASE (:LowCutoff - 1)
         PRINT *, "Good condition"
     CASE (LowCutoff : HighCutoff - 1)
         PRINT *, "Fair condition"
     CASE (HighCutoff:)
         PRINT *, "Poor condition"
  END SELECT

END PROGRAM Pollution_3
```

Figure 3.4   (cont.)

PRACTICE!

Assume that Code is an integer variable, Name is a character variable, and X is a real variable.

1. If Number has the value 99, tell what output is produced by the following CASE construct, or indicate why an error occurs:

```
    SELECT CASE(Number)
      CASE DEFAULT
        PRINT *, "default"
      CASE (99)
        PRINT *, Number + 99
      CASE (-1)
        PRINT *, Number - 1
    END SELECT
```

2. As in 1, but for Number = −1.

3. As in 1, but for Number = 50.

4. If the value of `Code` is the letter B, tell what output is produced by the following CASE construct, or indicate why an error occurs:

```
SELECT CASE (Code)
  CASE ("A", "B")
    PRINT *, 123
  CASE ("P" : "Z")
    PRINT *, 456
END SELECT
```

5. As in 4, but suppose the value of `Code` is the letter Q.

6. As in 4, but suppose the value of `Code` is the letter M.

7. If the value of X is 2.0, tell what output is produced by the following CASE construct, or indicate why an error occurs:

```
SELECT CASE (X)
  CASE (1.0)
    PRINT *, X + 1.0
  CASE (2.0)
    PRINT *, X + 2.0
END SELECT
```

8. Write a CASE construct that increases `Balance` by adding `Amount` to it if the value of the character variable `TransCode` is D; decrease `Balance` by subtracting `Amount` from it if `TransCode` is W; display the value of `Balance` if `TransCode` is P; and display an illegal-transaction message otherwise.

9. Write a CASE construct to assign a value to `Cost` corresponding to the value of `Distance` given in the following table:

DISTANCE	COST
0 through 100	5.00
More than 100 but not more than 500	8.00
More than 500 but less than 1000	10.00
1000 or more	12.00

10. Write a CASE construct to display the name of a month or an error message for a given value of the integer variable `Month`. Display an error message if the value of `Month` is less than 1 or greater than 12.

3.5 THE LOGICAL DATA TYPE

Recall that there are two **logical constants** in Fortran,

```
.TRUE.
```

and

```
.FALSE.
```

(Note the periods that must appear as part of these logical constants.) A **logical variable** is declared using a LOGICAL type statement of the form

```
LOGICAL :: list
```

where `list` is a list of variables being typed as logical. Like all type statements, this type statement must appear in the specification part of the program. For example,

```
LOGICAL :: RootExists, End_of_Data
```

declares that `RootExists` and `End_of_Data` are logical variables.

An assignment statement of the form

```
logical-variable = logical-expression
```

can be used to assign a value to a logical variable. Thus,

```
End_of_Data = .TRUE.
```

is a valid assignment statement; it assigns the value `.TRUE.` to `End_of_Data`. Likewise,

```
RootExists = Discriminant >= 0
```

is a valid assignment statement and assigns `.TRUE.` to `RootExists` if `Discriminant` is nonnegative and assigns `.FALSE.` otherwise.

Logical values can be displayed using list-directed output. A logical value is displayed as only a `T` or an `F`, usually preceded by a space. For example, if `A`, `B`, and `C` are logical variables that are true, false, and false, respectively, the statement

```
PRINT *, A, B, C, .TRUE., .FALSE.
```

produces

```
 T F F T F
```

as output.

Logical values can also be read using list-directed input. In this case, the input values consist of optional blanks followed by an optional period followed by `T` or `F`, which may be followed by other characters. The value true or false is assigned to the corresponding variable according to whether the first letter encountered is `T` or `F`. For example, for the statements

```
LOGICAL :: A, B, C
READ *, A, B, C
```

the following data could be entered:

```
.T., F, .FALSE
```

The values assigned to `A`, `B`, and `C` would be true, false, and false, respectively. This would also be the case if the following data were entered:

```
.T., FALL, FLASE
```

In the next example we consider the design of logical circuits. The program in Figure 3.5 that models a circuit for a binary half-adder uses logical variables `A` and `B` to represent inputs to the circuit and logical variables `Sum` and `Carry` to represent the outputs produced by the circuit.

Example: Logical Circuits

Arithmetic operations are implemented in computer hardware by logical circuits. The following circuit is a *binary half-adder* that adds two binary digits:

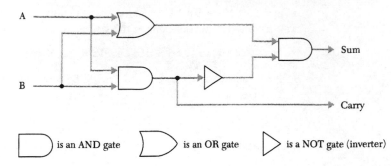

It contains four basic electronic components called **gates:** two AND gates, one OR gate, and one NOT gate (also called an *inverter*). The inputs to these gates are pulses of current applied to the lines leading into the gates, and the outputs are pulses of current on the lines emanating from the gates.

In circuit design, + is used to denote OR, · to denote AND, and an overbar to denote NOT. Using this notation, we can represent the output *Sum* in the circuit for a binary half-adder by

$$Sum = (A + B) \cdot \overline{(A \cdot B)}$$

and the output *Carry* by

$$Carry = A \cdot B$$

The program in Figure 3.5 implements a binary half-adder, using logical variables A, B, Sum, and Carry. The logical expressions for Sum and Carry are implemented by the Fortran logical expressions

```
Sum = (A .OR. B) .AND..NOT. (A .AND. B)
Carry = A .AND. B
```

Figure 3.5. A binary half-adder

```
PROGRAM Half_Adder
!-------------------------------------------------------------------
! Program to calculate the outputs from a logical circuit that
! represents a binary half-adder.  Variables used are:
!    A, B      : the two logical inputs to the circuit
!    Sum, Carry : the two logical outputs
!
! Input:   The two logical inputs A and B
! Output:  The two logical outputs Sum and Carry, which represent the
!          sum and carry that result when the input values are added
!-------------------------------------------------------------------

  IMPLICIT NONE
  LOGICAL :: A, B, Sum, Carry

  PRINT *, "Enter logical inputs A and B:"
  READ *, A, B
  Sum = (A .OR. B) .AND. .NOT. (A .AND. B)
  Carry = A .AND. B
  PRINT *, "Carry, Sum =", Carry, Sum

END PROGRAM Half_Adder
```

Sample runs:

```
Enter logical inputs A and B:
T T
Carry, Sum = T F

Enter logical inputs A and B:
T F
Carry, Sum = F T

Enter logical inputs A and B:
F T
Carry, Sum = F T

Enter logical inputs A and B:
F F
Carry, Sum = F F
```

Figure 3.5 (cont.)

The sample runs show the outputs produced for each possible combination of logical values for the two inputs. If we identify the binary digits 0 and 1 with false and true, respectively, the program's output can be interpreted as a demonstration that $1 + 1 = 10$ (Sum = 0, Carry = 1), $1 + 0 = 01$, $0 + 1 = 01$, and $0 + 0 = 00$. This program, therefore, correctly implements binary addition of one-bit numbers.

PRACTICE!

For Exercises 1–7, tell whether each statement is true or false:

1. If Okay is a logical variable, the statement Okay = .FALSE. will set it to false.
2. If Okay is a logical variable and Code has the value 6128, then the statement Okay = (Code = 6128) will set Okay to true.
3. If Okay is a logical variable and Alpha has the value 5, then the statement Okay = 1 < Alpha < 7 will set Okay to true.
4. If Okay is a logical variable and the character variable Logic has the value ".TRUE.", then the statement Okay = Logic will set Okay to true.
5. If the logical variable Okay has been set to true, then the statement PRINT *, Okay will display .TRUE..
6. FALSE, .FALSE., and FALLS are all legal input values for a logical variable in a READ statement.
7. If Fred T. Tarantula is input for the statement READ *, P, Q, R, the logical variables P, Q, and R will become false, true, and true, respectively.

In Exercises 8–16, assume that M and N are integer variables with the values –2 and 5, respectively, and that X, Y, and Z are real variables with the values –1.99, 5.5, and 9.99, respectively. Find the value assigned to the logical variable Okay, or indicate why an error occurs.

8. Okay = M <= N
9. Okay = 2 * ABS(M) <= 8
10. Okay = X * X < SQRT(Z)
11. Okay = NINT(Z) == (6 * N - 3)

12. Okay = Okay .AND. (N == 6)
13. Okay = .NOT. (X < Y)
14. Okay = .NOT. ((M <= N) .AND. (X + Z > Y))
15. Okay = .NOT. (M <= N) .OR..NOT. (X + Z > Y)
16. Okay = .NOT. ((M > N) .OR. (X < Z)) .EQV.
        ((M <= N) .AND. (X >= Z))

For Exercises 17–24, write an assignment statement that will set the logical variable Okay to true if the condition is true and to false otherwise.

17. X is strictly between 0 and 10.

18. X and Y are both positive.

19. X and Y are both negative, or both are positive.

20. $-1 \le X \le 1$.

21. X is neither less than 0 nor greater than 100.

22. W, X, Y, and Z are all equal to each other.

23. W, X, Y, and Z are in increasing order.

24. X is greater than 10, or Y is greater than 10, but not both.

KEY TERMS

Block	LOGICAL data type	Named construct
Compound logical expression	Logical IF statement	Relational operator
IF (block IF) construct	Logical operator	Selection structure
IF-ELSE IF construct	Logical variable	Simple logical expression
Logical constant	Multialternative selection structure	Truth table

PROGRAMMING POINTERS

Program Style and Design

1. *The statement sequence(s) within* IF *and* CASE *constructs should be indented:*

```
IF logical-expression          SELECT CASE(Selector)
    statement₁                 {
        ⋮                          CASE (label-list₁)
    statement                          statement-sequence₁
ELSE                               CASE (label-list₂)
    statement₁                         statement-sequence₂
        ⋮                                  ⋮
    statementₙ                     CASE (label-listₙ)
END IF                                 statement-sequenceₙ
                                   DEFAULT
                                       statement-sequenceₙ₊₁
                               }
```

2. *Multialternative selection structures can be implemented more efficiently with an* IF-ELSE IF *construct than with a sequence of* IF *statements. For example, using the statements*

```
IF (Score >= 90) Grade ="A"
IF ((Score >= 80) .AND. (Score < 90)) Grade = "B"
IF ((Score >= 70) .AND. (Score < 80)) Grade = "C"
IF ((Score >= 60) .AND. (Score < 70)) Grade = "D"
IF (Score < 60) Grade = "F"
```

is less efficient than using

```
IF (Score >= 90) THEN
    Grade = "A"
ELSE IF (Score >= 80) THEN
    Grade = "B"
ELSE IF (Score >= 70) THEN
    Grade = "C"
ELSE IF (Score >= 60) THEN
    Grade = "D"
ELSE
    Grade = "F"
END IF
```

Potential Problems

1. *Periods must be used in the logical operators* `.NOT.`, `.AND.`, `.OR.`, `.EQV.`, *and* `.NEQV.`.

2. *Parentheses must enclose the logical expression in an* `IF` *construct or in a logical* `IF` *statement.*

3. *Parentheses must enclose the selector and each label-list in a* `CASE` *construct.*

4. *Real quantities that are algebraically equal may yield a false logical expression when compared with* `==` *because most real values are not stored exactly. For example, even though the two real expressions* `X * (1.0 / X)` *and* `1.0` *are algebraically equal, the logical expression* `X * (1.0 / X) == 1.0` *is usually false. Thus, if two real values* `RealNumber_1` *and* `RealNumber_2` *are subject to roundoff error, it is usually not advisable to check whether they are equal. It is better to check whether the absolute value of their difference is small:*

```
IF (ABS(RealNumber_1 - RealNumber_2) < Tolerance) THEN
    ⋮
```

where Tolerance is some small positive real value such as `1E-6`.

5. *Each* `IF` *construct (but not logical* `IF` *statements) must be closed with an* `END IF` *statement.*

6. *Each* `CASE` *construct must be closed with an* `END SELECT` *statement.*

Programming Problems

SECTIONS 3.2 AND 3.3

1. Modify the program in Figure 3.1 for solving quadratic equations so that when the discriminant is negative, the complex roots of the equation are displayed. If the discriminant D is negative, these roots are given by

$$\frac{(-B) \pm \sqrt{-D}\,i}{2A}$$

where $i^2 = -1$.

2. Write a program that reads values for the coefficients A, B, C, D, E, and F of the equations

$$Ax + By = C$$
$$Dx + Ey = F$$

of two straight lines. Then determine whether the lines are parallel (their slopes are equal) or the lines intersect. If they intersect, determine whether the lines are perpendicular (the product of their slopes is equal to −1).

3. Suppose the following formulas give the safe loading L in pounds per square inch for a column with slimness ratio S:

$$L = \begin{cases} 16500 - .4755S^2 & \text{if } S < 100 \\ \dfrac{17900}{2 + (S^2/17900)} & \text{if } S \geq 100 \end{cases}$$

Write a program that reads a slimness ratio and then calculates the safe loading.

4. Suppose that a gas company bases its charges on consumption according to the following table:

GAS USED	RATE
First 70 cubic meters	$5.00 minimum cost
Next 100 cubic meters	5.0¢ per cubic meter
Next 230 cubic meters	2.5¢ per cubic meter
Above 400 cubic meters	1.5¢ per cubic meter

Meter readings are four-digit numbers that represent cubic meters. Write a program in which the meter reading for the previous month and the current meter reading are entered and then the amount of the bill is calculated. *Note:* The current reading may be less than the previous one; for example, the previous reading may have been 9897, and the current one is 0103.

SECTION 3.4

5. Proceed as in Problem 4 but use a CASE construct to determine the applicable rate.

6. A computer supply company discounts the price of each of its products depending on the number of units bought and the price per unit. The discount increases as the number of units bought and/or the unit price increases. These discounts are given in the following table:

NUMBER BOUGHT	0–10.00	UNIT PRICE (DOLLARS) 10.01–100.00	100.01–
1–9	0%	2%	5%
10–19	5%	7%	9%
20–49	9%	15%	21%
50–99	14%	23%	32%
100–	21%	32%	43%

Write a program that reads the number of units bought and the unit price and then calculates and prints the total full cost, the total amount of the discount, and the total discounted cost.

SECTION 3.5

7. In a certain region, pesticide can be sprayed from an airplane only if the temperature is at least 70° F, the relative humidity is between 15 and 35 percent, and the wind speed is at most 10 miles per hour. Write a program that accepts three numbers representing temperature, relative humidity, and wind speed; assigns the value true or false to the logical variable OkToSpray according to these criteria; and displays this value.

8. Write a program that reads triples of real numbers and assigns the appropriate value of true or false to the following logical variables:

`Triangle:`	True if the real numbers can represent lengths of the sides of a triangle and false otherwise (the sum of any two of the numbers must be greater than the third)
`Equilateral:`	True if `Triangle` is true and the triangle is equilateral (the three sides are equal)
`Isosceles:`	True if `Triangle` is true and the triangle is isosceles (at least two sides are equal)
`Scalene:`	True if `Triangle` is true and the triangle is scalene (no two sides are equal)

The output from your program should have a format like the following:

```
Enter 3 lengths:
2, 3, 3
Triangle is: T
Equilateral is: F
Isosceles is: T
Scalene is: F
```

4

Repetitive Execution

4.1 LOOP TYPES

In earlier chapters we noted that programs can be designed using three basic control structures: sequence, selection, and repetition. In the preceding chapters we described sequence and selection, and in this chapter we consider the third basic control structure, repetition. A **repetition structure** or **loop** makes possible the repeated execution of one or more statements, called the **body of the loop**.

There are two basic types of repetition:

1. *Repetition controlled by a counter* in which the body of the loop is executed once for each value of some control variable in a specified range of values

2. *Repetition controlled by a logical expression* in which the decision to continue or to terminate repetition is determined by the value of some logical expression

We will consider both types of loops in this chapter and illustrate how they are used in solving several problems.

4.2 COUNTER-CONTROLLED DO LOOPS

Fortran 90 provides one basic loop construct, the DO **construct**. There are two basic forms of this construct, one to implement counter-controlled loops and another to implement loops controlled by a logical expression. In this section we consider the first form; the second type of loop is considered in Section 4.4.

OBJECTIVES

In this chapter, you will

- See how repetition is implemented in Fortran.
- Learn to use counter-controlled DO loops and general DO loops.
- Apply repetition to some real-world examples.

70

DO constructs for counter-controlled loops have the following form:

```
DO control-variable = initial-value, limit, step-size
    statement-sequence
END DO
```

where `initial-value`, `limit`, and `step-size` are integer expressions with `step-size` nonzero; `step-size` may be omitted, in which case it is taken to be 1.

When this loop is executed:

1. The control variable is assigned the initial value.
2. The control variable is compared with the limit to see if it is
   - less than or equal to the limit, for a positive step size
   - greater than or equal to the limit, for a negative step size
3. If so, the sequence of statements, called the **body of the loop**, is executed, the step size is added to the control variable, and step 2 is repeated. Otherwise, repetition terminates.

Note that if the termination test in step 2 is satisfied initially, the body of the loop is never executed.

To illustrate, consider the DO loop

```
DO Number = 1, 9
    PRINT *, Number, Number**2
END DO
```

where `Number` is an integer variable. In this example, `Number` is the control variable, the initial value is 1, the limit is 9, and the step size is 1. When this DO loop is executed, the initial value 1 is assigned to `Number`, and the PRINT statement is executed. The value of `Number` is then increased by 1, and because this new value 2 is less than the limit 9, the PRINT statement is executed again. This repetition continues as long as the value of the control variable `Number` is less than or equal to the limit 9. Thus, the output produced by this DO loop is

```
1    1
2    4
3    9
4    16
5    25
6    36
7    49
8    64
9    81
```

If the step size in a DO loop is negative, the control variable is decremented rather than incremented, and repetition continues as long as the value of the control variable is greater than or equal to the limit.

The initial values of the control variable, the limit, and the step size are determined before repetition begins and cannot be changed during execution of the DO loop. Within the body of the DO loop, the values of variables that specify the initial value, the limit, and the step size may change, but this does not affect the number of repetitions.[1] Also, the state-

---

[1] The number of repetitions is calculated as the larger of the value 0 and the integer part of

$$\frac{\texttt{limit} - \texttt{initial-value} + \texttt{step-size}}{\texttt{step-size}}$$

ments within a DO loop may use the value of the control variable, but *they must not modify the value of the control variable.* An attempt to do so results in a compile-time error.

The initial value, the limit, and the step size in a DO construct may be variables or expressions. For example, suppose that Number, I, and Sum are integer variables. The statements

```
READ *, Number
DO I = 1, Number
   Sum = Sum + I
END DO
```

read a value for Number, which is the limit for the DO loop. The loop computes the sum

$$1 + 2 + \cdots + \text{Number.}$$

The body of a DO loop may contain another DO loop. In this case, the second DO loop is said to be **nested** within the first DO loop. For example, the nested DO loops

```
DO M = 1, Last_M
   DO N = 1, Last_N
      Product = M * N
      PRINT *, M, " ", N, " ", Product
   END DO
END DO
```

in the program in Figure 4.1 calculate and display a table of products of the form M * N for M ranging from 1 through Last_M and N ranging from 1 through Last_N for integer variables M, N, Last_M, and Last_N. In the sample run, both Last_M and Last_N are assigned the value 4. The control variable M is assigned its initial value 1, and the internal DO loop is executed with M = 1. This calculates and displays the first four products, 1 ° 1, 1 ° 2, 1 ° 3, and 1 ° 4. The value of M is then incremented by 1, and the preceding DO loop is executed again with M = 2. This calculates and displays the next four products, 2 ° 1, 2 ° 2, 2 ° 3, and 2 ° 4. The control variable M is then incremented to 3, producing the next four products, 3 ° 1, 3 ° 2, 3 ° 3, and 3 ° 4. Finally, M is incremented to 4, giving the last four products, 4 ° 1, 4 ° 2, 4 ° 3, and 4 ° 4.

Figure 4.1.   Printing a multiplication table

```
PROGRAM Multiplication_Table
!----------------------------------------------------------------------
! Program to calculate and display a list of products of two numbers.
! Variables used are:
!   M, N          : the two numbers being multiplied
!   Product       : their product
!   Last_M, Last_N : the last values of M and N
!
! Input:  Last_M and Last_N, the largest numbers to be multiplied
! Output: List of products M * N
!----------------------------------------------------------------------

  IMPLICIT NONE
  INTEGER :: M, N, Last_M, Last_N, Product

  PRINT *, "Enter the last values of the two numbers:"
  READ *, Last_M, Last_N
  PRINT *, "M N M * N"
  PRINT *, "============="
```

```
    DO M = 1, Last_M
       DO N = 1, Last_N
          Product = M * N
          PRINT *, M, " ", N, " ", Product
       END DO
    END DO

END PROGRAM Multiplication_Table
```

Sample run:
```
Enter the last values of the two numbers:
4, 4
M · N · M * N
==============
1 · 1 ·   1
1   2     2
1   3     3
1   4     4
2   1     2
2   2     4
2   3     6
2   4     8
3   1     3
3   2     6
3   3     9
3   4    12
4   1     4
4   2     8
4   3    12
4   4    16
```

Figure 4.1   (cont.)

PRACTICE!

1. Name and briefly describe the two basic types of repetition structures.

For Exercises 2–12, assume that I, J, and K are integer variables. Describe the output produced by the given program segment.

2.
```
DO I = 1, 5
    PRINT *, "Hello"
END DO
```

3.
```
DO I = 1, 5, 2
    PRINT *, "Hello"
END DO
```

4.
```
DO I = 1, 6
    PRINT *, I, I + 1
END DO
```

5.
```
DO I = 6, 1, -1
    PRINT *, I
    PRINT *
    PRINT , I**2
END DO
```

6.
```
DO I = 6, 6
    PRINT *, "Hello"
END DO
```

7.
```
DO I = 6, 5
    PRINT *, "Hello"
END DO
```

8.
```
DO I = -2, 3
    PRINT *, I, " squared = ", I * I
END DO
```

9.
```
DO I = 1, 5
   PRINT *, I
   DO J = I, 1, -1
      PRINT *, J
   END DO
END DO
```

10.
```
K = 5
DO I = -2, 3
   PRINT *, I + K
   K = 1
END DO
```

11.
```
DO I = 1, 3
   DO J = 1, 3
      DO K = 1, J
         PRINT *, I, J, K
      END DO
   END DO
END DO
```

12.
```
DO I = 1, 3
   DO J = 1, 3
      DO K = I, J
         PRINT *, I + J + K
      END DO
   END DO
END DO
```

13. What, if anything, is wrong with the following DO loop?

```
DO I = 1, 10
   PRINT *, I
   I = I + 1
END DO
```

In Exercises 14–16, assume that I, J, and Limit are integer variables and that Alpha and DeltaX are real variables. Describe the output produced, or explain why an error occurs.

14.
```
Alpha = -5.0
DeltaX = 0.5
DO I = 1, 5
   PRINT *, Alpha
   Alpha = Alpha + DeltaX
END DO
```

15.
```
PRINT *, "Values:"
DO I = 0, 2
   DO J = 1, I
      PRINT *, I, J
   END DO
END DO
PRINT *, "The end"
```

16.
```
Limit = 3
DO I = 1, Limit
   Limit = 1
   PRINT *, I, Limit
END DO
```

17. Write statements to print the first 100 positive integers.

18. Write statements to print the first 100 even positive integers.

19. Write statements to print all positive integers having at most three digits, the last of which is 0.

20. Write statements to read a value for the integer variable N and then print all integers from 1 through 1000 that are multiples of N.

21. Write statements to read a value for the integer variable N, and then read and find the sum of N real numbers.

APPLICATION: DEPRECIATION TABLES

PROBLEM

Depreciation is the decrease in the value over time of some asset due to wear and tear, decay, declining price, and so on. For example, suppose that a company purchases a new robot for $20,000 that will be used on its assembly line for 5 years. After that time, called the *useful life* of the robot, it can be sold at an estimated price of $5,000, which is the robot's *salvage value*. Thus, the value of the robot will have depreciated $15,000 over the 5-year period. A program is needed to calculate depreciation tables that display the depreciation in each year of an item's useful life.

Solution

Specification.   The input for this problem is the purchase price of an item, its useful life, and its salvage value. The output is a depreciation table. A specification for this problem is therefore as follows:

Input: The purchase price of an item
The item's useful life (in years)
The item's salvage value

Output: A depreciation table

Design.   A first version of an algorithm for solving this problem is:

1.   Get the purchase price, useful life, and salvage value of the item.

2.   Calculate the amount to depreciate: purchase price − salvage value.

3.   Generate a depreciation table.

Coding steps 1 and 2 is straightforward, but step 3 obviously needs refinement. Generating a table requires a loop, and a counter-controlled loop is appropriate here. We can rewrite step 3 as

3.   Repeat the following for each year from 1 to the end of the useful life:

Display the year number and the depreciation for that year.

We will use the following variables:

VARIABLES FOR DEPRECIATION PROBLEM	
Price	Purchase price of item
SalvageValue	Its salvage value
Amount	Amount to be depreciated
UsefulLife	Useful life in years
Year	Year in which depreciation is being calculated
Depreciation	Depreciation for that year

To complete the algorithm, we must describe how depreciation is to be calculated. There are many

A robotic arm. (Photo courtesy of The Stock Market.)

methods, but we will consider only one here: the *sum-of-the-years'-digits method*. To illustrate it, consider depreciating $15,000 over a 5-year period. To use this method, we first calculate the "sum of the years," $1 + 2 + 3 + 4 + 5 = 15$. In the first year, 5/15 of $15,000 ($5,000) is depreciated; in the second year, 4/15 of $15,000 ($4,000) is depreciated; and so on, giving the following depreciation table:

YEAR	DEPRECIATION
1	$5,000
2	$4,000
3	$3,000
4	$2,000
5	$1,000

Thus, to use this method, we must add another variable to our list of identifiers:

ANOTHER VARIABLE FOR DEPRECIATION PROBLEM

Sum: $1 + 2 + \cdots + UsefulLife$

Once this sum has been calculated, we can calculate depreciation for a given *Year* as

$$Depreciation = (UsefulLife - Year + 1) * Amount / Sum$$

We are now ready to give a complete algorithm for solving this problem. We must add statements to cal-culate *Sum*. These should be placed before the loop for generating the depreciation table, since it would be inefficient to calculate this sum over and over again for each year. Our final algorithm is as follows:

ALGORITHM FOR DEPRECIATION PROBLEM

Algorithm to generate depreciation tables using the sum-of-the-years'-digits method.

Input: *Price, UsefulLife,* and *SalvageValue*

Output: A depreciation table showing the year number and the amount to be depre-ciated in that year

1. Enter *Price, UsefulLife,* and *SalvageValue*.
2. Calculate *Amount* = *Price* − *SalvageValue*.
3. Set *Sum* to 0.
4. Repeat the following for *Year* ranging from 1 to *UsefulLife:* Add *Year* to *Sum*.
5. Repeat the following for *Year* ranging from 1 to *UsefulLife:*
   a. Calculate *Depreciation* = (*UsefulLife* − *Year* + 1) * *Amount* / *Sum*.
   b. Display Year and *Depreciation*.

Coding. The program in Figure 4.2 implements this algorithm. It uses DO loops to carry out the repetitions required in steps 4 and 5.

Figure 4.2. Calculating depreciation

```
PROGRAM Depreciation_Table
!-----------------------------------------------------------------------
! Program to calculate and display a depreciation table using the
! sum-of-the-years'-digits method of depreciation. Variables used are:
!     Price        : purchase price of item
!     SalvageValue : and its salvage value
!     Amount       : amount to be depreciated (Price - SalvageValue)
!     UsefulLife   : its useful life
!     Depreciation : amount of depreciation
!     Year         : number of year in depreciation table
!     Sum          : 1 + 2 + ... + UsefulLife
!
! Input: Price, SalvageValue, and UsefulLife
! Output: Table showing year number and depreciation for that year
!-----------------------------------------------------------------------

  IMPLICIT NONE
  REAL :: Price, SalvageValue, Amount, Depreciation
  INTEGER :: UsefulLife, Year, Sum
```

```
! Get the information about the item
PRINT *, "Enter purchase price, useful life, and salvage value:"
READ *, Price, UsefulLife, SalvageValue

! Calculate amount to be depreciated
Amount = Price - SalvageValue

! Calculate Sum for sum-of-the-years'-digits method
Sum = 0
DO Year = 1, UsefulLife
   Sum = Sum + Year
END DO


! Generate the depreciation table
PRINT *
PRINT *, "Year   Depreciation"
PRINT *, "===================="
DO Year = 1, UsefulLife
   Depreciation = (UsefulLife - Year + 1) * Amount / REAL(Sum)
   PRINT *, " ", Year, Depreciation
END DO

END PROGRAM Depreciation_Table
```

Figure 4.2   (cont.)

Execution and Testing.   This program was executed several times using test data for which the results were easy to check. It was then run with the data given in the problem:

```
Enter purchase price, useful life, and salvage value:
20000, 5, 5000

Year    Depreciation
====================
   1     5.0000000E+03
   2     4.0000000E+03
   3     3.0000000E+03
   4     2.0000000E+03
   5     1.0000000E+03
```

4.3 GENERAL DO LOOPS

The counter-controlled DO loop described in Section 4.2 is used to implement a repetition structure in which the number of iterations is determined before execution of the loop begins. For some problems, however, the number of iterations cannot be determined in advance and a more general repetition structure is required. Repetition in such loops is usually controlled by some logical expression, as pictured in Figure 4.3.

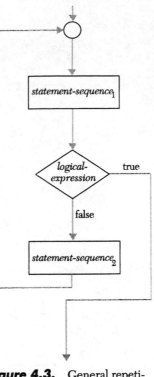

Figure 4.3.   General repetition structure

Fortran 90 provides a `DO-EXIT` **construct** that can be used to implement such repetition structures. It has the form

```
DO
    statement-sequence
    IF (logical-expression₁) EXIT
    statement-sequence
END DO
```

where either `statement-sequence₁` or `statement-sequence₂` may be omitted. The statements that make up the body of the loop are executed repeatedly until the `logical-expression` in the `IF` statement becomes true. Repetition is then terminated, and execution continues with the statement following the `END DO`. *Warning:* If the `logical-expression` never becomes true, an **infinite loop** results.

To illustrate the use of a general loop controlled by a logical expression, consider the following variation of the summation problem considered in Section 4.2:

For a given value of *Limit,* what is the smallest positive integer *Number* for which the sum

$$1 + 2 + \cdots + Number$$

is greater than *Limit,* and what is the value of this sum?

To solve this problem, we must perform the following steps:

1. Enter a value for *Limit.*
2. Initialize *Number* and *Sum* to 0.

3. Repeat the following:
    a. If *Sum.* > *Limit*, terminate repetition; otherwise continue with the following.
    b. Increment *Number* by 1.
    c. Add *Number* to *Sum.*
4. Display *Number* and *Sum.*

Note that the logical expression that controls repetition of the loop in step 3 is evaluated at the top of the loop. Thus, this loop is sometimes called a **pretest loop** or a "test-at-the-top" loop. If this logical expression is false initially, the statements that follow it will not be executed; such a loop is thus said to have **zero-trip** behavior. In the preceding summation algorithm, therefore, if the value −1 is entered for *Limit,* the loop will be exited immediately and execution will continue with the display instruction that follows the loop; the value 0 will be displayed for both *Number* and *Sum.*

A pretest loop can be implemented by a DO-EXIT construct of the form

```
DO
    IF (logical-expression) EXIT
    statement-sequence
END DO
```

For example,

```
DO
    IF (Sum > Limit) EXIT    ! Terminate repetition
    ! Otherwise continue with the following:
    Number = Number + 1
    Sum = Sum + Number
END DO
```

implements the loop in step 3 above.

Input Loops

One common use of loops is to read and process a set of data values. Because it may not be possible or practical to determine beforehand how many data values must be processed, a general loop should be used rather than a counter-controlled DO loop.

One of the easiest ways to implement input loops is by using a **test-in-the-middle loop** of the form.

Repeat the following:

1. Read a data value.
2. If the end of data was encountered, terminate repetition; otherwise continue with the following.
3. Process the data value.

In step 2, it must be possible to detect when the end of data occurred. One method is to use an IOSTAT = clause as described in the next chapter. For interactive input, another common method is to append to the data set an artificial data value called an **end-of-data flag** or **sentinel**, which is distinct from any possible data item. As each data item is read, it is checked to determine whether it is this end-of-data flag. If it is, repetition is terminated; otherwise it is processed as a regular data value. This technique for reading and processing data values is used in solving the mean-time-to-failure problem of the next section.

In the summation problem, we used a *pretest loop* in which the logical expression that controls repetition is evaluated *before* the body of the loop is executed. In the preceding discussion of input loops, we showed how a *test-in-the-middle loop* can be used to read and process data values. Sometimes, however, it is convenient to use a **posttest** or "test-at-the-bottom" loop, in which the termination test is made *after* the body of the loop is executed. Such a structure can be implemented in Fortran with a program segment of the form

```
DO
    statement-sequence
    IF (logical-expression) EXIT
END DO
```

Such loops can be used to implement input loops in which the user is asked at the end of each repetition whether there is more data to process. Such loops are sometimes called **query-controlled input loops**.

To illustrate a query-controlled input loop, we reconsider the problem of converting Celsius temperatures to Fahrenheit temperatures described in Section 2.6. The program developed there to solve this problem was designed to process only one temperature at a time. To process several temperatures, the program must be executed for each one. This program can be easily modified to process several temperatures by "wrapping" the statements within a loop that reads and processes a temperature and then asks the user if there is more data to be processed. Using such a query-controlled input loop, we can modify the algorithm given earlier as follows:

ALGORITHM FOR TEMPERATURE-CONVERSION PROBLEM

This algorithm converts temperatures on the Celsius scale to the corresponding temperatures on the Fahrenheit scale. Values are processed until the user indicates that there is no more data.

Input: Temperatures in degrees Celsius
           User responses

Output: Temperatures in degrees Fahrenheit

Repeat the following:

1. Enter *Celsius*.
2. Calculate *Fahrenheit* = 1.8 * *Celsius* + 32.
3. Display *Fahrenheit*.
4. Ask the user if there are more temperatures to process.
5. Read the user's *Response* (Y or N).
6. If *Response* = "N", terminate repetition.

The program in Figure 4.4 implements this algorithm; the query-controlled input loop is highlighted in color.

Figure 4.4. Temperature conversion-repetitive version

```
PROGRAM Temperature_Conversion_3
!-------------------------------------------------------------------------
! Program to convert temperatures on the Celsius scale to the
! corresponding temperatures on the Fahrenheit scale. A query-
! controlled input loop is used to process several temperatures.
! Variables used are:
! Celsius    : temperature on the Celsius scale
! Fahrenheit : temperature on the Fahrenheit scale
! Response   : user's response to the more-data query
!
! Input: Celsius, Response
! Output: Fahrenheit
!-------------------------------------------------------------------------
```

```
IMPLICIT NONE
REAL :: Celsius, Fahrenheit
CHARACTER(1) :: Response

! Query-controlled loop to process temperatures
DO
    ! Obtain Celsius temperature
    PRINT *, "Enter temperature in degrees Celsius:"
    READ *, Celsius

    ! Calculate corresponding Fahrenheit temperature
    Fahrenheit = 1.8 * Celsius + 32.0

    ! Display temperatures
    PRINT *, Celsius, "degrees Celsius =", &
            Fahrenheit, "degrees Fahrenheit"

    ! Ask user if there is more data
    PRINT *
    PRINT *, "More temperatures to convert (Y or N)?"
    READ *, Response
    IF (Response == "N") EXIT
END DO

END PROGRAM Temperature_Conversion_3
```

Sample run:

```
Enter temperature in degrees Celsius:
0
  0.0000000E+00 degrees Celsius = 32.0000000 degrees Fahrenheit

More temperatures to convert (Y or N)?
Y
Enter temperature in degrees Celsius:
11.193
 11.1929998 degrees Celsius = 52.1473999 degrees Fahrenheit

More temperatures to convert (Y or N)?
Y
Enter temperature in degrees Celsius:
-17.728
-17.7280006 degrees Celsius = 8.9599609E-02 degrees Fahrenheit

More temperatures to convert (Y or N)?
Y
Enter temperature in degrees Celsius:
49.1
 49.0999985 degrees Celsius = 1.2038000E+02 degrees Fahrenheit

More temperatures to convert (Y or N)?
N
```

Figure 4.4 (cont.)

The DO-CYCLE Construct

The EXIT statement causes repetition of a loop to terminate by transferring control to
the statement following the END DO statement. Sometimes it is necessary to terminate
only the current repetition and jump ahead to the next one. Fortran 90 provides the
CYCLE **statement** for this purpose.

To illustrate the use of CYCLE, suppose that in the temperature-conversion program in Figure 4.4, we wanted to process only temperatures of 0° C or above. For this, we need only add the statement

```
IF (Celsius < 0.0)
    PRINT *, "*** Temperature must be 0 or above ***"
    CYCLE
END IF
```

after the READ *, Celsius statement in the query-controlled input loop. If a negative value is entered for Celsius, a message will be displayed and the CYCLE statement will cause the rest of the loop body to be skipped. A new pass through the loop will begin so that a new value for Celsius will be entered.

Named DO Constructs

We noted in Section 3.4 that Fortran 90 permits naming IF and IF-ELSE IF constructs by attaching a label at the beginning and end of the construct. DO constructs can also be named in this way:

```
name: DO...
      :
END DO name
```

This is especially useful in the case of nested DO loops. It helps with determining which END DO is matched with which DO. Thus, the nested loops in the summation example of Section 4.2 could perhaps better be written as:

```
Outer: DO M = 1, Last_M
    Inner: DO N = 1, Last_N
        Product = M * N
        PRINT *, M, " ", N, " ", Product
    END DO Inner
END DO Outer
```

The name attached to a DO construct can also be attached to an EXIT or CYCLE statement within that construct. This causes control to transfer to the END DO having the same name. For example, suppose that a problem requires calculating A^N for several values of A and for several values of N for each A value. Suppose that entering 0 for A and N signals the end of input. Nested DO constructs of the following form could be used:

```
A_Loop: DO
    PRINT *, "Enter A:"
    READ *, A
    N_Loop: DO
        PRINT *, "Enter N:"
        READ *, N
        IF (N == 0) THEN
            IF (A == 0) EXIT A_Loop
            EXIT N_Loop
            PRINT *, A ** N
        END IF
    END DO N_Loop
END DO A_Loop
```

APPLICATION: MEAN TIME TO FAILURE

PROBLEM

One important statistic used in measuring the reliability of a component in a circuit is the *mean time to failure*, which can be used to predict the circuit's lifetime. This is especially important in situations in which repair is difficult or even impossible, such as for a computer circuit in a space satellite. Suppose that NASA has awarded an engineering laboratory a contract to evaluate the reliability of a particular component for a future space probe to Mars. As part of this evaluation, an engineer at this laboratory has tested several of these circuits and recorded the time at which each failed, now she would like a program to process this data and determine the mean time to failure.

Solution

Specification. The input for this problem is obviously a collection of failure times for the component being tested, and the output is clearly the average or mean of these times. To calculate this mean, we must know how many tests were conducted, but this information is not given in the statement of the problem. We cannot assume, therefore, that it is part of the input, and so the program will have to be flexible enough to process any number of data values. A specification of the input and output for this problem thus might be

Input:	A collection of numeric values (number unknown)
Output:	The number of values
	The mean of the values

Design. In developing algorithms to solve problems like this, one useful method is to begin by considering how the problem could be solved without using a computer, perhaps instead using pencil and paper and/or a calculator. To solve the problem in this manner, we enter the values one at a time, counting each value as it is entered and adding it to the sum of the preceding values. This procedure involves two quantities:

Space probe. (Photo courtesy of The Stock Market.)

1. A counter that is incremented by 1 each time a data value is entered
2. A running sum of the data values

DATA VALUE	COUNTER	SUM
	0	0.0
3.4	1	3.4
4.2	2	7.6
6.0	3	13.6
5.5	4	19.1
⋮	⋮	⋮

The procedure begins with 0 as the value of the counter and 0.0 as the initial value of the sum. At each stage, a data value is entered, the value of the counter is incremented by 1, and the data value is added to the sum, producing a new sum. These steps are repeated until eventually all the data values have been processed, and the sum is then divided by the counter to obtain the mean value. An initial algorithm for solving the problem thus is

1. Initialize a counter and a running sum to zero.
2. Repeatedly read a new data value, count it, and add it to the running sum.
3. After all the data has been processed, calculate the mean value and display the counter and the mean value.

Here, coding step 1 is straightforward, and only steps 2 and 3 require some refinement. Clearly, step 2 requires an input loop as described in the preceding section:

2. Repeat the following:
   a. Attempt to read a failure time.
   b. If the end of data is encountered, terminate repetition; otherwise, continue with the following.
   c. Increment the counter by 1.
   d. Add the failure time to the running sum.

After all of the data has been read and processed, the mean failure time is computed by dividing the final sum by the counter. If, however, there were no data values at all, steps c and d would be bypassed, and both the counter and the sum would be 0. The division operation required in step 3 to compute the mean failure time cannot be performed, because division by zero is not permitted. To guard against this error, we will check that the counter is nonzero before performing this division:

3. If the counter is nonzero, do the following:
   a. Divide the sum by the count to obtain the mean failure time.
   b. Display the count and the mean failure time.
   Else
       Display a "no data" message.

We can now write a complete algorithm for solving this problem. We will use the following variables:

VARIABLES FOR MEAN-TIME-TO-FAILURE PROBLEM	
FailureTime	Current failure time read
NumTimes	Number of failure-time readings
Sum	Sum of failure times
MeanFailureTime	Mean time to failure

A pseudocode description of this algorithm then is

ALGORITHM FOR MEAN-TIME-TO-FAILURE PROBLEM

Algorithm to read failure times, count them, and find the mean time to failure. Values are read until the end of data is encountered.

Input: A collection of failure times
Output: The mean time to failure and the number of failure times

1. Initialize *NumTimes* to 0 and *Sum* to 0.0.
2. Repeat the following:
   a. Attempt to read a *FailureTime*.
   b. If the end of data is encountered, terminate repetition; otherwise, continue with the following.
   c. Increment *NumTimes* by 1.
   d. Add *FailureTime* to the running *Sum*.
3. If *NumTimes* ≠ 0 do the following:
   a. Calculate *MeanFailureTime* = *Sum* / *NumTimes*.
   b. Display *NumTimes* and *MeanFailureTime*.
   Else
       Display a "no data" message.

Coding.   The program in Figure 4.5 implements the algorithm for solving this problem. Note that it uses a sentinel-controlled loop implemented as a DO-EXIT construct for the input loop in step 2.

Figure 4.5.   Mean time to failure

```fortran
PROGRAM Mean_Time_to_Failure
!-----------------------------------------------------------------------
! Program to read a list of failure times, count them, and find the
! mean time to failure. Values are read until an end-of-data flag
! is read. Identifiers used are:
! FailureTime      : the current failure time read
! EndDataFlag      : a constant -- the end-of-data flag
! NumTimes         : the number of failure-time readings
! Sum              : sum of failure times
! MeanFailureTime : the mean time to failure
!
! Input:  A list of failure times
! Output: Number of failure times read and their mean or a message
!         indicating that no failure times were entered
!-----------------------------------------------------------------------

  IMPLICIT NONE
  INTEGER :: NumTimes
  REAL :: FailureTime, Sum, MeanFailureTime
  REAL, PARAMETER :: EndDataFlag = -1.0

  ! Initialize Sum and NumTimes and give instructions to user
  Sum = 0.0
  NumTimes = 0
  PRINT *, "Enter failure time of", EndDataFlag, "to stop."

  ! Repeat the following
  DO
     PRINT *, "Enter failure time:"
     READ *, FailureTime

     ! If end-of-data, terminate repetition
     IF (FailureTime == EndDataFlag) EXIT

     ! Otherwise, continue with the following:
     NumTimes = NumTimes + 1
     Sum = Sum + FailureTime
  END DO

  ! Calculate and display mean time to failure
  IF (NumTimes /= 0) THEN
     MeanFailureTime = Sum / NumTimes
     PRINT *
     PRINT *, "Number of failure-time readings:", NumTimes
     PRINT *, "Mean time to failure:", MeanFailureTime
  ELSE
     PRINT *, "No failure times were entered."
  END IF
END PROGRAM Mean_Time_to_Failure
```

Execution and Testing.   Test runs with input data like the following indicate that the program is correct:

Test Run #1:

```
Enter failure time of -1.0000000 to stop.
Enter failure time:
-1.0
No failure times were entered.
-1.0
No failure times were entered.
```

Test Run #2:

```
Enter failure time of -1.0000000 to stop.
Enter failure time:
25.5
Enter failure time:
-1.0

Number of failure-time readings: 1
Mean time to failure: 25.5000000
```

Test Run #3:

```
Enter failure time of -1.0000000 to stop.
Enter failure time:
3.0
Enter failure time:
4.0
Enter failure time:
5.0
Enter failure time:
-1.0

Number of failure-time readings: 3
Mean time to failure: 4.0000000
```

It can then be used to calculate mean failure times for other data sets, such as the following:

```
Enter failure time of -1.0000000 to stop.
Enter failure time:
127
Enter failure time:
123.5
Enter failure time:
155.4
Enter failure time:
99
Enter failure time:
117.3
Enter failure time:
201.5
Enter failure time:
-1.0

Number of failure-time readings: 6
Mean time to failure: 1.3728334E+02
```

It can then be used to calculate mean failure times for other data sets, such as the following:

```
Enter failure time of -1.0000000 to stop.
Enter failure time:
127
Enter failure time:
123.5
Enter failure time:
155.4
Enter failure time:
99
Enter failure time:
117.3
Enter failure time:
201.5
Enter failure time:
-1.0

Number of failure-time readings: 6
Mean time to failure: 1.3728334E+02
```

PRACTICE!

1. What is the difference between a pretest and a posttest loop?

2. (True or false) A pretest loop is always executed at least once.

3. (True or false) A posttest loop is always executed at least once.

4. Assuming that Number is an integer variable, describe the output produced by the following loop:

   ```
   Number = 1
   DO
       IF (Number > 100) EXIT
       PRINT *, Number
       NUM = 2 * Number
   END DO
   ```

5. Assume that Number and Limit are integer variables, and consider the following program segment:

   ```
   READ *, Limit
   Number = 0
   DO
       IF (Number > Limit) EXIT
       PRINT *, Number
       Number = Number + 1
   END DO
   ```

   Describe the output produced for the following inputs:
   (a) 4   **(b)** -2

6. Assume that `Number` and `Limit` are integer variables, and consider the following program segment:

```
READ *, Limit
Number = 0
DO
    PRINT *, Number
    Number = Number + 1
    IF (Number > Limit) EXIT
END DO
```

Describe the output produced for the following inputs:
(a) 4   (b) -2

7. Write a loop to print the value of X and decrease X by 0.5 as long as X is positive.

8. Write a loop to read values for A, B, and C and print their sum, repeating this procedure while none of A, B, or C is negative.

9. Write a loop to calculate and print the squares of consecutive positive integers until the difference between a square and the preceding one is greater than 50.

10. Design an algorithm that uses a loop to count the number of digits in a given integer.

11. Write Fortran statements to implement the algorithm in Exercise 10.

12. Develop an algorithm to approximate the value of ex^a using the infinite series

$$e^x = \sum_{n=0}^{\infty} \frac{x^n}{n!}$$

For each of the problems described in Exercises 13–16, specify the input and output for the problem, make a list of variables you will use in describing a solution to the problem, and then design an algorithm to solve the problem.

13. A car manufacturer wants to determine average noise levels for the 10 different models of cars the company produces. Each can be purchased with one of five different engines. Design an algorithm to enter the noise levels (in decibels) that were recorded for each possible model and engine configuration and to calculate the average noise level for each model as well as the average noise level over all models and engines.

14. Dispatch Die-Casting currently produces 200 castings per month and realizes a profit of $300 per casting. The company now spends $2000 per month on research and development and has a fixed operating cost of $20,000 per month that does not depend on the amount of production. If the company doubles the amount spent on research and development, it is estimated that production will increase by 20 percent. The company president would like to know, beginning with the current status and successively doubling the amount spent on research and development, at what point the net profit will begin to decline.

15. Consider a cylindrical reservoir with a radius of 30.0 feet and a height of 30.0 feet that is filled and emptied by a 12–inch-diameter pipe. The pipe has a 1000.0–foot-long run and discharges at an elevation 20.0 feet lower than the bottom of the reservoir. The pipe has been tested and has a roughness factor of 0.0130.

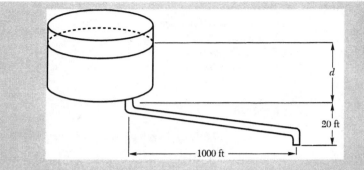

Several formulas have been developed experimentally to determine the velocity at which fluids flow through such pipes. One of these, the *Manning formula*, is

$$V = \frac{1.486}{N} R^{2/3} S^{1/2}$$

where

V = velocity in feet per second

N = roughness coefficient

R = hydraulic radius = $\dfrac{\text{cross-sectional area}}{\text{wetted perimeter}}$

S = slope of the energy gradient $\left(= \dfrac{d+20}{1000} \text{ for this problem} \right)$

The rate of fluid flow is equal to the cross-sectional area of the pipe multiplied by the velocity.

Design an algorithm to estimate the time required to empty the reservoir, given the reservoir's height, roughness coefficient, hydraulic radius, and pipe radius. Do this by assuming a constant flow rate for 5-minute segments.

16. A 100.0-pound sign is hung from the end of a horizontal pole of negligible mass. The pole is attached to the building by a pin and is supported by a cable, as shown in the following diagram. The pole and cable are each 6.0 feet long.

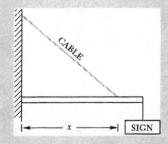

Design an algorithm to find the appropriate place (indicated by x in the diagram) to attach the cable to the pole so that the tension in the cable will be minimized. The equation governing static equilibrium tells us that

$$\text{tension} = \frac{100 \cdot 6 \cdot 6}{x\sqrt{36 - x^2}}$$

Calculate the tension for x starting at 1.0 feet and incrementing it by 0.1 feet until the approximate minimum value is located.

KEY TERMS

Body of the loop	Infinite loop	Query-controlled input loop
CYCLE statement	Loop	Repetition structure
DO construct	Nesting	Sentinel
DO-EXIT construct	Posttest	Test-in-the-middle loop
End-of-data flag	Pretest loop	Zero-trip behavior

PROGRAMMING POINTERS

Program Style and Design

1. *The body of a loop should be indented.*

```
DO variable = init, limit, step
    statement₁
        ⋮
    statementₙ
END DO

DO
    statement₁
        ⋮
    statementₙ
    IF (logical-condition) EXIT
    statementₙ₊₁
        ⋮
    statementₘ
END DO
```

2. *All programs can be written using the three control structures considered thus far: sequence, selection, and repetition.*

Potential Problems

1. *The control variable in a* DO *loop may not be modified within the loop. Modifying the initial value, limit, or step size does not affect the number of repetitions.*

2. *The statements within a general* DO *loop controlled by a logical expression must eventually cause the logical expression to become true, because otherwise an infinite loop will result.* For example, if X is a real variable, the statements

```
X = 0.0
DO
    IF (X == 1.0) EXIT
    PRINT *, X
    X = X + 0.3
END DO
```

will produce an infinite loop. Since the value of X is never equal to 1.0, repetition is not terminated. Changing the last statement in the loop to

```
X = X + 0.1
```

may also produce an infinite loop. Since X is initialized to 0 and 0.1 is added to X 10 times, X should have the value 1. However, the logical expression X == 1.0 may remain true because most real values are not stored exactly.

3. *Declarations initialize variables at compile time, not during execution.* This is important to remember when a program processes several sets of data and uses variables that must be initialized to certain values before processing each data set. To illustrate, consider the following program:

```
INTEGER :: Number, Sum = 0
CHARACTER(1) :: Response

DO ! Loop to process several data sets

   DO ! Input loop for current data set
      READ *, Number

         ! If end of current data set, terminate repetition
         IF (Number == -999) EXIT

         ! Otherwise continue with the following
      Sum = Sum + Number
   END DO

   PRINT *, "Sum =", Sum
   PRINT *
   PRINT *, "More data (Y or N)?"
   READ *, Response
   IF (Response == "N") EXIT

END DO
```

In the following sample run,

```
10
20
30
-999
Sum = 60

More data (Y or N)?
Y
15
125
-999
Sum = 200

More data (Y or N)?
N
```

the sum of the first data set is correctly displayed as 60, but the sum of the second data set is 140, and not 200 as shown. The error is caused by the fact that when the second set of numbers is processed, Sum is not reset to 0, because the initialization is done at compile time, not during execution. The obvious solution is to insert the statement

```
Sum = 0
```

between the two DO statements.

Programming Problems

SECTION 4.2

1. A certain product is to sell for Price dollars per item. Write a program that reads values for Price and the Number of items sold and then produces a table showing the total price of from 1 through TotalNumber units.

2. The mechanism shown below is part of a machine that a company is designing:

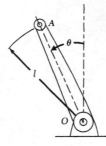

During operation, the rod OA will oscillate according to $\theta = \theta_0 \sin(2\pi t/\tau)$, where θ is measured in radians, θ_0 is the maximum angular displacement, τ is the period of motion, and t = time in seconds measured from $t = 0$ when OA is vertical. If l is the length OA, the magnitude of the acceleration of point A is given by

$$|a_A| = \frac{4\pi^2 l\theta_0}{\tau^2} \sqrt{\theta_0^2 \cos^4\left(\frac{2\pi t}{\tau}\right) + \sin^2\left(\frac{2\pi t}{\tau}\right)}$$

Write a program that will read values for θ_0, l, and τ and that will then calculate a table of values of t, θ and $|a_A|$ for $t = 0.0$ to 0.5 in steps of 0.05 (in seconds). Execute the program with $\tau = 2$ sec, $\theta_0 = \pi/2$, and $l = 0.1$ m.

3. Suppose that at a given time, genotypes AA, AB, and BB appear in the proportions x, y, and z, respectively, where $x = 0.25$, $y = 0.5$, and $z = 0.25$. If individuals of type AA cannot reproduce, the probability that one parent will donate gene A to an offspring is

$$p = \frac{1}{2}\left(\frac{y}{y+z}\right)$$

since $y/(y + z)$ is the probability that the parent is of type AB and $1/2$ is the probability that such a parent will donate gene A. Then the proportions x', y', and z' of AA, AB, and BB, respectively, in each succeeding generation are given by

$$x' = p^2, \qquad y' = 2p(1-p), \qquad z' = (1-p)^2$$

and the new probability is given by

$$p' = \frac{1}{2}\left(\frac{y'}{x'+z'}\right)$$

Write a program to calculate and print the generation number and the proportions of AA, AB, and BB under appropriate headings until the proportions of both AA and AB are less than some small positive value.

4. The sequence of *Fibonacci numbers* begins with the integers

$$1, 1, 2, 3, 5, 8, 13, 21, \ldots$$

where each number after the first two is the sum of the two preceding numbers. Write a program that reads a positive integer n and then displays the first n Fibonacci numbers.

5. One property of the Fibonacci sequence (see Problem 4) is that the ratios of consecutive Fibonacci numbers ($1/1$, $1/2$, $2/3$, $3/5$, $\ldots$) approach the "golden ratio"

$$\frac{\sqrt{5} - 1}{2}$$

Modify the program in Problem 4 to display Fibonacci numbers and the decimal values of the ratios of consecutive Fibonacci numbers.

6. If a loan of A dollars, which carries a monthly interest rate of R (expressed as a decimal), is to be paid off in N months, then the monthly payment P will be

$$P = A\left[\frac{R(1+R)^N}{(1+R)^N - 1}\right]$$

During this time period, some of each monthly payment will be used to repay that month's accrued interest, and the rest will be used to reduce the balance owed.

Write a program to print an *amortization table* that displays the payment number, the amount of the monthly payment, the interest for that month, the amount of the payment applied to the principal, and the new balance. Use your program to produce an amortization table for a loan of $50,000 to be repaid in 36 months at 1 percent per month.

SECTIONS 4.3 AND 4.4

7. Write a program to calculate all the Fibonacci numbers less than 5000 and the decimal values of the ratios of consecutive Fibonacci numbers (see Problem 4).

8. Write a program to read the data values shown in the following table, calculate the miles per gallon in each case, and print the values with appropriate labels:

MILES TRAVELED	GALLONS OF GASOLINE USED
231	14.8
248	15.1
302	12.8
147	9.25
88	7
265	13.3

9. Write a program to read a set of numbers, count them, and find and print the largest and smallest numbers in the list and their positions in the list.

10. Suppose that a ball dropped from a building bounces off the pavement and that on each bounce it returns to a certain constant percentage of its previous height. Write a program to read the height from which the ball was dropped and the percentage of rebound. Then let the ball bounce repeatedly, and print the height of the ball at the top of each bounce, the distance traveled during that bounce, and the total distance traveled thus far, terminating when the height of the ball is almost zero (less than some small positive value).

11. Write a program to read a set of numbers, count them, and calculate the mean, variance, and standard deviation of the set of numbers. The *mean* and *variance* of numbers $x_1, x_2, \ldots, x_n$ can be calculated using the following formulas:

$$\text{mean} = \frac{1}{n}\sum_{i=1}^{n} x_i \qquad \text{variance} = \frac{1}{n}\sum_{i=1}^{n} x_i^2 - \frac{1}{n^2}\left(\sum_{i=1}^{n} x_i\right)^2$$

The *standard deviation* is the square root of the variance.

5

Input/Output

5.1 FORMATTED OUTPUT

There are two output statements in Fortran, the `PRINT` statement and the `WRITE` statement. The `PRINT` **statement** is the simpler of the two and has the form

```
PRINT format-specifier, output-list
```

where `format-specifier` is one of the following:

1. `*` (an asterisk)
2. A character constant or a character variable (or expression or array) whose value specifies the format for the output
3. The label of a `FORMAT` statement

Each execution of a `PRINT` statement displays the values of the items in the `output-list` on a new line. If the output list is omitted, a blank line is displayed.

The `format-specifier` specifies the format in which values of the expressions in the output list are to be displayed. An asterisk (`*`) indicates list-directed output in which the format for the various types of expressions in the output list is machine-dependent. In the second type of format specifier, the formatting information is given as a character string that consists of format descriptors, separated by commas and enclosed in parentheses:

```
'(list of format descriptors)'    or
"(list of format descriptors)"
```

In the third case, the formatting information is supplied by a `FORMAT` **statement** whose label is specified. This statement has the form

OBJECTIVES

In this chapter, you will

- Learn how to use the `PRINT` statement.
- Study input using the `READ` statement.
- Find out how the WRITE statement is used for output.
- Learn more about the READ statement.
- Study input from and output to files.
- Apply input/output techniques to a device-monitoring problem.

> `label FORMAT (list of format descriptors)`

where `label` is an integer in the range 1 through 99999.

There are many format descriptors that may be used in format specifiers. A list of the most useful descriptors is given in Table 5.1. The most common of these are described in this section.[1]

For some Fortran compilers, the first character of each line of output directed to a printer is used to control the vertical spacing. If this character is one of the following, it is removed from the output line and is used to effect the appropriate printer control:

blank	Normal spacing: advance to the next line before printing.
0	Double spacing: skip one line before printing.
1	Advance to top of next page before printing.
+	Overprint the last line printed.

The details regarding how your particular system uses control characters (and whether it uses any others) can be obtained from system manuals, your instructor, or computer center personnel.

When control characters are in effect, it is important to pay attention to printer control, because otherwise the output may not be what was intended. To illustrate, consider the following statement:

```
PRINT '(I3)', N
```

TABLE 5-1 Format Description

FORMS		USE
Iw	Iw.m	Integer data
Bw	Bw.m	Integer data in binary form
Ow	Ow.m	Integer data in octal form
Zw	Zw.m	Integer data in hexadecimal form
Fw.d		Real data in decimal notation
Ew.d	Ew.dEe	Real data in exponential notation
ESw.d	ESw.dEe	Real data in scientific notation
ENw.d	ENw.dEe	Real data in engineering notation
Gw.d	Gw.dEe	General i/o descriptor
A	Aw	Character data
"x ... x"	'x ... x'	Character strings
Lw		Logical data
Tc	TLn	TRn	Tab descriptors
nX		Horizontal spacing
/		Vertical spacing
:		Format scanning control

w: a positive integer constant specifying the field width
m: a nonnegative integer constant specifying the minimum number of digits to be read/ displayed
d: a nonnegative integer constant specifying the number of digits to the right of the decimal point
e: a nonnegative integer constant specifying the number of digits in an exponent
x: a character
c: a positive integer constant representing a character position
n: a positive integer constant specifying the number of character positions

[1] For descriptions of the other format descriptors, see Chapter 5 of our more comprehensive text. *Fortran 90 for Engineers and Scientists.*

The format descriptor I3 specifies that the value to be printed is an integer and is to be printed in the first three positions of a line. If the value of N is 15, the three positions are filled with ƀ15 (where ƀ denotes a blank). If control characters are in effect, the blank in the first position is removed and is interpreted as a control character. This produces normal spacing and displays the value 15 in the first two positions of a new line:

> | 15

If, however, the value of N is 150, the first three positions are to be filled with 150. The character 1 in the first position is removed and interpreted as a control character. It is not printed, but instead the value 50 is printed at the top of a new page:

> ⌈ 50

When control characters are in effect, it is good practice to use the first print position of each output line to indicate explicitly what printer control is desired. This can be done by making the first descriptor of each format specifier one of the following:

1X or " " for normal spacing
"0" for double spacing
"1" for advancing to a new page
"+" for overprinting

For list-directed output, a blank will automatically be inserted at the beginning of each output line as a control character and will produce normal spacing.

The default output device for many systems is the screen and control characters are not normally in effect. We will assume that this is the case in this text:

In the examples in this text, control characters are *not* assumed. However, so that these examples do not need modification for systems in which control characters are in effect, we will use an appropriate format descriptor (e.g., 1X) at the beginning of each output format specifier.

Integer Output—The I Descriptor

Integer values that are output using an I descriptor are *right-justified* in fields of the specified sizes; that is, each value is displayed so that its last digit appears in the right-most position of the field. For example, if the values of the integer variables Number, L, and Kappa are

```
INTEGER :: Number = 3, L = 5378, Kappa = -12345
```

then the statements

```
PRINT '(1X, 2I5, I7, I10)', Number, Number - 3, L, Kappa
PRINT '(1X, 2I5.2, I7, I10.7)', Number, Number - 3, L, Kappa
PRINT '(1X, 2I5.0, I7, I10)', Number, Number - 3, L, Kappa
```

or

```
PRINT 30, Number, Number - 3, L, Kappa
PRINT 31, Number, Number - 3, L, Kappa
PRINT 32, Number, Number - 3, L, Kappa
30 FORMAT(1X, 2I5, I7, I10)
31 FORMAT(1X, 2I5.2, I7, I10.7)
32 FORMAT(1X, 2I5.0, I7, I10)
```

produce the following output:

```
|_____3____0____5378_____-12345
 ------------------------------
|____03___00____5378___-0012345
 ------------------------------
|_____3_____5378_____-12345
 ------------------------------
```

If an integer value (including a minus sign if the number is negative) requires more spaces than specified by a descriptor, the field is filled with asterisks. Thus, the statement

```
PRINT '(1X, 4I3)', Number, Number - 3, L, Kappa
```

will produce

```
|___3__0******
 -------------
```

Real Output—The F, E, ES, and EN Descriptors

Like integer values, real values are *right-justified* in their fields. For a descriptor Fw.d, w specifies the *total width of the field* in which to display a real value, and d is the number of digits to the right of the decimal point. If the value has more than d digits following the decimal point, it is *rounded* to d digits. If it has fewer than d digits, the remaining positions are filled with zeros.

For example, to display the values of the integer variables In and Out and the values of the real variables A, B, and C as given by

```
INTEGER :: In = 625, Out = -19
REAL :: A = 7.5, B = .182, C = 625.327
```

we can use the statement

```
PRINT '(1X, 2I4, 2F6.3, F8.3)', In, Out, A, B, C
```

The resulting output is

```
|__625_-19_7.500_0.182_625.327
 -----------------------------
```

As with the I descriptor, if the real number being output requires more spaces than specified by the descriptor, the entire field is *filled with asterisks*. For a descriptor Fw.d, one should have w ≥ d + 3 to allow for the sign of the number, the first digit, and the decimal point.

For output using an E descriptor, real values are usually displayed in *normalized form*—a minus sign, if necessary, followed by one leading zero, then a decimal point followed by d significant digits, and E with an appropriate exponent in the next four spaces for the first form or e spaces for the second form. For example, if the values of real variables A, B, C, and D are given by

```
REAL :: A = .12345E8, B = .0237, C = 4.6E-12, D = -76.1684E12
```

the statement

```
PRINT '(1X, 2E15.5, E15.4, E14.4)', A, B, C, D
```

produces output like the following:

```
|_____0.12345E+08____0.23700E-01____0.40600E-11___-0.7617E+14
 ------------------------------------------------------------
```

As with the F descriptor, a field is *asterisk-filled* if it is not large enough for the value. For a descriptor Ew.d, one should have w ≥ d + 7, or for the second form

`Ew.dEe`, `w ≥ d + e + 5`, to allow space for the sign of the number, a leading zero, a decimal point, and `E` with the exponent.

The **scientific descriptor** `ES` is used in the same manner as the `E` descriptor, except that values are normalized so that the mantissa is at least 1 but less than 10 (unless the value is zero). The **engineering descriptor** `EN` also is used in the same manner as the `E` descriptor, except that the exponent is constrained to be a multiple of 3, so that a nonzero mantissa is greater than or equal to 1 and less than 1000.

Character Output

Character constants may be displayed by including them in the list of descriptors of a format specifier. For example, if `X` and `Y` have the values 0.3 and 7.9, respectively, the statements

```
PRINT '(1X, "X =", F6.2, " Y =", F6.2)', X, Y
```

or

```
PRINT 70, X, Y
70 FORMAT(1X, "X =", F6.2, " Y =", F6.2)
```

produce as output

```
 X =  0.30 Y =   7.90
```

Character data may also be displayed by using an `A` format descriptor of the form `rA` or `rAw`. In the first form, the field width is determined by the length of the character value being displayed. In the second form, if the field width exceeds the length of the character value, that value is *right-justified* in the field. In contrast with numeric output, however, if the length of the character value exceeds the specified field width, the output consists of the *leftmost* w characters. For example, the preceding output would also be produced if the labels were included in the output list, as follows:

```
PRINT '(1X, A, F6.2, A, F6.2)', "X =", X, " Y =", Y
```

Positional Descriptors—X and T

Two format descriptors can be used to provide spacing in an output line. A descriptor of the form `nX` can be used to insert `n` blanks in an output line. A tab descriptor of the form `Tc` causes the next output field to begin at the specified position `c` on the current line.

To illustrate these descriptors, suppose that `Number` is an integer variable with value 141. The output statement

```
PRINT 75, "John Q. Doe", "CPSC", Number
```

together with either of the following `FORMAT` statements

```
75 FORMAT(1X, A11, 3X, A4, 2X, I3)
```

or

```
75 FORMAT(1X, A11, T16, A4, 2X, I3)
```

will produce the output

```
John Q. Doe   CPSC  141
```

Repeating Groups of Format Descriptors

As we have seen, it is possible to repeat some format descriptors by preceding them with a *repetition indicator*. For example, `3F10.2` is equivalent to `F10.2`, `F10.2`,

F10.2. It is also possible to repeat a group of descriptors by enclosing the group in parentheses and then placing a repetition indicator before the left parenthesis. For example, the format specifier

```
'(1X, A, F6.2, A, F6.2)'
```

can be written more compactly as

```
'(1X, 2(A, F6.2))'
```

The Slash (/) Descriptor

A single output statement can be used to display values on more than one line, with different formats, by using a slash (/) descriptor. The slash causes output to begin on a new line, and it can also be used with a repetition indicator to skip several lines. It is not necessary to use a comma to separate a slash descriptor from other descriptors. For example, consider the statements

```
PRINT 88, "Values", N, A, M, B, C, D
88 FORMAT(1X, A, 3/ 1X, 2(I10, F10.2) // 1X, 2E15.7)
```

If the values of N, A, M, B, C, and D are given by

```
N = 5173
A = 617.2
M = 7623
B = 29.25
C = 37.555
D = 5.2813
```

then the resulting output is

```
Values
----------------------------------------------
----------------------------------------------
----------------------------------------------
      5173    617.20        7623     29.25
----------------------------------------------
   0.3755500E+02  0.5281300E+01
```

Scanning the Format

If the values of all the items in the output list have been displayed before all the descriptors in the corresponding format specifier have been used, scanning of the format specifier continues. Values of character constants are displayed, and the positioning specified by slash, X, and T descriptors continues until one of the following is encountered:

1. The right parenthesis signaling the end of the list of format descriptors
2. An I, F, E, ES, EN, A, L, G, B, O, or Z descriptor
3. A colon

In cases 2 and 3, all remaining descriptors in the format specifier are ignored.

To illustrate, consider the statements

```
PRINT '(1X, I5, 3I6)', M, N
PRINT '(1X, F5.1, F7.0, F10.5)', A, B
PRINT '(1X, 5("  Item is", A10))', "Bumper", "Headlight"
PRINT '(1X, 5(: "  Item is", A10))', "Bumper", "Headlight"
```

If M and N are integer variables with values M = 7623 and N = 5173 and A and B are real variables with values given by A = 617.2 and B = 29.25, these statements produce the output

```
  7623   5173
  617.2    29.
    Item is     Bumper   Item is Headlight   Item is
    Item is     Bumper   Item is Headlight
```

If the list of descriptors is exhausted before the output list is, a new line of output is begun, and the format specifier or part of it is rescanned. If there are no internal parentheses within the format specifier, the rescanning begins with the first descriptor. For example, the statement

```
PRINT '(1X, 2I6)', N, N+1, N+2, N+3, N+4
```

produces the output

```
   5173   5174
   5175   5176
   5177
```

If the format specifier does contain internal parentheses, rescanning begins at the left parenthesis that matches the next-to-last right parenthesis; any repetition counter preceding this format group is in effect. Thus, the statements

```
PRINT 100, M, A, N, B, N + 1, B + 1.0, N + 2, B + 2.0
100 FORMAT(1X, I5, F10.3 / (1X, I10, F12.2))
```

produce the output

```
  7623    617.200
        5173          29.25
        5174          30.25
        5175          31.25
```

5.2 FORMATTED INPUT

We have seen that input is accomplished in Fortran by a READ **statement**. This statement has two forms, the simpler of which is

```
READ format-specifier, input-list
```

where the format specifiers and descriptors are essentially the same as those discussed for output in the preceding section. Character constants, however, may not appear in the list of format descriptors, and the colon separator is not relevant for input.

Integer Input

Integer data can be read using the I descriptor of the form rIw, where w indicates the width of the field, that is, the number of characters to be read. To illustrate, consider the following example:

```
INTEGER :: I, J, K
READ '(I6, I4, I7)', I, J, K
```

or

```
READ 5, I, J, K
5 FORMAT(I6, I4, I7)
```

If the data entered is

```
  -123  45   6789
------------------
```

the values assigned to I, J, and K are

```
I:  -123
J:  45
K:  6789
```

Had the data been entered as

```
-123    45      6789
--------------------
```

the same values would be assigned since *blanks within numeric fields are ignored* (unless the BZ descriptor is used to cause them to be interpreted as zeros). If the format specification were changed to

```
(I4, I2, I4)
```

the data should be entered as

```
-123456789
----------
```

with no intervening blanks.

Real Input

There are two ways that real data may be entered:

1. The numbers may be entered without decimal points.
2. The decimal point may be entered as part of the input value.

In the first case, the d specification in a format descriptor Fw.d automatically positions the decimal point so that there are d digits to its right. For example, if we wish to enter the following values for real variables A, B, C, D, and E,

```
A:  6.25
B:  -1.9
C:  75.0
D:  .182
E:  625.327
```

we can use the statement

```
READ '(F3.2, 2F3.1, F3.3, F6.3)', A, B, C, D, E
```

and enter the data in the following form:

```
625-19750182625327
------------------
```

Of course, we can use wider fields, for example,

```
(F4.2, 2F4.1, 2F8.3)
```

and enter the data in the form

```
 625 -19 750      182  625327
-----------------------------
```

In the second method of entering real data, the position of the decimal point in the value entered overrides the position specified by the descriptor. Thus, if the number to be read is 9423.68, an appropriate descriptor is F6.2 if the number is entered without a decimal point and F7.2, or F7.1, or F7.0, and so on, if the number is entered with a decimal point. For example, the preceding values for A, B, C, D, and E can be read using the statement

```
READ '(4F5.0, F8.0)', A, B, C, D, E
```

with the data entered in the following form:

```
 6.25 -1.9  75.  .182 625.327
```

Note that each field width must be large enough to accommodate the number entered, including the decimal point and the sign.

Real values entered in E notation can also be read using an F descriptor. The E, ES, and EN descriptors may also be used in a manner similar to that for the F descriptor.

Character Input

When a READ statement whose input list contains a character variable is executed, *all* characters in the field associated with the corresponding A descriptor are read. For example, if the line of data

```
Fourscore and seven years ago
```

is read by the statements

```
CHARACTER(6) :: Speech1, Speech2

READ '(2A)', Speech1, Speech2
```

the values assigned to Speech1 and Speech2 are

```
Speech1: Foursc
Speech2: ore an
```

Note that six characters were read for each of Speech1 and Speech2, because this is their declared length. If the following line of data

```
AB1''34;an,apple a day
```

is entered, the values assigned would be

```
Speech1: AB1''3
Speech2: 4;an,a
```

If the format specifier '(2A6)' were used, the same values would be assigned to Speech1 and Speech2. If, however, the format specifier '(A2, A12)' were used, the values assigned would be

```
Speech1: ABbbbb      (where b denotes a blank)
Speech2: an,app
```

Skipping Input Characters

The positional descriptors X and T may be used in the format specifier of a READ statement to skip over certain input characters. For example, if we wish to assign the following values to the integer variables I, J, and K:

```
I:    4
J:    56
$K:   137
```

by entering data in the form

```
I = 4    J = 56   K = 137
```

the following statements may be used:

```
READ '(3X, I2, 6X, I3, 5X, I4)', I, J, K
```

or

```
READ '(T4, I2, T12, I3, T20, I4)', I, J, K
```

Multiple Input Lines

A new line of data is required each time a READ statement is executed or whenever a slash (/) is encountered in the format specifier for the READ statement. This may be used to skip blank lines, remarks, and the like. For example, the following data

```
Amount to be produced
585.00
Reaction rate
(This assumes constant temperature)
5.75
```

can be read by a single READ statement, and the values 585.00 and 5.75 assigned to Amount and Rate, respectively, using

```
REAL :: Amount, Rate

READ '(/ F6.0 3/ F4.0)', Amount, Rate
```

PRACTICE!

Assuming that the following declarations and assignments

```
INTEGER :: Number = 12345
REAL :: Alpha = 87.6543
CHARACTER(25) :: Form_1 = '(1X, I10, F10.2, "---")', &
                 Title*8 = "Exercise"
```

have been made, describe the output that will be produced by the statements in Exercises 1–14. For Exercises 1–11, assume that control characters *are not in effect.*

1. PRINT *, "Computer science -- ", Title, " 5.2"

2. PRINT *, "Alpha =", Alpha, " Number =", Number

3. PRINT '(" Computer science -- Exercise", F4.1)', &
       3 * 2.1 - 1.1

4. PRINT '(1X, A, F4.1)', "Computer science", 5.2

5. PRINT 10, Title, 5.2
   10 FORMAT(" Computer science --", A2, F3.1)

6. PRINT 20, Number, Number + 1, Alpha, Alpha + 1,
   Alpha + 2
   20 FORMAT(1X, 2I7, F10.5, F10.3, F10.0)

```
 7. PRINT 30, Number, Alpha, Number + 1, Alpha + 1
    30 FORMAT(1X, I5, F7.4 / 1X, I5, E12.5)

 8. PRINT Form_1, Number, Alpha, Number + 1, Alpha + 1

 9. PRINT '(1X, I5, A2, I6 / 1X, 13("="))',
    Number, "=", 12345

10. PRINT 40, Number, Alpha, Number, Alpha
    40 FORMAT(/// 2(1X, I6 // 1X, F6.2) /// " ******")

11. PRINT 50, Number, Alpha, Number, Alpha, Number, Alpha
    50 FORMAT(1X, I6, F7.2, (1X, I5, F6.1))
```

For Exercises 12–14, assume that control characters *are in effect*.

```
12. PRINT '("Computer science -- ", A, F5.2)', Title, 5.2

13. PRINT 60, Number, Number + 1, Alpha, Alpha + 1,
    Alpha + 2
    60 FORMAT("0", 2I7, F10.5, F10.3, F10.0)

14. PRINT '(1X, I5, F7.4 / I5, E12.5)', &
            Number, Alpha, Number + 1, Alpha + 1
    PRINT '("+", TI5, I5, E12.5)', Number + 1, Alpha + 1
```

For the READ statements in Exercises 15–21, assuming the declarations

```
    INTEGER :: I, J
    REAL :: X, Y
    CHARACTER(20) :: Form_2 = '(I5, F6.0)', &
                     C*8
```

have been made, show how the data should be entered so that X, Y, I, J, and C are assigned the values 123.77, 6.0, 77, 550, and "Fortran", respectively:

```
15. READ *, I, J, X, Y

16. READ '(I3, F7.0, 2X, I5, T20, F5.0)', I, J, X, Y

17. READ Form_2, I, X, J, Y

18. READ 200, X, Y, I, J
    200 FORMAT(F5.2, 1X, F1.0, T4, I2, T9, I3)

19. READ 220, X, I, Y, J, C
    220 FORMAT(F6.2 / I5 // F6.0, I6 / A)

20. READ '(A, I2, F5.2)', C, I, X

21. READ '(A10, I10, F10.0)', C, I, X
```

5.3 THE WRITE STATEMENT AND THE GENERAL READ STATEMENT

5.3.1 The WRITE Statement

The WRITE **statement** has a more complicated syntax than the PRINT statement, but it is more general. It has the form

```
    WRITE (control-list) output-list
```

where `control-list` may include items selected from the following:

1. A **unit specifier**, which is an integer expression whose value designates the output device, or it may be an asterisk, indicating the standard output device (usually a monitor screen or a printer). The unit specifier may be given in the form

   `UNIT = unit-specifier` or simply `unit-specifier`

   In the second form, the unit specifier must be the first item in the control list.

2. A **format specifier** that may be of any of the forms allowed in the `PRINT` statement. It may be given in the form

   `FMT = format-specifier` or simply `format-specifier`

   In the second form, the format specifier must be the second item in the control list and the `UNIT` = clause must also be omitted for the unit specifier.

3. An `ADVANCE` = **clause** of the form

   `ADVANCE = character-expression`

   where the value of `character-expression` (after removing any trailing blanks and converting lower case to upper case) is one of the strings `"NO"` or `"YES"`.

4. Other items that are especially useful in file processing.

To illustrate, suppose that the values of `Gravity` and `Weight` are to be displayed on an output device having unit number 6. The statement

```
WRITE (6, *) Gravity, Weight
```

or any of several equivalent forms such as

```
WRITE (6, FMT = *) Gravity, Weight
WRITE (UNIT = 6, FMT = *) Gravity, Weight
WRITE (Output_Unit, *) Gravity, Weight
WRITE (UNIT = Output_Unit, FMT = *) Gravity, Weight
```

where `Output_Unit` is an integer variable with value 6, produce list-directed output to this device. If this device is the system's standard output device, the unit number 6 may be replaced by an asterisk in any of the preceding statements; for example,

```
WRITE (*, *) Gravity, Weight
```

and each of these is equivalent to the short form

```
PRINT *, Gravity, Weight
```

The `ADVANCE` = clause is used to specify whether output should advance to a new line after the current output has been completed. `ADVANCE` = `"NO"` causes non-advancing output, whereas `ADVANCE` = `"YES"` is the default condition and causes an advance to a new line of output after the `WRITE` statement has been executed.

The General `READ` Statement

The general form of the `READ` statement is

```
READ (control-list) input-list
```

where `control-list` may include items selected from the following:

1. A unit specifier (see the `WRITE` statement) indicating the input device
2. A format specifier (see the `WRITE` statement)
3. An `ADVANCE` = clause (see the `WRITE` statement)
4. An `IOSTAT` = clause to detect an input error or an end-of-file condition, as described in the next section
5. Other items that are particularly useful in processing files

For example, the statement

```
READ (5, *) Code, Time, Rate
```

or any of several equivalent forms such as

```
READ (UNIT = 5, FMT = *) CODE, TIME, RATE
READ (IN, *) CODE, TIME, RATE
```

where `In` has the value 5, can be use to read values for `Code`, `Time`, and `Rate`. Formatted input is also possible with the general `READ` statement.

5.4 FILE PROCESSING

Applications involving large data sets can be processed most conveniently if the data is stored in a file for later processing, for example, by a program as it reads input data from this file or by a printer as it produces a hard copy of the output. Files are usually stored on disks or on some other form of external (secondary) memory.

Opening Files

Before a file can be used in a Fortran program, a *unit number* must be connected to it and several items of information about the file must be supplied. This process is called *opening* the file and is accomplished using an `OPEN` **statement** of the form

```
OPEN (open-list)
```

where `open-list` includes

1. A unit specifier indicating a unit number connected to the file being opened; it has the same form as for the `WRITE` and `READ` statements.
2. A `FILE` = **clause** of the form

   ```
   FILE = character-expression
   ```

   where the value of `character-expression` (ignoring trailing blanks) is the name of the file to be connected to the specified unit number.
3. a `STATUS` = **clause** of the form

   ```
   STATUS = character-expression
   ```

   where the value of `character-expression` (ignoring trailing blanks and with lowercase letters converted to upper case) is one of

   ```
   "OLD"
   "NEW"
   "REPLACE"
   ```

   (or `"UNKNOWN"`). OLD means that the file already exists in the system. NEW means that the file does not yet exist and is being created by the program; execution of the OPEN statement creates an empty file with the specified name and changes its status to OLD. REPLACE creates a new file, replacing the old one if one already exists, and changes its status to OLD.

4. An ACTION = **clause** of the form

    ```
    ACTION = i-o-action
    ```

    where i-o-action is a character expression whose value (ignoring trailing blanks and case) is one of

    ```
    "READ"
    "WRITE"
    "READWRITE"
    ```

    The file will be opened for reading only, for writing only, or for both reading and writing, respectively. If this clause is omitted, the action is compiler-dependent, but normally the file will be opened for READWRITE.

5. A POSITION = **clause** of the form

    ```
    POSITION = character-expression
    ```

    where the value of character-expression (ignoring trailing blanks and with lowercase letters converted to upper case) is one of

    ```
    "REWIND"
    "APPEND"
    "ASIS"
    ```

    These specifiers position the file at its initial point, position it at the end of the file, or leave its position unchanged, respectively. If this clause is omitted, the position of the file will be left unchanged if the file is already open, and the file will be created and positioned at its initial point if the file does not exist.

6. An IOSTAT = **clause** of the form

    ```
    IOSTAT = status-variable
    ```

    where status-variable is an integer variable to which the value zero is assigned if the file is opened successfully and a positive value is assigned otherwise. A positive value usually represents the number of an appropriate error message in a list found in system manuals.

For example, to open a file named INFO.DAT from which data values are to be read, we might use the statement

```
OPEN (UNIT = 12, FILE = "INFO.DAT", STATUS = "OLD", &
      ACTION = "READ", POSITION = "REWIND", &
      IOSTAT = OpenStatus)
```

where OpenStatus is an integer variable. If the program containing this statement is to be used with various data files, it is better not to "hard wire" the file's name into the program. Instead we can declare a character variable to store the file's name, have the user input the name,

```
CHARACTER(12) :: FileName

WRITE (*, '(1X, A)', ADVANCE = "NO") &
      "Enter name of data file: "
READ *, FileName
```

and then use the following OPEN statement:

```
OPEN (UNIT = 12, FILE = FileName, STATUS = "OLD", &
      ACTION = "READ", POSITION = "REWIND", &
      IOSTAT = OpenStatus)
```

If the file is successfully opened, the status variable OpenStatus will be set to 0. If the file cannot be opened—for example, if INFO.DAT does not exist—OpenStatus will be assigned some positive value. In this case, an appropriate message can be displayed and program execution terminated:

```
IF (OpenStatus > 0) STOP "*** Cannot open file ***"
```

To open a new file named REPORT to which values are to be written, we might use the OPEN statement

```
OPEN (UNIT = 13, FILE = "REPORT", STATUS = "NEW", &
      ACTION = "WRITE", IOSTAT = OpenStatus)
```

to create the file. A WRITE statement such as

```
WRITE (13, '(1X, I3, F7.0, F10.2)') Code, Temperature, Pressure
```

might then be used to write the values of Code, Temperature, and Pressure to this file.

Other clauses that may be included in an OPEN statement are a BLANK = clause specifying how blanks in numeric fields are to be interpreted; a DELIM = clause specifying whether character strings written to the file are to be enclosed in delimiters; an ERR = clause specifying a statement to be executed if an error occurs; a FORM = clause specifying whether the file is formatted or unformatted; a PAD = clause specifying whether character inputs are to be padded with blanks; and a RECL = clause specifying the record length for a direct access file.

Closing Files

The CLOSE **statement** has a function opposite that of the OPEN statement and is used to disconnect a file from its unit number. It has the form

```
CLOSE (close-list)
```

where close-list must include a unit specifier and may include other items (an IOSTAT = clause, an ERR = clause, and a STATUS = clause). After a CLOSE statement is executed, the closed file may be reopened by using an OPEN statement; the same unit number may be connected to it, or a different one may be used. All files that are not explicitly closed by means of a CLOSE statement are automatically closed when an END statement or a STOP statement is executed.

File Input/Output

Once a file has been connected to a unit number, data can be read from or written to that file using the general forms of the READ and WRITE statements in which the unit number appearing in the control list is the same as the unit number connected to the file. To illustrate, suppose that the file INFO.DAT has been opened successfully for reading and we wish to read and process values for Code, Temperature, and Pressure from this file.

In the preceding section, we noted that the control list of a general READ statement may contain an IOSTAT = clause to detect an end-of-file condition or an input error. When a READ statement containing an IOSTAT = clause is executed, the status-variable is assigned:

1. A positive value (usually the number of an error message in a list found in the system manuals) if an input error occurs
2. A negative value if the end of data is encountered but no input error occurs
3. Zero if neither an input error nor the end of data occurs

For example, if `InputStatus` is an integer variable, an input loop of the following form can be used to read and process values for `Code`, `Temperature`, and `Pressure` from a file with unit number 12, terminating repetition when the end of the file is reached:

```
DO
    ! Read next data values
    READ (12, *, IOSTAT = InputStatus) Code, Temperature,
    Pressure

    ! If end of data, terminate repetition
    IF (InputStatus < 0) EXIT

    ! If input error, stop execution
    IF (InputStatus > 0) STOP "*** Input error ***"

    ! Otherwise continue processing data
    Count = Count + 1
        .
        .
    SumOfPressures + Pressure
END DO
```

Sometimes it is necessary to reposition a file so that, for example, data values that have already been read can be read again. To reposition a file at its beginning, we can use a REWIND **statement** of the form

```
REWIND unit-number
```

To reposition a file at the beginning of the preceding line, we can use a BACKSPACE **statement** of the form

```
BACKSPACE unit-number
```

If the file is at its initial point, these statements have no effect.

APPLICATION: TEMPERATURE AND VOLUME READINGS

PROBLEM

Suppose that a device monitoring a process records time, temperature, pressure, and volume and stores this data in a file. Each record in this file contains

Time in positions 1–4
Temperature in positions 5–8
Pressure in positions 9–12
Volume in positions 13–16

The value for time is an integer representing the time at which the measurements were taken. The values for temperature, pressure, and volume are real numbers but are recorded with no decimal point. Each must be interpreted as a real value having a decimal point between the third and fourth digits.

A program is to be designed to read the values for the temperature and volume, display these values in tabular form, and display the average temperature and the average volume.

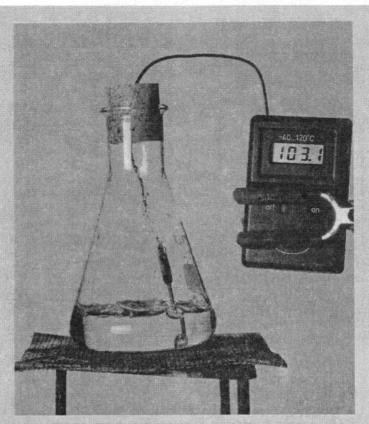

Monitoring temperature with a digital thermometer. (Photo courtesy of Photo Researchers, Inc.)

Solution

Specification.

Input (entered by the user): Name of the data file

Input (from the data file): Temperature and volume readings

Output (to the screen): Table of temperature and volume readings
Average temperature
Average volume

Design.
The following is an algorithm for solving this problem.

ALGORITHM FOR TEMPERATURE-VOLUME PROBLEM

1. Get the name of the file and open the file for input; if this fails, terminate execution.
2. Display headings for the table.
3. Initialize a counter, a sum of the temperature readings, and a sum of the volume readings to 0.

4. Do the following:
    a. Attempt to read a pair of temperature and volume readings from the file.
    b. If an input error occurred, terminate execution.
        If the end of the file was encountered, terminate repetition.
        Otherwise proceed with the following.
    c. Display the temperature and the volume.
    d. Increment the counter by 1.
    e. Add the temperature to the sum of the temperatures and the volume to the sum of the volumes.
5. Compute and display the average temperature and the average volume.

Coding.
The program in Figure 5.1 implements the preceding algorithm.

Figure 5.1. Temperature and volume readings

```fortran
PROGRAM Temperature_Volume_Readings
!----------------------------------------------------------------------
! Program to read temperatures and volumes from a file containing
! time, temperature, pressure, and volume readings made by some
! monitoring device. The temperature and volume measurements are
! displayed in tabular form, and the average temperature and the
! average volume are calculated and displayed.
! Variables used are:
!   FileName           : name of data file
!   OpenStatus         : status variable for OPEN statement
!   InputStatus        : status variable for READ statement
!   Temperature        : temperature recorded
!   Volume             : volume recorded
!   Count              : count of (Temperature, Volume) pairs
!   SumOfTemps         : sum of temperatures
!   SumOfVols          : sum of volumes
!   MeanTemperature    : mean temperature
!   MeanVolume         : mean volume
!
! Input (file):    Collection of temperature and volume readings
! Output (screen): Table of readings, average temperature, and
!                  average volume
!----------------------------------------------------------------------

  IMPLICIT NONE
  INTEGER :: Count = 0, OpenStatus, InputStatus
  CHARACTER(20) :: FileName
  REAL :: Temperature, Volume, SumOfTemps = 0.0, SumOfVols = 0.0, &
          MeanTemperature, MeanVolume

  ! Open the file as unit 15. If successful, set up the
  ! input and output formats, and display the table heading

  WRITE (*, '(1X, A)', ADVANCE = "NO") "Enter name of data file: "
  READ *, FileName
  OPEN (UNIT = 15, FILE = FileName, STATUS = "OLD", IOSTAT = OpenStatus)
  IF (OpenStatus > 0) STOP "*** Cannot open the file ***"

100 FORMAT(4X, F4.1, T13, F4.1)
110 FORMAT(1X, A11, A10)
120 FORMAT(1X, F8.1, F12.1)
  PRINT *
  PRINT 110, "Temperature", "Volume"
  PRINT 110, "===========", "======"

  ! While there is more data, read temperatures and volumes,
  ! display each in the table, and calculate the necessary sums

  DO
    READ (UNIT = 15, FMT = 100, IOSTAT = InputStatus) Temperature, Volume
    IF (InputStatus > 0) STOP "*** Input error ***"
    IF (InputStatus < 0) EXIT ! end of file
    PRINT 120, Temperature, Volume
    Count = Count + 1
```

```
        SumOfTemps = SumOfTemps + Temperature
        SumOfVols = SumOfVols + Volume
     END DO

   ! Find average temperature and average volume

     MeanTemperature = SumOfTemps / REAL(Count)
     MeanVolume = SumOfVols / REAL(Count)

     PRINT 130, "temperature", MeanTemperature, "volume", MeanVolume
130  FORMAT(//2(1X, "Average ", A, " is: ", F6.2 /))

     CLOSE (15)

   END PROGRAM Temperature_Volume_Readings
```

Figure 5.1 (cont.)

Execution and Testing. This program should be tested with several small data files to check its correctness. It can then be run with the data file described in the statement of the problem:

Listing of File fi15-1.dat:

```
1200034203221015
1300038803221121
1400044803241425
1500051303201520
1600055503181665
1700061303191865
1800067503232080
1900072103282262
2000076803252564
2100083503272869
2200088903303186
```

Execution of the program using this file produced the following output:

Sample Run:

```
Enter name of data file: fi15-1.dat


Temperature    Volume
===========    ======
   34.2        101.5
   38.8        112.1
   44.8        142.5
   51.3        152.0
   55.5        166.5
   61.3        186.5
   67.5        208.0
   72.1        226.2
   76.8        256.4
   83.5        286.9
   88.9        318.6

Average temperature is: 61.34
Average volume is: 196.11
```

KEY TERMS

ACTION = clause
ADVANCE = clause
BACKSPACE = statement
CLOSE statement
Control character
Engineering descriptor
FILE = clause
Format descriptor

Format specifier
FORMAT statement
IOSTAT = clause
OPEN statement
POSITION = clause
Positional descriptor
PRINT statement
READ statement

REWIND statement
Scientific descriptor
Slash descriptor
STATUS = clause
Unit specifier
WRITE statement

PROGRAMMING POINTERS

Program Style and Design

1. *Label all output produced by a program.* For example,

```
PRINT '(1X, "Rate =", F8.2, " Time =", F8.2)', &
Rate, Time
```

produces more informative output than

```
PRINT '(1X, 2F8.2)', Rate, Time
```

2. *Echo input values.* Input values, especially those read from a file, should be echoed; that is, they should be displayed as they are read (at least during program testing).

Potential Problems

1. *For some systems, the first position of each output line indicates explicitly what printer control is desired.* In some cases, control characters are always in effect; in others, they are not in effect unless a specific system command or compiler option is used.

2. *Formatted output of a numeric value produces a field filled with asterisks if the output requires more spaces than allowed by the specified field width.* For formatted output of real numbers with a descriptor of the form Fw.d, one should always have

```
w ≥ d + 3
```

For descriptors of the form Ew.d, ESw.d, and ENw.d, one should have

```
w ≥ d + 7
```

and for descriptors of the form Ew.dEe, ESw.dEe, and ENw.dEe,

```
w ≥ d + e + 5
```

3. *For formatted input with some compilers, blanks within a numeric field may be interpreted as zeros by some systems and ignored by others.* (The BZ and BN descriptors may be used to specify explicitly which interpretation is to be used.)

4. *For formatted input/output, characters are truncated or blanks are added, depending on whether the field width is too small or too large. For input, truncation occurs on the left, and blank padding on the right; for output, truncation occurs on the right, and blank padding on the left.* The acronyms sometimes used to remember this are

- **POT:** **P**adding on the left with blanks occurs for formatted **O**utput, or **T**runcation of rightmost characters occurs.
- **TIP:** **T**runcation of leftmost characters occurs for formatted **I**nput, or **P**adding with blanks on the right occurs.

These are analogous to the following acronym for assignment of character values:

- **APT:** For **A**ssignment (and list-directed input), both blank **P**adding and **T**runcation occur on the right.

Programming Problems

SECTION 5.1

1. Write a program that reads two three-digit integers and then calculates and displays their sum and their difference. The output should be formatted to appear as follows:

```
   456          456
 + 123        - 123
 -----        -----
   579          333
```

2. Write a program that reads two three-digit integers and then calculates and displays their product as well as the quotient and remainder that result when the first is divided by the second. The output should be formatted to appear as follows:

```
    739           61  R  7
                 ----
X    12        12 ) 739
------
   8868
```

3. Suppose that a certain culture of bacteria has a constant growth rate r, so that if there are n bacteria present, the next generation will have $n + r \cdot n$ bacteria. Write a program that reads the original number of bacteria, the growth rate, and an upper limit on the number of bacteria and then displays a table with appropriate headings that shows the generation number, the increase in the number of bacteria from the previous generation, and the total number of bacteria in that generation, for the initial generation number through the first generation for which the number of bacteria exceeds the specified upper limit.

SECTION 5.2

4. Angles are commonly measured in degrees, minutes ('), and seconds ("). There are 360 degrees in one complete revolution, 60 minutes in 1 degree, and 60 seconds in 1 minute. Write a program that reads two angular measurements, each in the form

   ```
   dddDmm'ss"
   ```

   where ddd, mm, and ss are the number of degrees, minutes, and seconds, respectively, and then calculates and displays their sum. Use this program to verify each of the following:

   ```
   74D29'13" + 105D8'16" = 179D37'29"
   7D14'55" + 5D24'55" = 12D39'50"
   20D31'19" + 0D31'30" = 21D2'49"
   122D17'48" + 237D42'12" = 0D0'0"
   ```

SECTIONS 5.3–5.5

5. Write a program that reads the time, temperature, pressure, and volume measurements from a data file like that described in Section 5.5, converts the time from military to ordinary time (e.g., 0900 is 9:00 A.M., 1500 is 3:00 P.M.), and displays a table like the following:

TIME	TEMPERATURE	PRESSURE	VOLUME
12:00 PM	34.2	32.2	101.5
⋮	⋮	⋮	⋮
10:00 PM	88.9	33.0	318.6

   Also, have the program calculate and display the maximum and minimum temperatures, the maximum and minimum pressures, the maximum and minimum volumes, and the times at which each of these maximum and minimum values occurred.

6. Write a program to search the file USERS.DAT (see Appendix B) to find and display the resource limit for a specified user's identification number.

7. Write a program to search the file INVENTOR.DAT (see Appendix B) to find an item with a specified stock number. If a match is found, display the unit price, the item name, and the number currently in stock; otherwise, display a message indicating that the item was not found.

8. At the end of each month, a report is produced that shows the status of each user's account in the file USERS.DAT (see Appendix B). Write a program to accept the current date and pro-

duce a report of the following form, in which the three asterisks (***) indicate that the user has already used 90 percent or more of the resources available to him or her, and xx is the current year.

```
            USER ACCOUNTS--06/30/xx

                    RESOURCE      RESOURCES
        USER-ID     LIMIT         USED
        -------     -----         ----
        10101       $750          $380.81
        1010        $650          $598.84***
                         :
```

6

Programming with Functions

6.1 HANDLING COMPLEX PROBLEMS: SUBPROGRAMS

For complex problems, it may not be possible to anticipate at the outset all the steps needed to solve the problem. In this case, it is helpful to divide the problem into a number of simpler problems, which are then considered individually and algorithms are designed to solve them. **Subprograms** can be written to implement each of these subalgorithms, and these subprograms can be combined to give a complete program that solves the original problem. In Fortran these subprograms are **functions** and **subroutines** whose execution is controlled by some other program unit, either the main program or some other subprogram. In this chapter we will consider how functions are written and used in this modular style of programming. In the next chapter, subroutines will be considered.

6.2 FUNCTIONS

The Fortran language provides many **intrinsic**, or **library**, **functions**. These intrinsic functions include the numeric functions introduced in Table 2.2 of Chapter 2 and a number of other numeric functions, as well as character and logical functions. See Appendix A for a list of these functions.

Function Subprograms

In some programs it is convenient for the user to define additional functions. Such **programmer-defined functions** are possible in Fortran, and once defined, they are used in the

OBJECTIVES

In this chapter, you will

- Learn to create programmer-defined functions.
- See how modules can be used to package subprograms together.
- Find out about external functions.
- Study recursion and how it is implemented in Fortran.
- Use functions in some real-world applications.

same way as library functions. They are written as **function subprograms**, which are separate program units whose syntax is similar to that of a Fortran (main) program:

> function heading
> specification part
> execution part
> END FUNCTION statement

The function heading is a FUNCTION **statement** of the form

> FUNCTION function-name (formal-argument-list)

or

> type-identifier FUNCTION function-name (formal-argument-list)

where the function-name may be any legal Fortran identifier, formal-argument-list is an identifier or a list (possibly empty) of identifiers separated by commas, and in the second form, type-identifier is the name of a type. This heading names the function and declares its arguments and, for the second form, the type of the value returned by the function. The variables in the formal-argument-list are called **formal** or **dummy arguments** and are used to pass information to the function subprogram.

The specification part of a function subprogram has the same form as the specification part of a Fortran program with the additional stipulation that it must declare

1. The type of the function value if this has not been included in the function heading.
2. The type of each formal argument. These declarations should also contain an INTENT **specifier** that tells how the arguments are to transfer information.

Similarly, the execution part of a function subprogram has the same form as the execution part of a Fortran program with the additional stipulation that it should include at least one statement that assigns a value to the identifier that names the function. Normally, this is done with an assignment statement of the form

> function-name = expression

The last statement of a function subprogram must be

> END FUNCTION function-name

(For external functions, this statement can be shortened to END.) The value of the function will be returned to the program unit that references it when this statement is encountered or when a RETURN **statement** of the form

> RETURN

is executed.

Example: Temperature Conversion

The formula for converting temperature measured in degrees Fahrenheit into degrees Celsius is

$$C = (F - 32)/1.8$$

where *F* is the Fahrenheit temperature to be converted and *C* is the corresponding Celsius temperature. Suppose we wish to define a function that performs this conversion.

A function subprogram to implement this function will have one formal argument representing a Fahrenheit temperature, and so an appropriate heading is

```
FUNCTION Fahr_to_Celsius(Temperature)
```

Since this function returns a real value, its name must be declared to be of type REAL in the function's specification part,

```
REAL :: Fahr_to_Celsius
```

or in the function's heading:

```
REAL FUNCTION Fahr_to_Celsius(Temperature)
```

(Note that double colons :: are not used in this case.) Since the formal argument Temperature must be of type REAL and will be used only to transfer information into the function, the specification part of this function subprogram must also contain the declaration

```
REAL, INTENT(IN) :: Temperature
```

The complete function subprogram is

```
!-Fahr_to_Celsius -----------------------------------------
! Function to convert a Fahrenheit temperature to Celsius
!
!   Accepts:  A Temperature in Fahrenheit
!   Returns:  The corresponding Celsius temperature
!----------------------------------------------------------

  FUNCTION Fahr_to_Celsius(Temperature)

    REAL :: Fahr_to_Celsius
    REAL, INTENT(IN) :: Temperature

    Fahr_to_Celsius = (Temperature - 32.0) / 1.8

  END FUNCTION Fahr_to_Celsius
```

This subprogram can be made accessible to a program, called the **main program**, in three ways:

1. It is placed in a subprogram section in the main program just before the END PROGRAM statement (as described later); in this case it is called an **internal subprogram**.
2. It is placed in a module (as described later) from which it can be imported into the program; in this case, it is called a **module subprogram**.
3. It is placed after the END PROGRAM statement of the main program, in which case it is called an **external subprogram**.

In this section we will use only internal subprograms. Module subprograms are described in Section 6.5 and external subprograms in Section 6.6.

Internal subprograms are placed in a subprogram section at the end of the main program (or at the end of an external subprogram). The program unit (main program or subprogram) that contains an internal subprogram is called a **host** for that subprogram. This subprogram section has the form

```
CONTAINS
   subprogram₁
   subprogram₂
       .
       .
   subprogramₙ
```

where each `subprogramᵢ` does not contain a subprogram section.

Figure 6.1 illustrates the use of an internal subprogram. In this example, program `Temperature_Conversion_1` is the main program (because its heading contains the keyword PROGRAM), and the function subprogram is named `Fahr_to_Celsius`.

Figure 6.1. Temperature conversions

```
PROGRAM Temperature_Conversion_1
!------------------------------------------------------------------
! Program to convert several Fahrenheit temperatures to the
! corresponding Celsius temperatures. The function Fahr_to_Celsius
! is used to perform the conversions. Identifiers used are:
!   Fahr_to_Celsius : internal function subprogram that converts
!                     Fahrenheit temperatures to Celsius
!   FahrenheitTemp  : a Fahrenheit temperature to be converted
!   CelsiusTemp     : the corresponding Celsius temperature
!   Response        : user response to "More data?" query
!
! Input:  FahrenheitTemp, Response
! Output: CelsiusTemp
!------------------------------------------------------------------

  IMPLICIT NONE
  REAL :: FahrenheitTemp, CelsiusTemp
  CHARACTER(1) :: Response

  DO
     ! Get a Fahrenheit temperature
     WRITE (*, '(1X, A)', ADVANCE = "NO") "Enter a Fahrenheit
     temperature: "
     READ *, FahrenheitTemp

     ! Use the function Fahr_to_Celsius to convert it to Celsius
     CelsiusTemp = Fahr_to_Celsius(FahrenheitTemp)

     ! Output the result
     PRINT '(1X, 2(F6.2, A))', FahrenheitTemp, &
           " in Fahrenheit is equivalent to ", CelsiusTemp, &
           " in Celsius"

     ! Check if more temperatures are to be converted
     WRITE (*, '(/ 1X, A)', ADVANCE = "NO") &
           "More temperatures to convert (Y or N)? "
     READ *, Response
     IF (Response /= "Y") EXIT
  END DO
```

```
CONTAINS

!- Fahr_to_Celsius -------------------------------------
! Function to convert a Fahrenheit temperature to Celsius
!
!    Accepts: A Temperature in Fahrenheit
!    Returns: The corresponding Celsius temperature
!-------------------------------------------------------

FUNCTION Fahr_to_Celsius(Temperature)

  REAL :: Fahr_to_Celsius
  REAL, INTENT(IN) :: Temperature

  Fahr_to_Celsius = (Temperature - 32.0) / 1.8

END FUNCTION Fahr_to_Celsius

END PROGRAM Temperature_Conversion_1
```

Sample Run:

```
Enter a Fahrenheit temperature: 32
 32.00 in Fahrenheit is equivalent to 0.00 in Celsius

More temperatures to convert (Y or N)? Y
Enter a Fahrenheit temperature: 212
212.00 in Fahrenheit is equivalent to 100.00 in Celsius

More temperatures to convert (Y or N)? Y
Enter a Fahrenheit temperature: -22.5
-22.50 in Fahrenheit is equivalent to -30.28 in Celsius

More temperatures to convert (Y or N)? N
```

Figure 6.1   (cont.)

Argument Association

The following diagram pictures the flow of control in the program in Figure 6.1:

When the program is run, execution proceeds from the beginning of the main program in the usual manner (1), until the assignment statement containing the reference to function `Fahr_to_Celsius` is reached (2). At that time, the actual argument `FahrenheitTemp` (3) in this reference is evaluated and copied to the formal argument `Temperature` of `Fahr_to_Celsius` (4). Control is transferred from the main program to the function subprogram `Fahr_to_Celsius`, which begins execution (5). The statement

```
Fahr_to_Celsius = (Temperature - 32.0) / 1.8
```

is evaluated, and since `Temperature` contains a copy of the value of `Fahrenheit-Temp`, the resulting value is the Celsius equivalent of `FahrenheitTemp`. When execution reaches the end of the function, control transfers back to the main program (6) and the value computed by the preceding expression is returned as the value of the function. In the main program, this value is then assigned to `CelsiusTemp` (7), and execution continues on through the remainder of the main program (8).

When a function is referenced, the intent is that the values of the actual arguments are passed to the formal arguments and these values are then used in computing the value of the function, but these values should not change while the function executes. *Including the* `INTENT(IN)` *attribute in a formal argument's declaration protects the corresponding actual argument by ensuring that the value of the formal argument cannot be changed while the function is being executed.*[1] Any attempt to change the value of the formal argument will result in a compile-time error. *If the* `INTENT(IN)` *clause is not used, the value of the formal argument may be changed in the function and the value of the corresponding actual argument will also change.* (See Potential Problem 4 in the Programming Pointers at the end of this chapter.)

Another consequence of this association between actual arguments and formal arguments is that *the number and type of the actual arguments must agree with the number and type of the formal arguments* (unless some arguments have been declared to be optional).[2] For example, the function reference in

```
CelsiusTemp = Fahr_to_Celsius(2.5, 1)
```

is not allowed, because the number of actual arguments does not match the number of formal arguments.

Local Identifiers—The Factorial Function

Some function subprograms require the use of constants and/or variables in addition to the formal arguments. These **local identifiers** are declared in the specification part of the subprogram.

To illustrate, we consider the *factorial function*. The factorial of a nonnegative integer n is denoted by $n!$ and is defined by

$$n! = \begin{cases} 1 & \text{if } n = 0 \\ 1 \times 2 \times 3 \times \cdots \times n & \text{if } n > 0 \end{cases}$$

---

[1] The `INTENT` attribute may also be used to specify other kinds of argument association, as described in Section 7.1.

[2] For a description of keyword and optional arguments, see Chapter 7 of our text *Fortran 90 for Engineers and Scientists*.

A function subprogram to define this integer-valued function will have one integer argument N, but it will also use a local variable I as a control variable in a DO loop that computes N!. The complete function subprogram is

```
!- Factorial -----------------------------------------------
! Function to calculate the factorial N! of N, which is
! 1 if N = 0, 1 * 2 * . . . * N if N > 0.
!
! Accepts:  Integer N
! Returns:  The integer N!
!
! Note:  I is a local integer variable used as a counter.
!------------------------------------------------------------

FUNCTION Factorial(N)

  INTEGER :: Factorial
  INTEGER, INTENT(IN) :: N
  INTEGER :: I

  Factorial = 1
  DO I = 2, N
     Factorial = Factorial * I
  END DO

END FUNCTION Factorial
```

Example: Poisson Probability Function

The program in Figure 6.2 uses the function subprogram Factorial in calculating values of the *Poisson probability function*, which is the probability function of a random variable, such as the number of radioactive particles striking a target in a given period of time, the number of flaws in a given length of magnetic tape, or the number of failures in an electronic device during a given time period. This function is defined by

$$P(n) = \frac{\lambda^n \cdot e^{-\lambda}}{n!}$$

where

λ = the average number of occurrences of the phenomenon per time period

n = the number of occurrences in that time period

For example, if the average number of particles passing through a counter during 1 millisecond in a laboratory experiment is 3 ($\lambda = 3$), then the probability that exactly 5 particles enter the counter ($n = 5$) in a given millisecond will be

$$P(5) = \frac{3^5 \cdot e^{-3}}{5!} = 0.1008$$

The program in Figure 6.2 reads values for NumOccurs and AveOccurs, uses the statement

```
Probability = Poisson(AveOccurs, NumOccurs)
```

to calculate the Poisson probability, and then displays this probability. The value of N! is obtained by the function Poisson from the function subprogram Factorial.

Figure 6.2. Poisson probability distribution

```
PROGRAM Poisson_Probability
!-----------------------------------------------------------------------
! Program to calculate the Poisson probability function using the
! function subprogram Poisson. Identifiers used are:
!   AveOccurs   : average # of occurrences of phenomenon per
!                 time period
!   NumOccurs   : number of occurrences in a time period
!   Probability : Poisson probability
!   NumProbs    : number of probabilities to calculate
!   I           : DO-loop control variable
!   Poisson     : internal function subprogram to calculate Poisson
!                 probability
!   Factorial   : internal function subprogram to calculate factorials
!
! Input:   NumProbs and values for AveOccurs and NumOccurs
! Output:  Poisson probabilities
!-----------------------------------------------------------------------

  IMPLICIT NONE
  REAL :: AveOccurs, Probability
  INTEGER :: NumProbs, I, NumOccurs

  PRINT *, "This program calculates Poisson probabilities."
  WRITE (*, '(1X, A)', ADVANCE = "NO") &
        "How many probabilities do you wish to calculate? "
  READ *, NumProbs

  DO I = 1, NumProbs
     WRITE (*, '(1X, A)', ADVANCE = "NO") &
           "Enter average # of occurrences per time period: "
     READ *, AveOccurs
     WRITE (*, '(1X, A)', ADVANCE = "NO") &
           "Enter # of occurrences for which to find probability: "
     READ *, NumOccurs
     Probability = Poisson(AveOccurs, NumOccurs)
     PRINT '(1X, "Poisson probability = ", F6.4 /)', Probability
  END DO

CONTAINS

  !-Poisson -------------------------------------------------------
  ! Function to calculate the Poisson probability
  !                         N   -Lambda
  !                 Lambda * e
  !       Poisson(N) = ------------------
  !                         N!.
  ! Function Factorial is called to calculate N!.
  !
  ! Accepts:  Real number Lambda and integer N
  ! Returns:  The poisson probability given by the formula above
  !-------------------------------------------------------------------

  FUNCTION Poisson(Lambda, N)
```

```
      REAL :: Poisson
      REAL, INTENT(IN) :: Lambda
      INTEGER, INTENT(IN) :: N

      Poisson = (Lambda ** N * EXP(-Lambda)) / REAL(Factorial(N))

END FUNCTION Poisson

!- Factorial -----------------------------------------------------------
! Function to calculate the factorial N! of N, which is 1 if N = 0,
! 1 * 2 * . . . * N if N > 0.
!
! Accepts: Integer N
! Returns: The integer N!
!
! Note:  I is a local integer variable used as a counter.
!-----------------------------------------------------------------------


FUNCTION Factorial(N)

   INTEGER :: Factorial
   INTEGER, INTENT(IN) :: N
   INTEGER :: I

   Factorial = 1
   DO I = 2, N
      Factorial = Factorial * I
   END DO

 END FUNCTION Factorial

END PROGRAM Poisson_Probability
```

Sample Run:

```
This program calculates Poisson probabilities.
How many probabilities do you wish to calculate? 2
Enter average # of occurrences per time period: 3
Enter # of occurrences for which to find probability: 5
Poisson probability = 0.1008

Enter average # of occurrences per time period: 4
Enter # of occurrences for which to find probability: 6
Poisson probability = 0.1042
```

Figure 6.2 (cont.)

The order in which subprograms are arranged is not important. Thus, in Figure 6.2, the subprogram Factorial could just as well precede the subprogram Poisson.

Scope

In a program that contains subprograms, there may be several points at which entities (variables, constants, subprograms, types) are declared—in the main program, in subprograms, or as described later, in modules. The portion of the program in which any of these items is *visible,* that is, where it is accessible and can be used, is called its **scope**.

There is one general scope principle:

Fundamental Scope Principle

The scope of an entity is the program or subprogram in which it is declared.

One scope rule that follows from the fundamental principle applies to items that are declared within a subprogram, that is, to the formal arguments of the subprogram and to the constants and variables declared in its specification part (and type identifiers, described in Chapter 9):

Scope Rule 1

An item declared within a subprogram is not accessible outside that subprogram.

Such items are therefore said to be **local** to that subprogram. For example, the scope of local variables I and N in function Factorial is this function subprogram; they cannot be accessed outside it.

Any item declared in the main program is called a **global entity** because it is accessible throughout the entire program, except within internal subprograms in which a local entity has the same name.

Scope Rule 2

A global entity is accessible throughout the main program and in any internal subprogram in which no local entity has the same name as the global item.

For example, in Figure 6.2, the variables AveOccurs, NumOccurs, Probability, Num-Probs, and I are global variables. All of them are accessible to the main program, and all but I are accessible to the function Factorial. The global variable I is not ac-cessible within Factorial because I is the name of a local variable within Factorial. A reference to the variable I within Factorial yields the value of the local variable I, whereas a reference to I outside the function gives the value of the global variable I. Thus, the same identifier I names two different variables that are associated with two different memory locations.

Scope rule 2 also applies to internal subprograms. For example, Factorial is global and thus can be referenced in either the main program or by Poisson. The function Poisson also is global and can thus be referenced in the main program. (It cannot be referenced within Factorial, however, because Poisson references Factorial, and thus Factorial would indirectly be referencing itself.)

Although global variables can be used to share data between the main program and internal subprograms or between internal subprograms, it is usually unwise to do so, since this practice reduces the independence of the various subprograms and thus makes modular programming more difficult. Changing the value of a global variable in one part of the program has the *dangerous side effect* of changing the value of that variable throughout the entire program, including all internal subprograms. Consequently, it is difficult to determine the value of that variable at any particular point in the program.

Statement labels are not governed by scope rule 2. Thus, the FORMAT statement in the main program in Figure 6.2 cannot be used within Poisson or Factorial because its statement label is not accessible to these subprograms.

The naming convention established by an IMPLICIT statement in the main program is also global. Thus, in Figure 6.2, the IMPLICIT NONE statement in the main program applies to both Poisson and Factorial so that it is not necessary to include it in these subprograms.

Saving the Values of Local Variables

The values of local variables in a subprogram are not retained from one execution of the subprogram to the next unless either

1. They are initialized in their declarations, or
2. They are declared to have the SAVE **attribute**.

To ensure that values of local uninitialized variables are saved from one execution of a subprogram to the next, we can specify that these variables have the SAVE attribute in their declarations

```
type, SAVE :: list-of-local-variables
```

or by using a SAVE **statement** of the form

```
SAVE list-of-local-variables
```

If the list is omitted, the values of all variables in the subprogram will be saved.

PRACTICE!

1. What are the two kinds of Fortran subprograms?
2. List the four parts of a function subprogram.
3. In the function heading FUNCTION Sum(A, B), A and B are called
    _____.
4. For a function whose heading is REAL FUNCTION Sum(A, B), the type of the values returned by the function is _____.
5. List the three ways that a subprogram can be made accessible to a program.
6. The part of a program in which a variable can be accessed is called the _____ of that variable.
7. (True or false) Function subprograms and the main program may use the same identifiers.

Exercises 8–11 deal with the following internal function:

```
FUNCTION What(N)

    INTEGER :: What
    INTEGER, INTENT(IN) :: N

    What = (N * (N + 1)) / 2

END FUNCTION What
```

8. If the statement Number1 = What(Number2) appears in the main program, Number2 is called a(n) _____ argument in this function reference.
9. If the statement Number = What(3) appears in the main program, the value assigned to Number will be _____.
10. (True or false) The value assigned to Number by the statement Number = What(5) in the main program will be 15.
11. (True or false) The statement N = 1 may be inserted in the function What.
12. Write a function that calculates values of $x^2 \sin x$.
13. Write a function Range that calculates the range between two integers, that is, the result of subtracting the smaller integer from the larger one.

14. Write a real-valued function Round that has a real argument Amount and an integer argument N and that returns the value of Amount rounded to N places. For example, the function references Round(10.536, 0), Round(10.536, 1), and Round(10.536, 2) should give the values 11.0, 10.5, and 10.54, respectively.

15. The number of bacteria in a culture can be estimated by

$$N \cdot e^{kt}$$

where N is the initial population, k is a rate constant, and t is time. Write a function to calculate the number of bacteria present at time t for given values of k and N.

16. Write a real-valued function NumericGrade that accepts a letter grade and returns the corresponding numeric value (A = 4.0, B = 3.0, C = 2.0, D = 1.0, F = 0.0).

17. Write a character-valued function LetterGrade that assigns a letter grade to an integer score using the following grading scale:

90–100:	A
80–89:	B
70–79:	C
60–69:	D
Below 60:	F

18. Write a function that calculates the sum $m + (m + 1) + \cdots + n$, for two given integers m and n.

19. Write a function Days_in_Month that returns the number of days in a given month and year. (See Exercise 20 of Section 3.4, which describes which years are leap years.)

20. Write a logical-valued function that determines if an integer is a perfect square.

21. The *greatest common divisor* (GCD) of two integers a and b, not both of which are zero, is the largest positive integer that divides both a and b. The *Euclidean algorithm* for finding this greatest common divisor of a and b, GCD(a, b), is as follows: if $b = 0$, GCD(a, b) is a. Otherwise, divide a by b to obtain quotient q and remainder r, so that $a = bq + r$. Then GCD(a, b) = GCD(b, r). Replace a by b and b by r and repeat this procedure. Because the remainders are decreasing, a remainder of 0 will eventually result. The last nonzero remainder is then GCD(a, b). For example:

$1260 = 198 \cdot 6 + 72$	GCD(1260, 198) = GCD(198, 72)
$198 = 72 \cdot 2 + 45$	= GCD(72, 54)
$72 = 54 \cdot 1 + 18$	= GCD(54, 18)
$54 = 18 \cdot 3 + 0$	= 18

Note: If either a or b is negative, replace it with its absolute value.
Write a function subprogram to calculate the GCD of two integers.

22. A *prime number* is an integer $n > 1$ whose only positive divisors are 1 and n itself. Write a logical-valued function that determines whether n is a prime number.

PROBLEM

Write a program to approximate the area under the graph of a nonnegative function $y = f(x)$ from $x = a$ to $x = b$, thus obtaining an approximate value for the integral

$$\int_a^b f(x)dx$$

Solution

One common method for approximating this integral is to divide the interval $[a, b]$ into n subintervals each of length $x = (b - a)/n$ using $n - 1$ equally spaced points $x_1, x_2, \ldots, x_{n-1}$. Locating the corresponding points on the curve and connecting consecutive points using line segments forms n trapezoids:

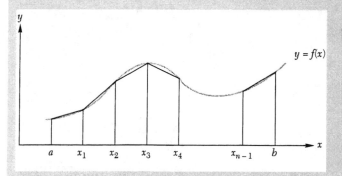

The sum of the areas of these trapezoids is approximately the area under the graph of f.

The bases of the first trapezoid are $y_0 = f(a)$ and $y_1 = f(x_1)$, and thus its area is

$$\frac{1}{2}\Delta x(y_0 + y_1)$$

Similarly, the area of the second trapezoid is

$$\frac{1}{2}\Delta x(y_1 + y_2)$$

where $y_2 = f(x_2)$, and so on. The sum of the areas of the n trapezoids is

$$\frac{1}{2}\Delta x(y_0 + y_1) + \frac{1}{2}\Delta x(y_1 + y_2) +$$
$$\frac{1}{2}\Delta x(y_2 + y_3) + \cdots + \frac{1}{2}\Delta x(y_{n-1} + y_n)$$

where $y_0, y_1, \ldots, y_{n-1}, y_n$ are the values of the function f at $a, x_1, \ldots, x_{n-1}, b$, respectively. Combining terms, we can write this sum more simply as

$$\Delta x\left(\frac{y_0 + y_n}{2} + y_1 + y_2 + \cdots + y_{n-1}\right)$$

or, written more concisely using Σ (sigma) notation,

$$\Delta x\left(\frac{y_0 + y_n}{2} + \sum_{i=1}^{n-1} y_i\right)$$

which is then an approximation of the area under the curve.

The following algorithm uses this *trapezoidal method* to approximate the integral of some given function F.

ALGORITHM FOR TRAPEZOIDAL APPROXIMATION OF AN INTEGRAL

Algorithm to approximate the integral of a function F over an interval $[A, B]$ using the trapezoidal method.

Input: The endpoints A, B of the interval and the number N of subintervals to use

Output: Approximate value of the integral of F from A to B

1. Read A, B, and N.

2. Calculate $DeltaX = \dfrac{B - A}{N}$.

3. Set X equal to A.

4. Set Sum equal to 0.

5. Do the following for I ranging from 1 to $N - 1$:
   a. Add $DeltaX$ to X.
   b. Calculate $Y = F(X)$.
   c. Add Y to Sum.

6. Calculate $Sum =$
$$DeltaX \cdot \left(\frac{F(A) + F(B)}{2} + Sum\right).$$

7. Display N and Sum.

The program in Figure 6.3 implements the preceding algorithm and uses it to approximate

$$\int_0^1 (x^2 + 1)dx$$

A function subprogram is used to define the integrand

$$f(x) = x^2 + 1$$

Figure 6.3. Trapezoidal approximation of an integral

```fortran
PROGRAM Approximate_Integration
!---------------------------------------------------------------------------
! Program to approximate the integral of a function over the interval
! [A,B] using the trapezoidal method.  Identifiers used are:
!   A, B   : the endpoints of the interval of integration
!   N      : the number of subintervals
!   I      : counter
!   DeltaX : the length of the subintervals
!   X      : a point of subdivision
!   Y      : the value of the function at X
!   Sum    : the approximating sum
!   F      : the integrand (internal function)
!
! Input:  A, B, and N
! Output: Approximation to integral of F on [A, B]
!---------------------------------------------------------------------------

  IMPLICIT NONE
  REAL :: A, B, DeltaX, X, Y, Sum
  INTEGER :: N, I

  PRINT *, "Enter the interval endpoints and the # of subintervals:"
  READ *, A, B, N

  ! Calculate subinterval length
  ! and initialize the approximating Sum and X

  DeltaX = (B - A) / REAL(N)
  X = A
  Sum = 0.0

  ! Now calculate and display the sum

  DO I = 1, N - 1
     X = X + DeltaX
     Y = F(X)
     Sum = Sum + Y
  END DO

  Sum = DeltaX * ((F(A) + F(B)) / 2.0 + Sum)

  PRINT '(1X, "Approximate value using", I4, &
        " subintervals is", F10.5)', N, Sum

CONTAINS

  !-F(X)---------------
  ! The integrand
  !--------------------

  FUNCTION F(X)
```

```
        REAL :: F
        REAL, INTENT(IN) :: X

        F = X**2 + 1.0

      END FUNCTION F

    END PROGRAM Approximate_Integration
```

Sample Runs:

```
Enter the interval endpoints and the # of subintervals:
0, 1, 10
Approximate value using  10 subintervals is   1.33500

Enter the interval endpoints and the # of subintervals:
0, 1, 50
Approximate value using  50 subintervals is   1.33340

Enter the interval endpoints and the # of subintervals:
0, 1, 100
Approximate value using 100 subintervals is   1.33335
```

Figure 6.3 (cont.)

APPLICATION: ROAD CONSTRUCTION

PROBLEM

The Cawker City Construction Company has contracted to build a highway for the state highway commission. Several sections of this highway must pass through hills from which large amounts of dirt must be excavated to provide a flat and level roadbed. For example, one section that is 1000 feet in length must pass through a hill whose height (in feet) above the roadbed has been measured at equally spaced distances and tabulated as follows:

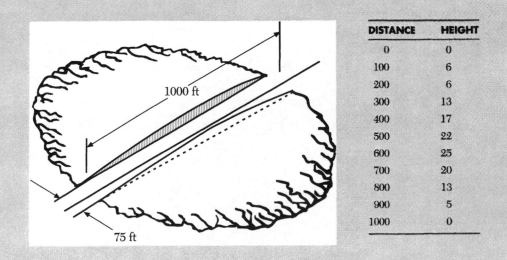

DISTANCE	HEIGHT
0	0
100	6
200	6
300	13
400	17
500	22
600	25
700	20
800	13
900	5
1000	0

Freeway construction (F3 Freeway, Oahu, HI). (Photo courtesy of Tony Stone Images)

In estimating the construction costs, the company needs to know the volume of dirt that must be excavated from the hill.

Solution

Specification The input to this problem consists of the length of the section of road to be constructed, the width of the road, and the estimates of the hill's height at equally spaced points along this section. The output is the volume of dirt that must be re-moved. Thus, we have the following specification for the problem:

Input: The length of a section of road
The width of the road
A list of heights at equally spaced points along this section

Output: The volume of dirt to be removed

Design To estimate the volume of dirt to be removed, we will assume that the height of the hill does not vary from one side of the road to the other. The volume can then be calculated as

Volume = (cross-sectional area of the hill)
× (width of the road)

and the cross-sectional area of the hill can be calculated as an integral:

$$\text{Cross-sectional area of the hill} = \int_0^{1000} h(x)dx$$

where $h(x)$ is the height of the hill at a distance x feet along the section of road. Since the value of $h(x)$ is known at equally spaced points along the road, the trapezoidal method can be used to approximate this integral.

An algorithm for solving this problem is then straightforward.

ALGORITHM FOR HIGHWAY CONSTRUCTION PROBLEM

Algorithm to approximate the volume of dirt to be removed in constructing a section of highway through a hill.

Input: Length and width of the road section and heights of the hill at equally spaced points

Output: Volume of dirt to be removed

1. Obtain the length and width of the section of highway.

2. Use the trapezoidal method to approximate the integral for the cross-sectional area of the hill.

3. Compute the volume of dirt to be removed:

4. Volume = (cross-sectional area of the hill) × (width of the road)

Coding The program in Figure 6.4 implements this algorithm. The number of equally spaced points at which height measurements have been made and the heights themselves are read from a data file. The length and width of the section of highway are entered from the keyboard. Note that the coding of the trapezoidal method from Figure 6.3 has been modified so that function values are read from a file rather than computed using a function subprogram.

Figure 6.4. Road construction

```
PROGRAM Road_Construction
!------------------------------------------------------------------------
! Program to approximate the volume of dirt to be removed in
! constructing a section of highway through a hill. Identifiers
! used are:
!   Length     : length of the section of road
!   Width      : width of the road
!   FileName   : name of data file containing hill information
!   NumPoints  : the number of points where height of hill was measured
!   DeltaX     : distance between points
!   I          : counter
!   Y          : the height of the hill
!   Sum        : sum approximating the integral for cross-sectional area
!                of the hill
!
! Input (keyboard): Length, Width
! Input (file):     NumPoints and values of Y (heights of hill)
! Output:           Volume of dirt to be removed
!------------------------------------------------------------------------

  IMPLICIT NONE
  REAL :: Length, Width, Delta_X, Y, Sum
  INTEGER :: NumPoints, I
  CHARACTER(20) :: FileName

  ! Get road information and name of data file containing hill information

  PRINT *, "Enter length and width of section of road (in feet):"
  READ *, Length, Width
  PRINT *, "Enter name of file containing hill information:"
  READ *, FileName

  ! Open the data file, read the number of points at which height of hill
  ! was measured, and compute the distance between these points

  OPEN (UNIT = 10, FILE = FileName, STATUS = "OLD", &
        ACTION = "READ", POSITION = "REWIND")
  READ (10, *) NumPoints
  Delta_X = Length / REAL(NumPoints - 1)

  ! Initialize the approximating Sum
  READ (10, *) Y
  Sum = Y / 2.0
```

```
        ! Now calculate Sum, which approximates cross-sectional area of hill
      DO I = 1, NumPoints - 2
         READ (10, *) Y
         Sum = Sum + Y
      END DO

      READ (10, *) Y
      Sum = Sum + Y / 2.0
      Sum = Delta_X * Sum

      PRINT *, "Volume of dirt to be removed is approximately"
      PRINT *, Sum * Width, "cubic feet."

   END PROGRAM Road_Construction
```

Figure 6.4   (cont.)

Execution and Testing   The program was executed with several simple data files to verify its correctness. It was then executed using a file containing the data given in the statement of the problem:

Listing of File fil6-4.dat:

```
   11              22
   0               25
   6               20
   10              13
   13              5
   17              0
```

Run of Program:

```
   Enter length and width of section of road (in feet): 1000, 75
   Enter name of file containing hill information: fil6-4.dat
   Volume of dirt to be removed is approximately
   9.8250000E+05 cubic feet.
```

PRACTICE!

1. The current i passing through a capacitor is given by

$$i(t) = 10 \sin^2\left(\frac{t}{\pi}\right) \quad \text{(amps)}$$

where t denotes time in seconds. Assume that the capacitance C is 5 F (farads). The voltage across the capacitor is given by

$$v(T) = \frac{1}{C}\int_0^T i(t)dt \quad \text{(volts)}$$

Find the value of $v(T)$ for $T = 1, 2, 3, 4$, and 5 seconds.

2. The circumference C of an ellipse with major axis $2a$ and minor axis $2b$ is given by

$$C = 4a\int_0^{\pi/2} \sqrt{1 - \left(\frac{a^2 - b^2}{a^2}\right)\sin^2\Phi}\ d\Phi$$

Assume that a room has the shape of an ellipse with $a = 20$ m, $b = 10$ m, and height $h = 5$ m. Find the total area $A = hC$ of the wall.

3. The fraction f of certain fission neutrons having energies above a certain threshold energy E° can be determined by the formula

$$f = 1 - 0.484 \int_0^E e^{-E} \sin(h\sqrt{2E})dE$$

Find the value of f for $E^\circ = 0.5, 1.0, 1.5, 2.0, 2.5,$ and 3.0. Compare the results.

4. A particle with mass $m = 20$ kg is moving through a fluid and is subjected to a viscous resistance

$$R(v) = -v^{3/2}$$

where v is its velocity. The relation between time t, velocity v, and resistance R is given by

$$t = \int_{v_0}^{v(t)} \frac{m}{R(v)} dv \qquad \text{(seconds)}$$

where v_0 is the initial velocity. Assuming that $v_0 = 15$ m/sec, find the time T required for the particle to slow down to $v(T) = 7.5$ m/sec.

5. Suppose that a spring has been compressed a distance x_c:

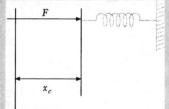

If $F(x)$ is the external force, then the absorbed energy can be expressed as

$$E = \int_0^{x_c} F(x)dx$$

Assume that

$$F(x) = \frac{1}{2}e^{x^2}\sin^2(3x^2) \qquad \text{(Newtons)}$$

and $x_c = 1$ cm. Compute the absorbed energy.

6.3 INTRODUCTION TO MODULES

In the preceding sections, we have seen that subprograms are separate program units written to perform specific computations. Often these are computations that arise in a variety of applications, and it is convenient to be able to use them in different programs. Fortran 90 provides modules that can be used to package together related subprograms (and other items). In this section we describe the composition of modules and how they can be used to build such libraries of subprograms.

Modules

A **module** is a program unit used to package together type declarations, subprograms, and definitions of new data types as described in Chapter 9. A simple form of a module that contains only subprograms is

```
MODULE name
CONTAINS
    subprogram₁
    subprogram₂
        ⋮
    subprogramₙ
END MODULE name
```

It packages the subprograms, called **module subprograms**, together into a **library** that can be used in any other program unit.

Example: A Temperature-Conversion Library

The temperature conversion performed by the function `Fahr_to_Celsius` in the program of Figure 6.1 is a conversion that may be useful in other applications. It is an integral part of the program, and copying it for use in another program is inconvenient. Putting this and related temperature-conversion subprograms in a module makes it possible to reuse them as needed. Figure 6.5 gives a partial listing of the contents of such a module.

As noted earlier, a module can also contain type declarations and other items besides subprograms. For example, declarations of temperature-related constants such as

```
REAL, PARAMETER :: HeatOfFusion = 79.71, &
                   HeatOfVaporization = 539.55
```

could be added to the module `Temperature_Library`.

Figure 6.5.   A temperature-conversion module

```
MODULE Temperature_Library
!-------------------------------------------------------------------------
! Module that contains the following subprograms for processing
! temperatures on various scales:
!    Fahr_to_Celsius: a Fahrenheit-to-Celsius conversion function
!    Celsius_to_Fahr: a Celsius-to-Fahrenheit conversion function
!    . . .
!-------------------------------------------------------------------------

  IMPLICIT NONE

CONTAINS

  !-Fahr_to_Celsius ------------------------------------------------------
  ! Function to convert a Fahrenheit temperature to Celsius.
  !   Accepts: A Temperature in Fahrenheit
  !   Returns: The corresponding Celsius temperature
  !-----------------------------------------------------------------------

  FUNCTION Fahr_to_Celsius(Temperature)

    REAL :: Fahr_to_Celsius
    REAL, INTENT(IN) :: Temperature
```

```
     Fahr_to_Celsius = (Temperature - 32.0) / 1.8

END FUNCTION Fahr_to_Celsius

!-Celsius_to_Fahr-----------------------------------------------------
! Function to convert a Celsius temperature to Fahrenheit.
! Accepts: A Temperature in Celsius
! Returns: The corresponding Fahrenheit temperature
!---------------------------------------------------------------------

FUNCTION Celsius_to_Fahr(Temperature)

  REAL :: Celsius_to_Fahr
  REAL, INTENT(IN) :: Temperature

  Celsius_to_Fahr = 1.8 * Temperature + 32.0

END FUNCTION Celsius_to_Fahr

! ... Other temperature-related subprograms can be added ...

END MODULE Temperature_Library
```

Figure 6.5 (cont.)

Using a Module

Once a module has been written, its contents can be made available to any other program unit by placing in that program unit a USE **statement** of the form

```
    USE module-name
```

at the beginning of the specification part of a program unit. All identifiers declared in the specified module are *imported* into the program unit and can be used throughout it.

The USE statement may also have the form

```
    USE module-name ONLY: list
```

where list is a list of identifiers declared in that module and renamings of these identifiers of the form

```
    new-identifier => identifier
```

In this form, only the identifiers listed are imported. These identifiers or their new names may then be used in the program unit containing this USE statement.

Figure 6.6 is a modification of the program in Figure 6.1 that imports the contents of the module Temperature_Library and uses the function Fahr_to_Celsius to perform conversions of several Fahrenheit temperatures to Celsius. Note that the USE statement could be replaced by

```
    USE Temperature_Library, ONLY: Fahr_to_Celsius
```

Translation of a source program to produce an executable program consists of two separate steps:

1. **Compilation**, in which the source program is translated to an equivalent machine-language program, called an *object program*, which is stored in an *object file*. (UNIX object files have the extension .o, DOS object files have the extension .OBJ.)
2. **Linking**, in which any references to functions contained in a module are linked to their definitions in that module, creating an *executable program*, which is stored in an *executable file*.

Figure 6.6. Temperature conversions

```
PROGRAM Temperature_Conversion_2
!-----------------------------------------------------------------------
! Program to convert several Fahrenheit temperatures to the
! corresponding Celsius temperatures.  The function Fahr_to_Celsius
! from module Temperature_Library is used to perform the conversions.
! Identifiers used are:
!   Fahr_to_Celsius : module function subprogram that converts
!                     Fahrenheit temperatures to Celsius
!   FahrenheitTemp  : a Fahrenheit temperature to be converted
!   CelsiusTemp     : the corresponding Celsius temperature
!   Response        : user response to "More data?" query
!
! Imported: Fahr_to_Celsius from module Temperature_Library
! Input:    FahrenheitTemp, Response
! Output:   CelsiusTemp
!-----------------------------------------------------------------------

  USE Temperature_Library

  IMPLICIT NONE
  REAL :: FahrenheitTemp, CelsiusTemp
  CHARACTER(1) :: Response

  DO
     ! Get a Fahrenheit temperature
     WRITE (*, '(1X, A)', ADVANCE = "NO") "Enter a Fahrenheit temperature: "
     READ *, FahrenheitTemp

     ! Use the module function Fahr_to_Celsius to convert it to Celsius
     CelsiusTemp = Fahr_to_Celsius(FahrenheitTemp)

     ! Output the result
     PRINT '(1X, 2(F6.2, A))', FahrenheitTemp, &
           " in Fahrenheit is equivalent to ", CelsiusTemp, " in Celsius"

     ! Check if more temperatures are to be converted
     WRITE (*, '(/ 1X, A)', ADVANCE = "NO") &
           "More temperatures to convert (Y or N)? "
     READ *, Response
     IF (Response /= "Y") EXIT
  END DO

END PROGRAM Temperature_Conversion_2
```

Since modules also need to be compiled, translation of a program that uses a module may require three separate actions:

1. Separate compilation of the program's source file, creating an object file
2. Separate compilation of the module, creating a different object file
3. Linking the function calls in the program's object file to the function definitions in the module's object file, creating an executable program

It makes no difference whether the source program or the module is compiled first, but *both source programs and modules must be compiled before linking can be performed.* The following diagram illustrates this process:

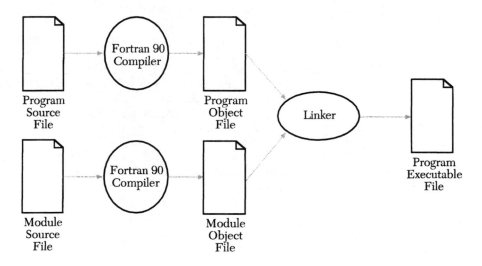

For some compilers, these three steps can be accomplished with a single command. For example, for the NAGware f90 Compiler (UNIX), the command

```
f90 fig6-8.f90 fig6-9.f90 -o fig6-9
```

will compile the module `fig6-8.f90` and the source program `fig6-9.f90` and link the resulting object files together to form the executable file `fig6-9`. If the module has already been compiled separately using the command

```
f90 -c fig6-8.f90
```

to create the object file `fig6-8.o`, then compiling the source program and linking the resulting object file with the module's object file can be accomplished using the command

```
f90 fig6-8.o fig6-9.f90 -o fig6-9
```

If both the module and the source program have been compiled separately,

```
f90 -c fig6-8.f90
f90 -c fig6-9.f90
```

the object files `fig6-8.o` and `fig6-9.o` can be linked using the command

```
f90 fig6-8.o fig6-9.o -o fig6-9
```

6.4 EXTERNAL FUNCTIONS

In Section 6.2 we noted that function subprograms can be classified in three ways:

1. Internal subprograms
2. Module subprograms
3. External subprograms

In the preceding sections, we have described internal and module functions in detail, and in this section we consider external subprograms.

External Subprograms

A subprogram can be made accessible to a program unit by attaching it after the END statement of the program unit; in this case it is called an **external subprogram**. Figure 6.7 illustrates. The function subprogram Fahr_to_Celsius is an external subprogram attached to program Temperature_Conversion_3. Note that Fahr_to_Celsius is *declared in both the main program and the subprogram.*

Figure 6.7. Temperature conversions

```fortran
PROGRAM Temperature_Conversion_3
!---------------------------------------------------------------------
! Program to convert several Fahrenheit temperatures to the
! corresponding Celsius temperatures.  The function Fahr_to_Celsius
! is used to perform the conversions.  Identifiers used are:
!   Fahr_to_Celsius : external function subprogram that converts
!                     Fahrenheit temperatures to Celsius
!   FahrenheitTemp  : a Fahrenheit temperature to be converted
!   CelsiusTemp     : the corresponding Celsius temperature
!   Response        : user response to "More data?" query
!
! Input: FahrenheitTemp, Response
! Output: CelsiusTemp
!---------------------------------------------------------------------

  REAL :: Fahr_to_Celsius
  REAL :: FahrenheitTemp, CelsiusTemp
  CHARACTER(1) :: Response

  DO
     ! Get a Fahrenheit temperature
     WRITE (*, '(1X, A)', ADVANCE = "NO") "Enter a Fahrenheit temperature: "
     READ *, FahrenheitTemp

     ! Use the external function Fahr_to_Celsius to convert it to Celsius
     CelsiusTemp = Fahr_to_Celsius(FahrenheitTemp)

     ! Output the result
     PRINT '(1X, 2(F6.2, A))', FahrenheitTemp, &
           " in Fahrenheit is equivalent to ", CelsiusTemp, " in Celsius"
```

```
            ! Check if more temperatures are to be converted
            WRITE (*, '(/ 1X, A)', ADVANCE = "NO") &
                   "More temperatures to convert (Y or N)? "
            READ *, Response
            IF (Response /= "Y") EXIT
         END DO

END PROGRAM Temperature_Conversion_3

!- Fahr_to_Celsius -----------------------------------------
! Function to convert a Fahrenheit temperature to Celsius
!    Accepts:  A Temperature in Fahrenheit
!    Returns:  The corresponding Celsius temperature
!----------------------------------------------------------

FUNCTION Fahr_to_Celsius(Temperature)

   IMPLICIT NONE
   REAL :: Fahr_to_Celsius
   REAL, INTENT(IN) :: Temperature

   Fahr_to_Celsius = (Temperature - 32.0) / 1.8

END FUNCTION Fahr_to_Celsius
```

Figure 6.7 (cont.)

Interfaces

A main program and external subprograms are separate, independent program units. Neither the main program nor any subprogram can access any of the items declared locally in any other subprogram, nor can an external subprogram access any of the items declared in the main program. The only way that information is passed from one program unit to another is by means of the arguments and the function name.

Since internal subprograms are contained within a host, the compiler can check each reference to the subprogram to determine if it has the correct number and types of arguments (and other properties) and for a function subprogram, whether the value returned is used correctly. Similarly, module subprograms are referenced in statements within that module or in statements that follow a USE statement for that module, and the compiler can check that the arguments and result returned are used correctly. In both cases, the subprogram has an **explicit interface**. An external subprogram is separate from the main program and from other program units, however, and the compiler may not be able to check whether references to it are correct. Consequently, external subprograms are said to have **implicit interfaces**.

To ensure that a compiler can perform the necessary consistency checks, it is desirable that external subprograms have explicit interfaces. Some compilers even require them for all external subprograms.

Interface blocks can be used to provide these explicit interfaces. They have several different forms and uses, but the form needed for external subprograms is

```
INTERFACE
   interface-body
END INTERFACE
```

where `interface-body` consists of:

1. The subprogram heading (except that different names may be used for the formal arguments)
2. Declarations of the argument and the result type in the case of a function
3. An `END FUNCTION` (or `END SUBROUTINE`) statement

Figure 6.8 illustrates the use of an interface block to provide an explicit interface for the function `Fahr_to_Celsius`.

Figure 6.8. Temperature conversions

```
PROGRAM Temperature_Conversion_4
!-------------------------------------------------------------------
! Program to convert several Fahrenheit temperatures to the
! corresponding Celsius temperatures. The function Fahr_to_Celsius
! is used to perform the conversions. Identifiers used are:
!   Fahr_to_Celsius : external function subprogram that converts
!                     Fahrenheit temperatures to Celsius
!   Fahrenheit Temp : a Fahrenheit temperature to be converted
!   CelsiusTemp     : the corresponding Celsius temperature
!   Response        : user response to "More data?" query
!
! Input:   FahrenheitTemp, Response
! Output:  Celsius Temp
!-------------------------------------------------------------------

  IMPLICIT NONE

  INTERFACE
    FUNCTION Fahr_to_Celsius (Temperature)
      REAL :: Fahr_to_Celsius
      REAL, INTENT(IN) :: Temperature
    END FUNCTION Fahr_to_Celsius
  END INTERFACE

  REAL :: FahrenheitTemp, CelsiusTemp
  CHARACTER(1) :: Response

  DO
    ! Get a Fahrenheit temperature
    WRITE (*, '(1X, A)', ADVANCE = "NO") "Enter a Fahrenheit temperature:"
    READ *, FahrenheitTemp

    !Use the function Fahr_to_Celsius to convert it to Celsius
    CelsiusTemp = Fahr_to_Celsius(FahrenheitTemp)

    ! Output the result
    PRINT '(1X, 2(F6.2, A))', FahrenheitTemp, &
          " in Fahrenheit is equivalent to ", CelsiusTemp, " in Celsius"

    ! Check if more temperatures are to be converted
    WRITE (*, '(/ 1X, A)', ADVANCE = "NO") &
          "More temperatures to convert (Y or N)? "
```

```
        READ *, Response
      IF (Response /= "Y") EXIT
   END DO

END PROGRAM Temperature_Conversion_4

!-Fahr_to_Celsius-------------------------------------------
! Function to convert a Fahrenheit temperature to Celsius
!   Accepts:  A Temperature in Fahrenheit
!   Returns:  The corresponding Celsius temperature
!-----------------------------------------------------------

FUNCTION Fahr_to_Celsius (Temperature)

  IMPLICIT NONE
  REAL :: Fahr_to_Celsius
  REAL, INTENT(IN) :: Temperature

  Fahr_to_Celsius = (Temperature - 32.0) / 1.8

END FUNCTION Fahr_to_Celsius
```

Figure 6.8   (cont.)

6.5 INTRODUCTION TO RECURSION

All of the examples of function references considered thus far have involved a main program referencing a subprogram or one subprogram referencing another subprogram. In fact, a subprogram may even reference itself, a phenomenon known as **recursion**. In this section, we show how recursion is implemented in Fortran 90.

To illustrate the basic idea of recursion, we consider the problem of calculating the factorial function. The first definition of the factorial $n!$ of a nonnegative integer n that one usually learns is

$$n! = 1 \times 2 \times \cdots \times n, \quad \text{for } n > 0$$

and that $0!$ is 1. In calculating a sequence of consecutive factorials, however, it would be foolish to calculate each one using this definition, that is, to multiply together the numbers from 1 through n each time; for example,

$$0! = 1$$
$$1! = 1$$
$$2! = 1 \times 2 = 2$$
$$3! = 1 \times 2 \times 3 = 6$$
$$4! = 1 \times 2 \times 3 \times 4 = 24$$
$$5! = 1 \times 2 \times 3 \times 4 \times 5 = 120$$

It is clear that once one factorial has been calculated, it can be used to calculate the next one; for example, given the value $4! = 24$, we can use this value to calculate $5!$ simply by multiplying the value of $4!$ by 5:

$$5! = 5 \times 4! = 5 \times 24 = 120$$

and this value can then be used to calculate $6!$:

$$6! = 6 \times 5! = 6 \times 120 = 720$$

and so on. Indeed, to calculate $n!$ for any positive integer n, we need only know the value of $0!$,

$$0! = 1$$

and the fundamental relation between one factorial and the next:

$$n! = n \times (n - 1)!$$

This approach to calculating factorials leads to the following recursive definition of $n!$:

$$0! = 1$$

$$\text{For } n > 0, n! = n \times (n - 1)!$$

Another classic example of a function that can be calculated recursively is the power function that calculates x^n, where x is a real value and n is a nonnegative integer. The first definition of x^n that one learns is usually an iterative (nonrecursive) one:

$$x^n = \underbrace{x \times x \times \cdots \times x}_{n \ x\text{'s}}$$

and later one learns that x^0 is defined to be 1. (For convenience, we assume here that x^0 is 1 also when x is 0, although in this case it is usually left undefined.)

In calculating a sequence of consecutive powers of some number, however, it would again be foolish to calculate each one using this definition, that is, to multiply the number by itself the required number of times; for example,

$$3.0^0 = 1$$
$$3.0^1 = 3.0$$
$$3.0^2 = 3.0 \times 3.0 = 9.0$$
$$3.0^3 = 3.0 \times 3.0 \times 3.0 = 27.0$$
$$3.0^4 = 3.0 \times 3.0 \times 3.0 \times 3.0 = 81.0$$
$$3.0^5 = 3.0 \times 3.0 \times 3.0 \times 3.0 \times 3.0 = 243.0$$
$$\vdots$$

Once again, the value of this function for a given integer can be used to calculate the value of the function for the next integer. For example, to calculate 3.0^4, we can simply multiply the value of 3.0^3 by 3.0:

$$3.0^4 = 3.0 \times 3.0^3 = 3.0 \times 27.0 = 81.0$$

Similarly, we can use the value of 3.0^4 to calculate 3.0^5:

$$3.0^5 = 3.0 \times 3.0^4 = 3.0 \times 81.0 = 243.0$$

and so on. We need only know the value of 3.0^0,

$$3.0^0 = 1$$

and the fundamental relation between one power of 3.0 and the next:

$$3.0^n = 3.0 \times 3.0^{n-1}$$

This suggests the following recursive definition of x^n:

$$x^0 = 1$$

$$\text{For } n > 0, x^n = x \times x^{n-1}$$

In general, a function is said to be *defined recursively* if its definition consists of two parts:

1. An **anchor** or **base case**, in which the value of the function is specified for one or more values of the argument(s)
2. An **inductive** or **recursive step**, in which the function's value for the current value of the argument(s) is defined in terms of previously defined function values and/or argument values

We have seen two examples of such recursive definitions of functions, the factorial function

$$0! = 1 \qquad \text{(the anchor or base case)}$$
$$\text{For } n > 0, n! = n \times (n - 1)! \qquad \text{(the inductive or recursive step)}$$

and the power function

$$x^0 = 1 \qquad \text{(the anchor or base case)}$$
$$\text{For } n > 0, x^n = x \times x^{n-1} \qquad \text{(the inductive or recursive step)}$$

In each definition, the first statement specifies a particular value of the function, and the second statement defines its value for n in terms of its value for $n - 1$.

Subprograms may be declared to be recursive by attaching the word RECURSIVE at the beginning of the subprogram heading. For a recursive function, a RESULT **clause** must also be attached at the end of the function heading to specify a variable that will be used to return the function result rather than the function name. *The type of the function is specified by declaring the type of this result variable* instead of the name of the function.

To illustrate, consider the factorial function again. The recursive definition of this function can be implemented as a recursive function in Fortran in a straightforward manner:

```
!-Factorial ----------------------------------------------
!   Function to calculate factorials (recursively).
!
!     Accepts:  integer n >= 0
!     Returns:  n!
!----------------------------------------------------------

RECURSIVE FUNCTION Factorial(n) RESULT (Fact)

  INTEGER :: Fact              ! Result variable
  INTEGER, INTENT(IN) :: n

  IF (n == 0) THEN
    Fact = 1
  ELSE
    Fact = n * Factorial(n - 1)
  END IF

END FUNCTION Factorial
```

When this function is referenced, the inductive step

```
  ELSE
      Fact = n * Factorial(n - 1)
```

causes the function to reference itself repeatedly, each time with a smaller argument, until the anchor case

```
  IF (n == 0) THEN
      Fact = 1
```

is reached.

For example, consider the reference `Factorial(5)` to calculate 5!. Since the value of n, which is 5, is not 0, the inductive step generates another reference to `Factorial` with argument n - 1 = 4. Before execution of the original function reference is suspended, the current value 5 of the argument n is saved so that the value of n can be restored when execution resumes. This might be pictured as follows:

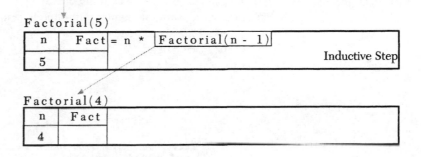

Since the value 4 of n in this function reference is not 0, the inductive step in this second reference to `Factorial` generates another reference to `Factorial` with argument 3. The inductive step in this function reference with argument n = 3 generates another reference to `Factorial` with argument 2, which in turn generates another reference with argument 1, which in turn generates another reference with argument 0:

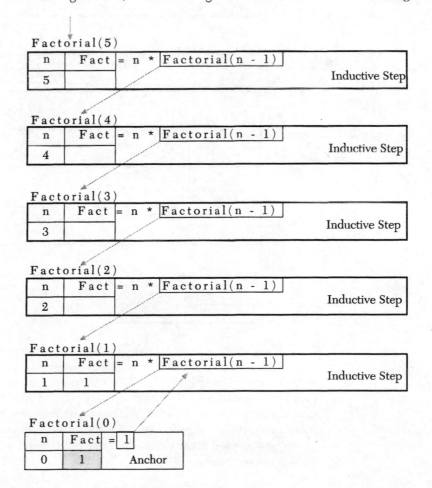

Because the anchor condition is now satisfied in this last function reference, no additional references are generated; instead the value 1 is assigned to `Fact`.

The function reference with argument 0 is thus completed, and the value 1 is returned as the value for `Factorial(0)`. Execution of the preceding function is resumed. The value of the argument n is restored, and the expression `n * Factorial(n - 1) = 1 * Factorial(0) = 1 * 1 = 1` is calculated and returned as the value of `Factorial(1)`. Execution of `Factorial` with argument 1 is thus complete, and execution of the preceding reference is resumed. The value of n is restored, and the value of `n * Factorial(n - 1) = 2 * Factorial(1) = 2 * 1 = 2` is calculated for `Factorial(2)`. This *back-tracking* continues until 120 is returned as the value for `Factorial(5)`:

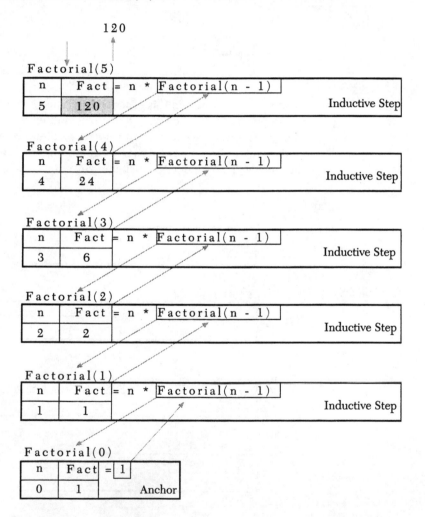

Many problems can be solved with equal ease using either a recursive or a nonrecursive algorithm. For some problems, however, recursion is the most natural and straightforward technique. The following is an example of such a problem. For these problems, nonrecursive algorithms may not be obvious, may be more difficult to develop, and may be less readable than recursive ones. For such problems, the simplicity of the recursive algorithms compensates for any inefficiency. Unless the programs are to be executed many times, the extra effort required to develop nonrecursive solutions is not warranted.

Example: Street Network

Consider a network of streets laid out in a rectangular grid, for example,

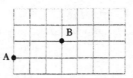

In a *northeast path* from one point in the grid to another, one may go only to the north (up) and to the east (right). For example, there are four northeast paths from A to B in the preceding grid:

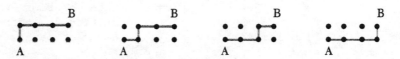

To count the paths, we might proceed (recursively) as follows. To get from A to B, there are two ways to begin:

Case 1:   Go one block north (up); call this point A1 .

Case 2:   Go one block east (right); call this point A2 .

In either case, we must count paths on a smaller grid. In the first case, there are the same number of columns separating A_1 and B, but there is one less row. In the second case, there are the same number of rows separating A2 and B, but there is one less column. This suggests the following inductive step in a recusive solution to the problem:

Number of paths from A to B

= (Number of paths from A_1 to B) + (Number of paths from A_2 to B)

The function `Number_of_Paths` in Figure 6.9 uses this recursive approach to count the number of northeast paths from one point to another in a rectangular grid. The anchor case is that in which points A and B coincide.

Figure 6.9.   Counting paths in a street network

```
PROGRAM Path_Counter
!-----------------------------------------------------------------------
! Program to count "northeasterly" paths from a given starting point
! in a network of streets to a specified ending point. Identifiers
! used are:
!   StartRow, StartColumn : coordinates of starting point
!   EndRow, EndColumn     : coordinates of ending point
!   Number_of_Paths       : recursive function to count paths
!
! Input:  StartRow, StartColumn, EndRow, EndColumn
! Output: Number of northeast paths
!-----------------------------------------------------------------------

 IMPLICIT NONE
 INTEGER :: StartRow, StartColumn, EndRow, EndColumn

 PRINT *, "Enter the starting coordinates (row then column):"
 READ *, StartRow, StartColumn
```

```
        PRINT *, "Enter the ending coordinates (row then column):"
        READ *, EndRow, EndColumn

        PRINT *, "There are", &
                 Number_of_Paths(EndRow - StartRow, &
                                 EndColumn - StartColumn), " paths"

CONTAINS

   ! Number_of_Paths ----------------------------------------------------
   ! A recursive function to calculate the number of northeasterly paths
   ! in a network of streets. Identifiers used are:
   !   NumRows, NumColumns : number of rows and columns from starting
   !                         position to ending position
   !   Num_Paths           : number of paths
   !
   ! Accepts: Number_of_Rows, Number_of_Columns
   ! Returns: Num_Paths
   !---------------------------------------------------------------------

   RECURSIVE FUNCTION &
     Number_of_Paths(NumRows, NumColumns) RESULT (Num_Paths)

     INTEGER, INTENT(IN) :: NumRows, NumColumns
     INTEGER :: Num_Paths

     IF ((NumRows == 0) .OR. (NumColumns == 0)) THEN
        Num_Paths = 1
     ELSE
        Num_Paths = Number_of_Paths(NumRows - 1, NumColumns) &
                  + Number_of_Paths(NumRows, NumColumns - 1)
     END IF

   END FUNCTION Number_of_Paths

END PROGRAM Path_Counter
```

Sample Runs:

```
Enter the starting coordinates (row then column): 0, 1
Enter the ending coordinates (row then column): 3, 2
There are 4 paths

Enter the starting coordinates (row then column): 1, 1
Enter the ending coordinates (row then column): 1, 1
There are 1 paths

Enter the starting coordinates (row then column): 0, 1
Enter the ending coordinates (row then column): 7, 4
There are 120 paths

Enter the starting coordinates (row then column): 0, 0
Enter the ending coordinates (row then column): 7, 4
There are 330 paths
```

Figure 6.9 (cont.)

PRACTICE!

1. _____ is the phenomenon of a subprogram referencing itself.

2. Describe what it means to say that a function is defined recursively.

3. A function subprogram is declared to be recursive by attaching the word _____ at the beginning of the function heading.

4. For a recursive function, a _____ clause must be attached at the end of the function heading to specify that an identifier other than the function name will be used for the function result.

5. (True or false) A nonrecursive function for computing some value may execute more rapidly than a recursive function that computes the same value.

6. For the following recursive function, find `F(5)`.

```
RECURSIVE FUNCTION F(N) RESULT (F_value)

   INTEGER :: F_Value
   INTEGER, INTENT(IN) :: N

   IF (N == 0) THEN
      F_Value = 0
   ELSE
      F_Value = N + F(N - 1)
   END IF

END FUNCTION F
```

7. For the function in Exercise 6, find `F(0)`.

8. For the function in Exercise 6, suppose + is changed to * in the inductive step. Find `F(5)`.

For Exercises 9–11, determine what is calculated by the given recursive functions.

9.
```
RECURSIVE FUNCTION F(X, N) RESULT (F_Value)

   REAL :: F_Value
   REAL, INTENT(IN) :: X
   INTEGER, INTENT(IN) :: N

   IF (N == 0) THEN
      F_Value = 0
   ELSE
      F_Value = X + F(X, N - 1)
   END IF

END FUNCTION F
```

10.
```
RECURSIVE FUNCTION F(N) RESULT (F_Value)

   INTEGER :: F_Value
   INTEGER, INTENT(IN) :: N

   IF (N < 2) THEN
      F_Value = 0
   ELSE
      F_Value = 1 + F( N / 2)
   END IF

END FUNCTION F
```

```
11. RECURSIVE FUNCTION F(N) RESULT (F_Value)

       INTEGER :: F_Value
       INTEGER, INTENT(IN) :: N

       IF (N == 0) THEN
          F_Value = 0
       ELSE
          F_Value = F(N / 10) + MOD(N, 10)
       END IF

    END FUNCTION F
```

12. Write a recursive function that computes x^n for a real value x and a nonnegative integer n.

13. Write a recursive function that returns the number of digits in a nonnegative integer.

14. Write a recursive function that computes the greatest common divisor of two integers (see Exercise 21 of Section 6.2).

KEY TERMS

Anchor (base) case	Inductive (recursive) step	Programmer-defined function
Compilation	INTENT specifier	RECURSIVE Keyword
CONTAINS Keyword	Interface block	Recursion
Explicit interface	Internal subprogram	RESULT clause
External subprogram	Intrinsic (library) function	RETURN statement
Formal (dummy) argument	Library	SAVE attribute
Function	Linking	SAVE statement
FUNCTION statement	Local identifier	Scope
Function subprogram	Local item	Subprogram
Global entity	Main program	Subprogram section
Host	Module	Subroutine
Implicit interface	Module subprogram	USE statement

PROGRAMMING POINTERS

Program Style and Design

1. *Subprograms should be documented in the same way that the main program is.* The documentation should include a brief description of the processing carried out by the subprograms, the values passed to them, the values returned by them, and what the arguments and local variables represent.

2. *Subprograms are separate program units, and the program format should reflect this fact.* In this text, we
   - Insert one or more blank lines before and after each subprogram to set it off from other program units.
   - Follow the stylistic standards described in earlier chapters when writing subprograms.

3. *An INTENT(IN) clause should be used in the declaration of each argument of a function subprogram to specify that values will only be passed to that argument and not returned by it.* This protects the argument by ensuring that its value is not changed within the subprogram.

4. *Programs for solving complex problems should be designed in a modular fashion.* The problem should be divided into simpler subproblems so that subprograms can be written to solve each of them.

Potential Problems

1. *The number of actual arguments in a reference to a function must be the same as the number of formal arguments (unless some arguments have been declared to be optional—see Footnote 2 in Section 6.2); also, the type of each actual argument must agree with the type of the corresponding formal argument.*

2. *The argument checking described in Potential Problem 1 is done automatically by the compiler for module functions and internal functions. Interface blocks may be used to ensure that similar checking is done for external functions.*

3. *The type of an external function must be declared both in the function subprogram and in the program unit that references the function.*

4. *If a formal argument is not declared to have the* INTENT(IN) *attribute and its value is changed in a subprogram, the value of the corresponding actual argument also changes.* For example, if the function F is defined by the function subprogram

```
FUNCTION F(X, Y)

REAL :: F
REAL :: X, Y

F = X ** 2 - 2.5 * Y + 3.7 * Y ** 2
X = 0

END FUNCTION F
```

then when the function is referenced in the main program by a statement such as

```
Alpha = F(Beta, Gamma)
```

where Alpha, Beta, and Gamma are real variables, the value of the function is assigned to Alpha, but Beta is set equal to zero, since it corresponds to the formal argument X, whose value is changed in the subprogram.

Programming Problems

SECTION 6.2

1. Write a program that inputs several pairs of integers, calls the function Range in Exercise 13 of Section 6.2 to calculate the range between each pair, and displays this range.

2. Write a program that inputs real numbers, calls the function Round in Exercise 14 of Section 6.2 to round each real value to a specified number of places, and displays the rounded value.

3. Write a program that reads values for an initial population of bacteria, a rate constant, and a time (e.g., 1000, 0.15, 100), calls the function from Exercise 15 of Section 6.2 to calculate the number of bacteria at that time, and displays this value.

4. Write a logical-valued function that determines whether a character is one of the digits 0 through 9. Use it in a program that reads several characters and checks to see whether each is a digit.

5. If an amount of A dollars is borrowed at an annual interest rate r (expressed as a decimal) for y years, and n is the number of payments to be made per year, then the amount of each payment is given by

$$\frac{r \cdot A/n}{1 - \left(1 + \frac{r}{n}\right)^{-n \cdot y}}$$

Write a function to calculate these payments. Use it in a program that reads several values for the amount borrowed, the interest rate, the number of years, and the number of payments per year and displays the corresponding payment for each set of values.

6. Write a program that reads several test scores and displays for each the corresponding letter grade and the numeric value of that grade. Use the functions `NumericGrade` and `LetterGrade` from Exercises 16 and 17 of Section 6.2.

7. Write a program that reads several pairs of integers `Number_1` and `Number_2` and, for each pair, calls the function from Exercise 18 of Section 6.2 to calculate the sum of the integers from `Number_1` through `Number_2` and displays this sum.

8. Write a program that reads several integers and, for each, displays a message indicating whether it is a perfect square. Use the function from Exercise 20 of Section 6.2 to determine if a number is a perfect square.

9. Write a program that reads several integers, uses the function from Exercise 22 of Section 6.2 to determine whether each is a prime, and displays each number with the appropriate label "is prime" or "is not prime."

Applications

10. If the angle between a force and a path of motion changes during displacement, the work done by the force F (newtons) in moving an object from $s = a$ to $s = b$ (meters) along the line is given by

$$W = F \int_a^b \cos(\theta(s)) ds \quad \text{(joules)}$$

where $\theta(s)$ is the angle at a distance s from the initial point a. Write a program that asks the user to enter values for a, b, and F, that reads a value for n and the value of $\theta(s)$ at n equally spaced points along the path of motion from a data file, and that then uses the trapezoidal method to approximate this integral. The program should then compute and display the work done. Run your program using a force of 10.38 N, $a = 0.0$ m, $b = 30.0$ m, and the following angles at points $a, a + \Delta s, a + \Delta s, \ldots, b$: 0.5, 1.4, 0.75, 0.9, 1.3, 1.48, 1.5, 1.6 (all in radians).

11. Proceed as in Problem 10, but suppose both the angle and the force vary. In this case, the work done is given by

$$W = \int_a^b F(s) \cos(\theta(s)) ds$$

where $F(s)$ is the angle at a distance s from the initial point a. Write a program that asks the user to enter values for a and b, that reads a value for n and the values of $F(s)$ and $\theta(s)$ at n equally spaced points along the path of motion from a data file, and that then uses the trapezoidal method to approximate this integral. The program should then compute and display the work done. Run your program using $a = 20.0$ m, $b = 50.0$ m, and the following pairs of values for $F(s)$ and $\theta(s)$ at points $a, a + \Delta s, a + 2\Delta s, \ldots, b$ (all in newtons and radians):

F(s)	θ(s)
0.0	0.60
4.3	0.87
7.8	1.02
9.9	0.99
12.5	1.20
16.3	0.98
18.4	0.86
21.7	0.43

F(s)	θ(s)
25.4	0.23
22.3	0.14
20.9	0.15
18.7	0.08

SECTION 6.3

12. Design and test a module for converting weights from the U.S. system to the metric system. Some useful conversion formulas are: 16 ounces = 1 pound, 2000 pounds = 1 ton, 1 ounce = 28.349523 grams, 1 kilogram = 1000 grams.

13. Design and test a module for converting lengths from the U.S. system to the metric system. Some useful conversion formulas are: 12 inches = 1 foot, 3 feet = 1 yard, 1 mile = 5280 feet, 1 inch = 2.540005 centimeters, 1 meter = 100 centimeters, 1 kilometer = 1000 meters.

14. Design and test a module for converting volumes from the U.S. system to the metric system. Some useful conversion formulas are: 2 pints = 1 quart, 4 quarts = 1 gallon, 1 pint = 0.4731631 liters, 1 kiloliter = 1000 liters.

SECTION 6.4

15. Write a program to test the recursive power function of Exercise 12 in Section 6.4.

16. Write a program to test the recursive digit-counter function of Exercise 13 in Section 6.4.

17. Write a program to test the recursive greatest common divisor function of Exercise 14 in Section 6.4.

7

Programming with Subroutines

7.1 SUBROUTINE SUBPROGRAMS

Subroutine subprograms have many features in common with function subprograms:

- They are program units designed to perform particular tasks under the control of some other program unit.
- They have the same basic form: each consists of a heading, a specification part, an execution part, and an END statement.
- They may be internal, module, or external subprograms.
- The scope rules described in Section 6.1 apply to both functions and subroutines.
- They may be used as arguments of other subprograms (see Section 7.3).
- They may be recursive (see Section 7.4).

They differ, however, in the following respects:

- Functions are designed to return a single value to the program unit that references them. Subroutines often return more than one value, or they may return no value at all but simply perform some task such as displaying a list of instructions to the user.
- Functions return values via function names; subroutines return values via arguments.
- A function is referenced by using its name in an expression, whereas a subroutine is referenced by a CALL statement.

OBJECTIVES

In this chapter, you will

- Learn to create subroutines.
- Read about using subprograms as arguments for other subprograms
- Apply the concepts learned to nuclear reactor and artificial intelligence examples.

The form of a subroutine subprogram is

```
    subroutine heading
    specification part
    execution part
    END SUBROUTINE statement
```

The *subroutine heading* is a SUBROUTINE **statement** of the form

```
    SUBROUTINE subroutine-name(formal-argument-list)
```

or for a recursive subroutine,

```
    RECURSIVE SUBROUTINE subroutine-name(formal-argument-list)
```

where the list of formal arguments is as described for function subprograms in Chapter 6. A subroutine is referenced by a CALL **statement** of the form

```
    CALL subroutine-name(actual-argument-list)
```

This statement calls the named subroutine. Execution of the current program unit is suspended; the actual arguments are associated with the corresponding formal arguments; and execution of the subroutine begins. When execution of the subroutine is completed, execution of the original program unit resumes with the statement following the CALL statement.

Example: Displaying an Angle in Degrees

As a simple illustration, suppose we wish to develop a subroutine that accepts from the main program an angular measurement in degrees, minutes, and seconds and displays it as an equivalent number of degrees. For example, the value 100° 30′ 36″ is to be displayed as

```
100 degrees, 30 minutes, 36 seconds
is equivalent to
100.510 degrees
```

This subroutine will have three formal arguments, all of type INTEGER, the first representing the number of degrees, the second the number of minutes, and the third the number of seconds. Thus, an appropriate heading for this subroutine is

```
SUBROUTINE PrintDegrees(Degrees, Minutes, Seconds)
```

where Degrees, Minutes, and Seconds must be declared of type INTEGER in the specification part of the subroutine. The complete subroutine is shown in the program of Figure 7.1 as an internal subprogram. It is referenced by the CALL statement

```
CALL PrintDegrees(NumDegrees, NumMinutes, NumSeconds)
```

which causes the values of the actual arguments NumDegrees, NumMinutes, and NumSeconds to be passed to the formal arguments Degrees, Minutes, and Seconds, respectively, and initiates execution of the subroutine. When the end of the subroutine is reached, execution resumes with the statement following this CALL statement in the main program.

Figure 7.1. Displaying an angle in degrees

```fortran
PROGRAM Angles_1
!-----------------------------------------------------------------------
! Program demonstrating the use of a subroutine PrintDegrees to
! display an angle in degrees.  Variables used are:
!   NumDegrees : degrees in the angle measurement
!   NumMinutes : minutes in the angle measurement
!   NumSeconds : seconds in the angle measurement
!   Response   : user response to more-data question
!
! Input:  NumDegrees, NumMinutes, NumSeconds, Response
! Output: Equivalent measure in degrees (displayed by PrintDegrees)
!-----------------------------------------------------------------------

  IMPLICIT NONE
  INTEGER :: NumDegrees, NumMinutes, NumSeconds
  CHARACTER(1) :: Response

  ! Read and convert angles until user signals no more data
  DO
     WRITE (*, '(1X, A)', ADVANCE = "NO") &
           "Enter degrees, minutes, and seconds: "
     READ *, NumDegrees, NumMinutes, NumSeconds
     CALL PrintDegrees(NumDegrees, NumMinutes, NumSeconds)
     WRITE (*, '(/ 1X, A)', ADVANCE = "NO") "More angles (Y or N)? "
     READ *, Response
     IF (Response /= "Y") EXIT
  END DO

CONTAINS

  !-PrintDegrees---------------------------------------------------------
  ! Subroutine to display a measurement of Degrees, Minutes, Seconds
  ! as the equivalent degree measure.
  !
  ! Accepts: Degrees, Minutes, Seconds
  ! Output:  Values of Degrees, Minutes, and Seconds and the
  !          equivalent degree measure
  !-----------------------------------------------------------------------

  SUBROUTINE PrintDegrees(Degrees, Minutes, Seconds)

    INTEGER, INTENT(IN) :: Degrees, Minutes, Seconds

    PRINT 10, Degrees, Minutes, Seconds, &
              REAL(Degrees) + REAL(Minutes)/60.0 + REAL(Seconds)/3600.0
    10 FORMAT (1X, I3, " degrees", I3, " minutes", I3, " seconds" &
              / 1X, "is equivalent to" / 1X, F7.3, " degrees")

  END SUBROUTINE PrintDegrees

END PROGRAM Angles_1
```

Sample run:

```
Enter degrees, minutes, and seconds: 100, 30, 36
100 degrees 30 minutes 36 seconds
is equivalent to
100.510 degrees
```

```
More angles (Y or N)? Y
Enter degrees, minutes, and seconds: 360, 0, 0
360 degrees 0 minutes 0 seconds
is equivalent to
360.000 degrees

More angles (Y or N)? Y
Enter degrees, minutes, and seconds: 1, 1, 1
  1 degrees 1 minutes 1 seconds
is equivalent to
  1.017 degrees

More angles (Y or N)? N
```

Figure 7.1   (cont.)

Example of a Subroutine That Returns Values: Converting Coordinates

The subroutine in the preceding example does not return values to the main program; it only displays the information passed to it. As an illustration of a subroutine that does return values to the main program, consider the problem of converting the polar coordinates (r, θ) of a point P to rectangular coordinates (x, y). The first polar coordinate r is the distance from the origin to P, and the second polar coordinate θ is the angle from the positive x-axis to the ray joining the origin with P.

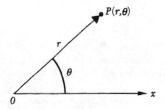

The formulas that relate the polar coordinates to the rectangular coordinates for a point are

$$x = r \cos\theta$$
$$y = r \sin\theta$$

Because the subprogram that performs this conversion must return *two* values (x and y), it is natural to use a subroutine like that in the program in Figure 7.2. The main program reads values for RCoord and TCoord, calls the subroutine Convert_to_ Rectangular with the statement

```
CALL Convert_to_Rectangular(RCoord, TCoord, XCoord, YCoord)
```

to calculate the corresponding rectangular coordinates XCoord and YCoord, and then displays these coordinates.

Figure 7.2.   Converting polar coordinates to rectangular coordinates

```
PROGRAM Polar_to_Rectangular
!-------------------------------------------------------------------------
! This program accepts the polar coordinates of a point and displays
! the corresponding rectangular coordinates.  The internal subroutine
! Convert_to_Rectangular is used to effect the conversion.
```

```fortran
      ! Variables used are:
      !   RCoord, TCoord : polar coordinates of a point
      !   XCoord, YCoord : rectangular coordinates of a point
      !   Response       : user response to more-data question
      !
      ! Input:  RCoord, TCoord, and Response
      ! Output: XCoord and YCoord
      !--------------------------------------------------------------------

        IMPLICIT NONE
        REAL :: RCoord, TCoord, XCoord, YCoord
        CHARACTER(1) :: Response

        ! Read and convert coordinates until user signals no more data
        DO
           WRITE (*, '(1X, A)', ADVANCE = "NO") &
                 "Enter polar coordinates (in radians): "
           READ *, RCoord, TCoord
           CALL Convert_to_Rectangular(RCoord, TCoord, XCoord, YCoord)
           PRINT *, "Rectangular coordinates:", XCoord, YCoord
           WRITE (*, '(/ 1X, A)', ADVANCE = "NO") &
                 "More points to convert (Y or N)? "
           READ *, Response
           IF (Response /= "Y") EXIT
        END DO

      CONTAINS

        !-Convert_to_Rectangular----------------------------------------------
        ! Subroutine to convert polar coordinates (R, Theta) to rectangular
        ! coordinates (X, Y).
        !
        ! Accepts: Polar coordinates R and Theta (in radians)
        ! Returns: Rectangular coordinates X and Y
        !--------------------------------------------------------------------

        SUBROUTINE Convert_to_Rectangular(R, Theta, X, Y)

          REAL, INTENT(IN) :: R, Theta
          REAL, INTENT(OUT) :: X, Y

          X = R * COS(Theta)
          Y = R * SIN(Theta)

        END SUBROUTINE Convert_to_Rectangular

      END PROGRAM Polar_to_Rectangular
```

Sample run:
```
Enter polar coordinates (in radians): 1.0, 0
Rectangular coordinates:   1.0000000   0.0000000E+00

More points to convert (Y or N)? Y
Enter polar coordinates (in radians): 0, 1.0
Rectangular coordinates:   0.0000000E+00   0.0000000E+00
```
Figure 7.2 (cont.)

```
More points to convert (Y or N)? Y
Enter polar coordinates (in radians): 1.0, 1.57
Rectangular coordinates:    7.9627428E-04   0.9999997

More points to convert (Y or N)? Y
Enter polar coordinates (in radians): 4.0, 3.14159
Rectangular coordinates:   -4.0000000   1.0140727E-05

More points to convert (Y or N)? N
```

Figure 7.2 (cont.)

Argument Association

When the CALL statement

```
CALL Convert_to_Rectangular(RCoord, TCoord, XCoord, YCoord)
```

in the program in Figure 7.2 is executed, the values of the actual arguments RCoord and TCoord are passed to the formal arguments R and Theta, respectively:

ACTUAL ARGUMENTS		FORMAL ARGUMENTS
Rcoord	$\longrightarrow$	R
Tcoord	$\longrightarrow$	Theta
XCoord		X
YCoord		Y

R and Theta have been declared to be IN arguments because the intent is that values are only to be passed to them and used within the subroutine. They are not intended to return new values to the calling program unit, and thus no new values may be assigned to them within the subroutine.

The formal arguments X and Y are declared to have the INTENT(OUT) **attribute** because they are intended only to pass values back to the calling program unit. Thus, after values for X and Y are calculated and execution of the subroutine is complete, these values are passed back to the corresponding actual arguments XCoord and YCoord:

ACTUAL ARGUMENTS		FORMAL ARGUMENTS
Rcoord	$\longrightarrow$	R
Tcoord	$\longrightarrow$	Theta
XCoord	$\longleftarrow$	X
YCoord	$\longleftarrow$	Y

A formal argument may also be declared to have the INTENT(INOUT) **attribute.** Such arguments can be used to pass information both to and from the subroutine:

```
actual-argument<———————>formal-argument
```

Because both OUT and INOUT arguments are intended to pass values back to the calling program unit, the corresponding actual arguments must be variables.

PRACTICE!

1. What are the two kinds of Fortran subprograms?
2. List the four parts of a subroutine subprogram.

3. In the subroutine heading SUBROUTINE Display(A, B), A and B are called _____.

4. List three differences between subroutine subprograms and function subprograms.

Exercises 5–10 refer to the following internal subroutine Calculate:

```
SUBROUTINE Calculate(Alpha, Number_1, Number_2)
  REAL, INTENT(IN) :: Alpha
  INTEGER, INTENT(OUT) :: Number_1
  INTEGER, INTENT (INOUT) :: Number_2
      :
END SUBROUTINE Calculate
```

Also, assume that the following declarations have been made in the main program:

```
INTEGER :: Code, Id_Number
REAL :: Rate
```

Tell if the given statement is a valid reference to Calculate.

5. Rate = Calculate(2.45, Code, Id_Number)

6. CALL Calculate(Rate + 0.5, 0, Code - Id_Number)

7. CALL Calculate(Rate, Id_Number)

8. CALL Calculate(Rate, Code, Id_Number)

9. CALL Calculate

10. CALL Calculate(Rate, Rate, Rate)

11. Write a subroutine that displays the name of a month whose number (1–12) is passed to it.

12. Write a subroutine Switch that interchanges the values of two integer variables. For example, if A has the value 3 and B has the value 4, then the statement CALL Switch(A, B) causes A to have the value 4 and B the value 3.

13. Write a subroutine that accepts a measurement in centimeters and returns the corresponding measurement in yards, feet, and inches (1 cm = 0.3937 in).

14. Write a subroutine that accepts a weight in grams and returns the corresponding weight in pounds and ounces (1 g = 0.35274 oz).

15. Write a subroutine that accepts a time in military format and returns the corresponding time in the usual representation in hours, minutes, and A.M./P.M. For example, a time of 100 should be returned as 1 hour, 0 minutes, and A.M.; a time of 1545 should be returned as 3 hours, 45 minutes, and P.M.

16. Write a subroutine that accepts a time in the usual representation in hours, minutes, and one of the strings A.M. or P.M., and returns the corresponding military time. (See Exercise 15.)

APPLICATION: SHIELDING A NUCLEAR REACTOR

In many problems, the process being studied involves **randomness**, for example, Brownian motion, the arrival of airplanes at an airport, and the number of defective parts a machine manufactures. Computer programs that **simulate** such processes use **random number generators** to introduce randomness into the values produced during execution.

Fortran 90 provides the subroutine RANDOM_SEED to initialize the random number generator RANDOM_NUMBER, which is a subroutine that produces random real numbers uniformly distributed over the range 0 to 1. The numbers produced by such a generator can be used to generate random real numbers in other ranges or to generate random integers. For example, if RandomNumber is a random number in the range 0 to 1, the value of the expression

        A + (B - A) * RandomNumber

will be a random real number in the range A to B, and the value of the expression

        M + INT(K * RandomNumber)

will be a random integer in the range M through M + K - 1.

PROBLEM

When the enriched uranium fuel of a nuclear reactor is burned, high-energy neutrons are produced. Some of these are retained in the reactor core, but most of them escape. Since this radiation is dangerous, the reactor must be shielded. The problem is to simulate neutrons entering the shield and to determine what percentage of them get through it.

Solution

Specification   To model the shielding in such a way that we can simulate the paths of neutrons that enter it, we will make the simplifying assumption that neutrons entering the shield follow random paths by moving forward, backward, left, or right with equal likelihood, in jumps of one unit. We will also assume that losses of energy occur only when there is a change of direction, and that after a certain number of such direction changes, the neutron's energy is dissipated and it dies within the shield, provided that it has not already passed back inside the reactor core or outside through the shield.

Making these simplifying assumptions, we can specify the problem as follows:

Input: Thickness of the shield
         Limit on the number of direction changes
         Number of neutrons

Output: Percentage of neutrons that reach the outside

Design   To simulate the paths the neutrons take, we will generate random integers with values 1, 2, 3, or 4,

(a)   (b)

Nuclear power plant at Three Mile Island. (Photos courtesy of (a) Tony Stone Images, (b) Stock Boston)

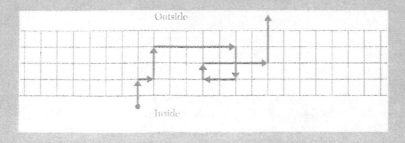

corresponding to movement forward, backward, to the left, or to the right, respectively. If the net movement in the forward direction equals the thickness of the shield, the neutron escapes. If it becomes 0, the neutron returns back inside the reactor. If the number of direction changes reaches a specified limit, the neutron dies within the shield. We repeat this some given number of times and calculate the percentage of neutrons that escape.

The following algorithm describes this simulation more precisely. It uses the following variables:

VARIABLES FOR SHIELDING PROBLEM

Thickness	Thickness of shield
DirectionChangeLimit	Limit on number of direction changes (before energy is dissipated)
NewDirection	A random integer 1, 2, 3, or 4 representing direction
OldDirection	Previous direction of neutron
NumDirectionChanges	Number of changes of direction
Forward	Net units traveled in the forward direction
NumNeutrons	Number of neutrons simulated
NumEscaped	Number of neutrons escaping through the shield

ALGORITHM FOR SHIELDING PROBLEM

Algorithm to simulate neutrons entering a shield and to determine how many reach the outside. The neutrons are assumed to move forward, backward, left, and right with equal likelihood and to die within the shield if a certain number of direction changes occur. A random number generator is assumed.

Input: Thickness of the shield, limit on the number of direction changes, and number of particles

Output: Percentage of particles that reach the outside

1. Read *Thickness*, *DirectionChangeLimit*, and *NumNeutrons*.
2. Initialize *NumEscaped* to 0.
3. Do the following for $I = 1$ to *NumNeutrons*:
   a. Initialize *Forward* to 0, *OldDirection* to 0, and *NumDirectionChanges* to 0.
   b. Repeat the following until particle reaches the outside of the shield (*Forward* $\geq$ *Thickness*), returns inside the reactor (*Forward* $\leq$ 0), or dies within the shield (*NumDirectionChange* $\geq$ *Direction-ChangeLimit*):
      i. Generate a random integer 1, 2, 3, or 4 for the direction *NewDirection*.
      ii. If *NewDirection* $\neq$ *OldDirection*, increment *NumDirectionChanges* by 1 and set *OldDirection* equal to *New-Direction*.
      iii. If *NewDirection* = 1, increment *Forward* by 1.
         Else if *NewDirection* = 2, decrement *Forward* by 1.
   c. If *Forward* $\geq$ *Thickness*, increment *NumEscaped* by 1.
4. Display 100 ° *NumEscaped* / *NumNeutrons*.

Coding

The program in Figure 7.3 implements this algorithm. It uses the intrinsic subroutine RANDOM_NUMBER to generate random real numbers in the range 0 to 1, which are then transformed into random integers 1, 2, 3, or 4, corresponding to the four directions forward, backward, left, and right, respectively.

Figure 7.3. Simulate shielding of nuclear reactor

```
PROGRAM Shielding_a_Nuclear_Reactor
!-------------------------------------------------------------------
! This program uses a random number generator to simulate neutrons
! entering a shield and to determine what percentage reaches the
! outside. The neutrons are assumed to move forward, backward, left
! and right with equal likelihood and to die within the shield if a
! certain number of changes of direction have occurred. Identifiers
! used are:
```

```fortran
!     Thickness            : thickness of shield
!     DirectionChangeLimit : limit on # of direction changes before
!                            energy dissipated
!     RandomReal           : a random real number in the range 0 to 1
!     NewDirection         : a random integer 1, 2, 3, or 4
!                            representing direction
!     OldDirection         : previous direction of neutron
!     NumDirectionChanges  : number of changes of direction
!     Forward              : net units traveled forward
!     NumNeutrons          : number of neutrons simulated
!     NumEscaped           : number of neutrons reaching outside of
!                            shield
!     I                    : loop control variable
!
! Input:   Thickness, DirectionChangeLimit, and NumNeutrons
! Output:  Percentage of neutrons that reach the outside
!------------------------------------------------------------------------

  IMPLICIT NONE
  REAL :: RandomReal
  INTEGER :: Thickness, DirectionChangeLimit, NewDirection, &
             OldDirection, NumDirectionChanges, Forward, &
             NumNeutrons, NumEscaped, I

  PRINT *, "Enter thickness of shield, limit on # of direction"
  PRINT *, "changes, and the number of neutrons to simulate:"
  READ *, Thickness, DirectionChangeLimit, NumNeutrons

  NumEscaped = 0

  ! Begin the simulation

  CALL RANDOM_SEED
  DO I = 1, NumNeutrons
     Forward = 0
     OldDirection = 0
     NumDirectionChanges = 0

     ! Repeat the following until neutron reaches outside of
     ! shield, returns inside reactor, or dies within shield

     DO
        CALL RANDOM_NUMBER(RandomReal)
        NewDirection = 1 + INT(4 * RandomReal)
        IF (NewDirection /= OldDirection) THEN
           NumDirectionChanges = NumDirectionChanges + 1
           OldDirection = NewDirection
        END IF
        IF (NewDirection == 1) THEN
           Forward = Forward + 1
        ELSE IF (NewDirection == 2) THEN
           Forward = Forward - 1
```

Figure 7.3 (cont.)

```
              END IF
              IF ((Forward >= Thickness) .OR. (Forward <= 0) .OR. &
                   (NumDirectionChanges >= DirectionChangeLimit)) EXIT
          END DO

          IF (Forward >= Thickness) NumEscaped = NumEscaped + 1

      END DO

      PRINT '(1X, F5.2, "% of the neutrons escaped")', &
            100 * REAL(NumEscaped) / REAL(NumNeutrons)

  END PROGRAM Shielding_a_Nuclear_Reactor
```

Figure 7.3 (cont.)

Execution and Testing

The following are four sample runs of the program. The first two are test runs. In the first test case, the neutron will move only once, since each first move is interpreted as a change of direction and the limit on the number of direction changes is 1. Since each of the four possible moves is equally likely, we would expect 25 percent of the neutrons to escape, and the result produced by the program is consistent with this value. In the second test case, the shielding is 100 units thick and the limit on the number of direction changes is small. Thus we expect almost none of the neutrons to escape through the shield.

Sample run #1:

```
    Enter thickness of shield, limit on # of direction changes,
    and the number of neutrons to simulate:
    1, 1, 1000
    25.80% of the neutrons escaped
```

Sample run #2:

```
    Enter thickness of shield, limit on # of direction changes,
    and the number of neutrons to simulate:
    100 5 1000
    0.00% of the neutrons escaped
```

Sample run #3:

```
    Enter thickness of shield, limit on # of direction changes,
    and the number of neutrons to simulate:
    4, 5, 100
    3.00% of the neutrons escaped
```

Sample run #4:

```
    Enter thickness of shield, limit on # of direction changes,
    and the number of neutrons to simulate:
    8, 10, 500
    0.20% of the neutrons escaped
```

7.2 SUBPROGRAMS AS ARGUMENTS

In our examples of subprograms thus far, the actual arguments have been constants, variables, or expressions, but Fortran also permits functions and subroutines as arguments for other subprograms. In this case, the function or subroutine must be a *module* subprogram, an *external* subprogram, or an *instrinsic* subprogram. Also, no INTENT attribute is used for a formal argument that is a subprogram.

Module Subprograms as Arguments

To illustrate the use of a module function as an argument, consider a subroutine `Integrate` that approximates the definite integral

$$\int_a^b f(x)\,dx$$

using the trapezoidal method of Section 6.3. We wish to use this subprogram in another program to calculate the integral of the function `Integrand(x)`, defined by `Integrand(x)` = e^{x^2}, for $0 \le x \le 1$. The program in Figure 7.4 imports this function from the module `Integrand_Function` and passes it along with the interval endpoints A and B to the subroutine `Integrate`, which displays the approximate value of the integral

$$\int_A^B e^{x^2}\,dx$$

Figure 7.4. Trapezoidal approximation of an integral—version 2

```
PROGRAM Definite_Integral_2
!-------------------------------------------------------------------
! Program to approximate the integral of a function over the interval
! [A,B] using the trapezoidal method.  This approximation is calculated
! by the subroutine Integrate; the integrand, the interval of
! integration, and the # of subintervals are passed as arguments to
! Integrate.  The function Integrand is imported from the module
! Integrand_Function.   Identifiers used are:
!   A, B       : endpoints of interval of integration
!   Integrate : subroutine to approximate integral of F on [A, B]
!   Integrand : the integrand
!   Number_of_Subintervals : # of subintervals into which [A, B] is cut
!
! Input:  A, B, and Number_of_Subintervals
! Output: Approximation to integral of F on [A, B]
!-------------------------------------------------------------------

  USE Integrand_Function ! module containing Integrand

  IMPLICIT NONE
  REAL :: A, B
  INTEGER :: Number_of_Subintervals

  WRITE (*, '(1X, A)', ADVANCE = "NO") &
        "Enter the interval endpoints and the # of subintervals: "
  READ *, A, B, Number_of_Subintervals

  CALL Integrate(Integrand, A, B, Number_of_Subintervals)

CONTAINS

  ! Integrate ------------------------------------------------------
  ! Subroutine to calculate the trapezoidal approximation of the
  ! integral of the function F over the interval [A,B] using N
  ! subintervals. Local variables used are:
  !     I     : counter
  !     DeltaX : the length of the subintervals
  !     X     : a point of subdivision
  !     Y     : the value of the function at X
  !     Sum   : the approximating sum
  !
  !Accepts: Function F, endpoints A and B, and number N of subintervals
  !Output:  Approximate value of integral of F over [A, B]
  !-------------------------------------------------------------------
```

```
  SUBROUTINE Integrate(F, A, B, N)

    REAL, INTENT(IN) :: A, B
    INTEGER, INTENT(IN) :: N
    REAL :: F, DeltaX, X, Y, Sum
    INTEGER :: I

    ! Calculate subinterval length
    ! and initialize the approximating sum and X

    DeltaX = (B - A) / REAL(N)
    X = A
    Sum = 0.0

    ! Now calculate the approximating sum
    DO I = 1, N - 1
       X = X + DeltaX
       Y = F(X)
       Sum = Sum + Y
    END DO
    Sum = DeltaX * ((F(A) + F(B)) / 2.0 + Sum)
    PRINT 10, Number_of_Subintervals, Sum
    10 FORMAT (1X, "Trapezoidal approximate value using", I4, &
                 " subintervals is", F10.5)

  END SUBROUTINE Integrate

END PROGRAM Definite_Integral_2
```

Sample run:

```
Enter the interval endpoints and the # of subintervals: 0, 1, 100
Trapezoidal approximate value using 100 subintervals is 1.46270
```

Figure 7.4 (cont.)

Here `Integrand_Function` is a module like that shown in Figure 7.5 which contains the function `Integrand`.

Figure 7.5. A module function

```
MODULE Integrand_Function
  !-----------------------------------------------------------------------
  ! Module containing a function Integrand
  !-----------------------------------------------------------------------

  CONTAINS
    FUNCTION Integrand(X)

       REAL :: Integrand
       REAL, INTENT(IN) :: X

       Integrand = EXP(X**2)

    END FUNCTION Integrand

END MODULE Integrand_Function
```

External Subprograms as Arguments

If an external function is to be passed as an argument to some other subprogram, it must be declared to have the EXTERNAL attribute. This can be done by using an EXTERNAL specifier in its type declaration,

```
type, EXTERNAL :: function-name
```

or by using a separate EXTERNAL **statement** of the form

```
EXTERNAL list of external subprogram names
```

Only the second form can be used for subroutines, because they are not declared (since they have no type associated with them).

For example, the program in Figure 7.4 can be easily modified to use an external function, as shown in Figure 7.6. We indicate that Integrand is an external function by including the EXTERNAL specifier in its type declaration in the main program.

Figure 7.6. Trapezoidal approximation of an integral—version 3

```
PROGRAM Definite_Integral_3
!-------------------------------------------------------------------------
! Program to approximate the integral of a function over the interval
! [A,B] using the trapezoidal method.  This approximation is calculated
! by the subroutine Integrate; the integrand, the interval of
! integration, and the # of subintervals are passed as arguments to
! Integrate.  Identifiers used are:
!   A, B       : endpoints of interval of integration
!   Integrate : subroutine to approximate integral of F on [A, B]
!   Integrand : the integrand
!   Number_of_Subintervals : # of subintervals into which [A, B] is cut
!
!   Input:   A, B, and Number_of_Subintervals
!   Output:  Approximation to integral of F on [A, B]
!-------------------------------------------------------------------------
  IMPLICIT NONE
  REAL :: A, B
  REAL, EXTERNAL :: Integrand
  INTEGER :: Number_of_Subintervals

  WRITE (*, '(1X, A)', ADVANCE = "NO") &
       "Enter the interval endpoints and the # of subintervals: "
  READ *, A, B, Number_of_Subintervals

  CALL Integrate(Integrand, A, B, Number_of_Subintervals)

CONTAINS

  !-------------------------------------------------------------------------
  !         Insert subroutine Integrate (see Figure 7.5) here
  !-------------------------------------------------------------------------

END PROGRAM Definite_Integral_3

! Integrand ---------------------------------------------------------------
!                            The integrand
!-------------------------------------------------------------------------
```

```
FUNCTION Integrand(X)

  REAL :: Integrand
  REAL, INTENT(IN) :: X
  Integrand = EXP(X**2)

END FUNCTION Integrand
```

Figure 7.6 (cont.)

Intrinsic Subprograms as Arguments

To approximate the integral of the sine function from 0 to 0.5, we can simply change the definition of `Integrand` to

```
Integrand = SIN(X)
```

and reexecute the program in Figure 7.4 or 7.6. An alternative is to remove the USE statement in Figure 7.4, or delete the function subprogram `Integrand` in Figure 7.6, and pass the intrinsic function `SIN` as an argument to `Integrate`. In this case we must indicate that it is an intrinsic function by using an `INTRINSIC` **statement** of the form

```
INTRINSIC list of intrinsic subprogram names
```

as in the program in Figure 7.7, or by using an `INTRINSIC` specifier in a type declaration:

```
type, INTRINSIC :: function-name
```

Figure 7.7. Trapezoidal approximation of an integral—version 4

```
PROGRAM Definite_Integral_4
!-------------------------------------------------------------------
! Program to approximate the integral of a function over the interval
! [A,B] using the trapezoidal method.  This approximation is calculated
! by the subroutine Integrate; the integrand, the interval of
! integration, and the # of subintervals are passed as arguments to
! Integrate.  Identifiers used are:
!   A, B       : endpoints of interval of integration
!   Integrate : subroutine to approximate integral of F on [A, B]
!   Number_of_Subintervals : # of subintervals into which [A, B] is cut
!
! Input: A, B, and Number_of_Subintervals
! Output: Approximation to integral of F on [A, B]
!-------------------------------------------------------------------

  IMPLICIT NONE
  REAL :: A, B
  INTRINSIC SIN
  INTEGER :: Number_of_Subintervals

  WRITE (*, '(1X, A)', ADVANCE = "NO") &
        "Enter the interval endpoints and the # of subintervals: "
  READ *, A, B, Number_of_Subintervals

  CALL Integrate(SIN, A, B, Number_of_Subintervals)
```

```
CONTAINS

   !-------------------------------------------------------------------
   !           Insert subroutine Integrate (see Figure 7.5) here
   !-------------------------------------------------------------------

END PROGRAM Definite_Integral_4
```

Sample run:

```
Enter the interval endpoints and the # of subintervals: 0, 0.5, 50
Trapezoidal approximate value using 50 subintervals is 0.12242
```

Figure 7.7   (cont.)

In our discussion of Fortran's intrinsic functions, in most cases we have used the *generic* names of these functions. These generic names simplify references to the functions, because the same function may be used with more than one type of argument. Some intrinsic functions may, however, also be referenced by *specific* names, as indicated in Appendix A. These specific names—but not the generic names—of the Fortran intrinsic functions may be used as arguments in a subprogram reference.

Interface Blocks

When an external subprogram is used in a program, the actual arguments must be associated correctly with the corresponding formal arguments, and for a function, the value returned by the function must be used appropriately. As we noted in Section 6.4, in some cases the compiler does not have enough information about the arguments to ensure that the subprogram is being used correctly.

To illustrate the problem, suppose that in the program in Figure 7.6, the function subprogram Integrand was changed to

```
! Integrand --------------------------------------------------------
!                              The integrand
!-------------------------------------------------------------------

FUNCTION Integrand(X, Y)

   REAL :: Integrand
   REAL, INTENT(IN) :: X, Y

   Integrand = X ** 2 + 3 * X * Y + Y ** 2

END FUNCTION Integrand
```

Most compilers would not detect any errors even though this function with two arguments is passed to the formal argument F of the subroutine Integrate, which assumes that F is a function with only one argument.

The problem is that the only information specified for the function Integrand is that it is a real-valued function; the number of arguments and their types are not specified. Consequently, the compiler cannot detect the incorrect usage of Integrand. The information needed by the compiler can be given using an interface block, as illustrated in Figure 7.8.

Note that the EXTERNAL attribute is not specified for the function Integrand. In general, interface blocks and EXTERNAL specifiers cannot both be used to declare subprograms, nor can interface blocks be used for module subprograms or intrinsic subprograms.

Figure 7.8. Trapezoidal approximation of an integral—version 5

```fortran
PROGRAM Definite_Integral_5
!-------------------------------------------------------------------------
! Program to approximate the integral of a function over the interval
! [A,B] using the trapezoidal method.  This approximation is calculated
! by the subroutine Integrate; the integrand, the interval of
! integration, and the # of subintervals are passed as arguments to
! Integrate.  Identifiers used are:
!   A, B        : endpoints of interval of integration
!   Integrate : subroutine to approximate integral of F on [A, B]
!   Integrand : the integrand
!   Number_of_Subintervals : # of subintervals into which [A, B] is cut
!
! Input:  A, B, and Number_of_Subintervals
! Output: Approximation to integral of F on [A, B]
!-------------------------------------------------------------------------

  IMPLICIT NONE
  REAL :: A, B

  INTERFACE
    FUNCTION Integrand(X)
      REAL :: Integrand
      REAL, INTENT(IN) :: X
    END FUNCTION Integrand
  END INTERFACE

  INTEGER :: Number_of_Subintervals

  WRITE (*, '(1X, A)', ADVANCE = "NO") &
        "Enter the interval endpoints and the # of subintervals: "
  READ *, A, B, Number_of_Subintervals

  CALL Integrate(Integrand, A, B, Number_of_Subintervals)

CONTAINS

    !-------------------------------------------------------------------
    !         Insert subroutine Integrate (see Figure 7.5) here
    !-------------------------------------------------------------------

END PROGRAM Definite_Integral_5

! Integrand -----------------------------------------------------------
!                         The integrand
!---------------------------------------------------------------------

FUNCTION Integrand(X)

  REAL :: Integrand
  REAL, INTENT(IN) :: X

  Integrand = EXP(X**2)

END FUNCTION Integrand
```

PROFESSIONAL SUCCESS: HINTS FOR DEBUGGING COMPILE-TIME ERRORS

Programs do not generally compile successfully on the first attempt. Only perfectly executed code can be translated by the compiler from Fortran 90 to object (machine) code; any command that can not be translated will be flagged as a compile-time error. First attempts at compiling can in fact be pretty discouraging, as the error reports generated by the compiler may be longer than the program itself! The cause of this is that compilers generally sweep through programs sequentially, and report each error detected by line number. Once the compiler has detected an initial error, it may misinterpret some of the program state-

ments that follow, and list them as errors even if they are, in fact, correct. The debugging process should therefore concentrate on finding and correcting only the first error listed, which will be located either at or above the line number reported by the compiler. Once that error has been located and fixed, the program should be recompiled. While there still may be errors, the new report generated will likely contain many fewer than the that used during the previous debugging cycle. This process of alternately compiling and debugging the source code should be repeated until an error-free report is produced.

°All "Profesional Success" boxed material contributed by Jack Leifer, University of South Carolina—Aiken.

PRACTICE!

1. (True or false) An internal subprogram may not be passed as an argument to another subprogram.

2. (True or false) An intrinsic subprogram may not be passed as an argument to another subprogram.

3. An external subprogram passed as an argument to another subprogram must have the _____ attribute.

4. What three items comprise a complete declaration of a function?

5. Write an interface block for the following function:

```
FUNCTION F(X, Y, N)

   REAL :: F
   REAL, INTENT(IN) :: X, Y
   INTEGER, INTENT(IN) :: N

   F = X**N + Y**N

END FUNCTION F
```

APPLICATION: ARTIFICIAL INTELLIGENCE

Artificial intelligence (AI) is concerned with designing computer systems that exhibit characteristics associated with human intelligence; for example, learning, deductive reasoning, problem solving, language understanding, and recognizing visual images. Areas currently studied in AI include

- Expert systems: Designing systems that use a knowledge base of information obtained from a human expert in some area and logical

rules to answer questions, analyze problems, and provide advice, much as a human expert would. Successful expert systems include MYCIN for medical consultations, DENDRAL for chemical inference, PROSPECTOR for dealing with geological data, and XCON for configuring computer systems.

- Pattern recognition: Recognizing speech, handwriting, patterns of amino acids in DNA strands, and so on.

- Computer vision: Designing machines that can accept input in visual form and can recognize and classify the images they receive.

- Robotics: Attempting to build machines that have sensing capabilities (vision, force, touch), can manipulate objects (grasp them, pick them up, put them down), and solve various object- and space-oriented problems (moving without bumping into things, fitting parts together).

- Search techniques: Searching large data sets in problems such as airline scheduling and routing, in which the number of possible search paths is so large that it is not feasible to examine them all.

- Game playing: Devising programs that solve puzzles and play board games such as tic-tac-toe, chess, and checkers.

Recursion is an important technique in many of these areas of AI. In fact, it is the basic control structure in the programming language LISP, which is one of the major programming languages in AI. We will consider one problem from the area of game playing that can easily be solved using recursion, but for which a nonrecursive solution is quite difficult.

PROBLEM

The *Towers of Hanoi* problem is to solve the puzzle shown in the following figure, in which one must move the disks from the left peg to the right peg according to the following rules:[1]

1. When a disk is moved, it must be placed on one of the three pegs.

2. Only one disk may be moved at a time, and it must be the top disk on one of the pegs.

3. A larger disk may never be placed on top of a smaller one.

Solution

The Towers of Hanoi puzzle is easy to solve for a small number of disks, but it becomes more difficult as the number of disks grows to seven, eight, and beyond. The puzzle can be solved easily, however, for any number of disks using recursion:

If there is one disk,

    Anchor step:
    Move it from Peg A to Peg C, solving the puzzle.

Else do the following:

Inductive step:

1. Move the topmost $N - 1$ disks from Peg A to Peg B, using C as an auxiliary peg.

2. Move the large disk remaining on Peg A to Peg C.

3. Move the $N - 1$ disks from Peg B to Peg C, using Peg A as an auxiliary peg.

This scheme is implemented by the recursive subroutine Move in the program of Figure 7.9, which solves the Towers of Hanoi puzzle:

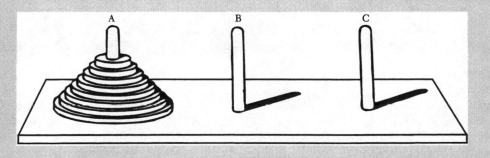

[1] Legend has it that the priests in the Temple of Bramah were given a puzzle consisting of a golden platform with three golden needles on which were placed 64 golden disks. Time was to end when they had successfully finished moving the disks to another needle, following the given rules. (Query: If the priests moved one disk per second and began their work in year 0, when would time end?)

Figure 7.9.   Towers of Hanoi

```fortran
PROGRAM Towers_of_Hanoi
!------------------------------------------------------------------------
! Program to solve the Towers of Hanoi puzzle recursively, using
! subroutine Move. Identifiers used are:
!   Peg_1, Peg_2, Peg_3 : labels for the pegs
!   Number_of_Disks      : number of disks
!   Move                 : subroutine to move the disks
!
!  Input:   Number_of_Disks
!  Output:  User prompts and a sequence of moves that solves
!           the puzzle
!------------------------------------------------------------------------

  CHARACTER(*), PARAMETER :: Peg1 = "A", Peg2 = "B", Peg3 = "C"
  INTEGER :: Number_of_Disks

  WRITE (*, '(1X, A)', ADVANCE = "NO") "Enter number of disks: "
  READ *, Number_of_Disks
  PRINT *
  CALL Move(Number_of_Disks, Peg1, Peg2, Peg3)

CONTAINS

  !--Move-------------------------------------------------------------
  ! Recursive subroutine to move N disks from StartPeg to EndPeg using
  ! AuxPeg as an auxiliary peg.  Variables used are:
  !   N        : number of disks
  !   StartPeg : peg containing the disks
  !   EndPeg   : peg to which disks are to be moved
  !   AuxPeg   : extra peg used to store disks being moved
  !
  ! Accepts: N, StartPeg, AuxPeg, EndPeg
  ! Output : A sequence of moves that solves the puzzle
  !-------------------------------------------------------------------

  RECURSIVE SUBROUTINE Move(N, StartPeg, AuxPeg, EndPeg)

    INTEGER, INTENT(IN) :: N
    CHARACTER(*), INTENT(IN) :: StartPeg, AuxPeg, EndPeg

    IF (N == 1) THEN ! Anchor
       PRINT *, "Move disk from ", StartPeg, " to ", EndPeg

    ELSE                  ! Inductive step
       ! Move n - 1 disks from StartPeg to AuxPeg
       ! using EndPeg as an auxiliary peg
       CALL Move(N - 1, StartPeg, EndPeg, AuxPeg)

       ! Move disk from StartPeg to EndPeg}
       CALL Move(1, StartPeg, " ", EndPeg)
```

```
          ! Move n - 1 pegs from AuxPeg to EndPeg
          ! using StartPeg as an auxiliary peg
        CALL Move(N - 1, AuxPeg, StartPeg, EndPeg)
    END IF

  END SUBROUTINE Move

END PROGRAM Towers_of_Hanoi
```

Sample run:

```
    Enter number of disks: 4

    Move disk from A to B
    Move disk from A to C
    Move disk from B to C
    Move disk from A to B
    Move disk from C to A
    Move disk from C to B
```

```
    Move disk from A to B
    Move disk from A to C
    Move disk from B to C
    Move disk from B to A
    Move disk from C to A
    Move disk from B to C
    Move disk from A to B
    Move disk from A to C
    Move disk from B to C
```

Figure 7.9   (cont.)

PRACTICE!

Exercises 1–4 assume the following recursive subroutine S:

```
    RECURSIVE SUBROUTINE S(Num)

      INTEGER, INTENT(IN) :: Num
      IF (1 <= Num .AND. Num <= 8) THEN
        CALL S(Num - 1)
        WRITE (*, '(I1)', ADVANCE = "NO") Num
      ELSE
        PRINT *
      END IF

    END SUBROUTINE S
```

1. What output is produced by each of the following subroutine calls?
   (a) CALL S(3)   (b) CALL S(7)   (c) CALL S(10)

2. If Num - 1 is replaced by Num + 1 in the procedure, what output will be produced by the subroutine calls in Exercise 1?

3. If the WRITE statement and the recursive call to S are interchanged, what output will be produced by the calls in Exercise 1?

4. If a copy of the WRITE statement is inserted before the recursive call to S, what output will be produced by the calls in Exercise 1?

5. Trace the execution of Move(4, "A", "B", "C") far enough to produce the first five moves. Does your answer agree with the program output in Figure 7.9? Do the same for Move(5, "A", "B", "C").

KEY TERMS

CALL statement	Randomness	Return Statement
EXTERNAL statement	Random number generator	Simulation
INTENT attribute	RANDOM_Number Subprogram	SUBROUTINE statement
INTRINSIC statement	Recursion	Subroutine subprogram

PROGRAMMING POINTERS

Program Style and Design

1. *Subprograms should be documented in the same manner as the main program.* The documentation should include a brief description of the processing carried out by the subprograms, the values passed to them, the values returned by them, and what the arguments and local variables represent.

2. *Subprograms are separate program units, and the subprogram format should reflect this fact.* In this text, we
   - Insert a blank comment line before and after each subprogram to set it off from other program units.
   - Follow the stylistic standards described in earlier chapters when writing subprograms.

3. *In the formal argument list of a subroutine, it is usually considered good practice to list arguments whose values are passed to the subroutine (IN arguments) before arguments whose values are returned by the subroutine (OUT and INOUT arguments).*

Potential Problems

1. *When a subprogram is referenced, the number of actual arguments must be the same as the number of formal arguments, and the type of each actual argument must agree with the type of the corresponding formal argument* (unless some arguments have been declared to be optional[2]).

2. *Information is shared among different program units only via the arguments and the function name for function subprograms.* Thus, if the value of a variable in one program unit is needed by another program unit, it must be passed as an argument, as this variable is not otherwise accessible to the other program unit. One consequence is that *local variables*—those not used as arguments—as well as statement labels in one program unit may be used in another program unit without conflict.

3. *When control returns from a subprogram, local variables in that subprogram do not retain their values unless they are initialized in their declarations or are declared to have the SAVE attribute.*

4. *Failure to declare the INTENT of formal arguments can lead to subtle errors.* For example, if a subroutine is defined by

```
SUBROUTINE Subber(NumItems, Sum)

   INTEGER :: NumItems, Sum, I

   Sum = 0
   DO I = 1, NumItems
      Sum = Sum + I
   END DO
   NumItems = 0

END SUBROUTINE Subber
```

then when the subroutine is called by a statement such as

```
CALL Subber(Count, Total)
```

---

[2] For a description of keyword and optional arguments, see Chapter 7 of our text *Fortran 90 for Engineers and Scientists*.

where `Count` and `Total` are integer variables, the value of `Total` will change to the value of `Sum`. However, the value of `Count` will also be changed (to 0) since it is associated with the formal argument `NumItems`, whose value is changed in the subprogram—this was probably not intended. For some compilers, the value of a constant might be changed in this manner!

5. *Local variables that are initialized in a subprogram retain their values from one subprogram reference to the next.*

6. *Programmer-defined subprograms used as actual arguments in a subprogram reference must be module subprograms or external subprograms that are declared to have the EXTERNAL attribute in the program unit that contains that reference.*

7. *Specific names, but not generic names, of intrinsic functions may be used as actual arguments in a subprogram reference, provided that they are declared to have the INTRINSIC attribute in the program unit that contains that reference.*

Programming Problems

SECTION 7.1

1. Write a program that reads the number of a month and calls the subprogram of Exercise 11 of Section 7.1 to display the name of the month.

2. Write a program that reads several pairs of integers and for each pair calls the subprogram `Switch` in Exercise 12 of Section 7.1 to interchange their values, and then displays their values.

3. Write a program that reads several measurements in centimeters and for each measurement calls the subprogram of Exercise 13 of Section 7.1 to find the corresponding measurement in yards, feet, and inches, and then displays this converted measurement.

4. Write a program that reads several weights in grams and for each measurement calls the subprogram of Exercise 14 of Section 7.1 to find the corresponding weight in pounds and ounces, and then displays this converted weight.

5. Write a program that reads several times in military format and for each time calls the subprogram of Exercise 15 of Section 7.1 to find the corresponding hours-minutes-A.M./P.M. representation, and then displays this representation.

6. Write a program that reads several times in hours-minutes-A.M./P.M. format and for each time calls the subprogram of Exercise 16 of Section 7.1 to find the corresponding military representation and then displays this representation.

7. Write a subroutine `Print_Stick_Number` to produce "stick numbers" like those on a calculator display for the digits 0, 1, 2, and 3, respectively:

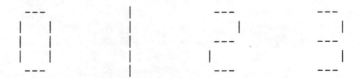

Write a program to test your subroutines.

8. Extend the subroutine from Problem 7 to display any digit. Write a program to read an integer and call the subroutine to display each digit of the integer.

9. Write a program that reads the diameters and heights of several right circular cylinders and displays the circumference, total surface area (including the ends), and the volume of each. The circumference, surface area, and volume should be calculated and returned by a subroutine.

10. Write a program that reads a positive integer and then calls a subprogram that displays its prime factorization, that is, a subprogram that expresses a positive integer as a product of primes or indicates that it is a prime (see Exercise 22 of Section 6.2 for the definition of a prime number).

APPLICATION

11. Modify the shield program in Figure 7.3 to allow the particle to travel in any direction rather than simply left, right, forward, or backward. Choose a direction (angle) at random, and let the particle travel a fixed (or perhaps random) distance in that direction.

12. The famous *Buffon Needle problem* is as follows: a board is ruled with equidistant parallel lines, and a needle whose length is equal to the distance between these lines is dropped at random on the board. What is the probability that it crosses one of these lines? The answer to this problem is $2/\pi$. Write a program to simulate this experiment and obtain an estimate for π.

13. Consider a quarter circle inscribed in a square whose sides have length 1:

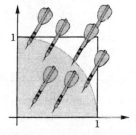

Imagine throwing q darts at this square and counting the total number p that hit within the quarter circle. For a large number of throws, we would expect

$$\frac{p}{q} \approx \frac{\text{area of the circle}}{\text{area of square}} = \frac{\pi}{4}$$

Write a program to approximate π using this method. To simulate throwing the darts, generate two random numbers X and Y and consider point (X,Y) as being where the dart hits.

APPLICATION

14. Write and test a recursive subroutine `PrintReverse` that accepts an integer and displays it in reverse order.

15. Write and test a recursive subroutine that displays a nonnegative integer with commas in the correct locations. For example, it should display 20131 as 20,131.

16. Write a recursive subroutine to find the prime factorization of a positive integer (see Problem 10).

8

Arrays

8.1 EXAMPLE: PROCESSING A LIST OF FAILURE TIMES

Consider again the mean-time-to-failure problem from Section 4.5. In this problem, a number of components in a circuit were tested and the time at which each component failed was recorded. As a measure of the reliability of a component, the mean of these failure times was calculated. This computation required processing the list of failure times only once. Suppose now that we wish to analyze these failure times using a program to

1. Find the mean time to failure.
2. Print a list of failure times greater than the mean.
3. Sort the failure times so that they are in ascending order.

Clearly, this will require processing the list several times.

To solve this problem efficiently, we need a **data structure** to store and organize the entire collection of failure times. This should be a structure that allows a data value to be stored or retrieved directly by specifying its location in the structure, so that it takes no longer to access the value in location 50 than to access that in location 5. And we prefer that the structure be stored in main memory so that storage and retrieval are fast. One such data structure is a **one-dimensional array**, in which a fixed number of data values, all of the same type, are organized in a sequence and direct access to each value is possible by specifying its position in this sequence.

If an array is to be used in a Fortran program to solve the mean-time-to-failure problem, a sequence of 50

OBJECTIVES

In this chapter, you will

- Learn about one-dimensional and higher-dimensional arrays.
- Examine the similarities and differences between compile-time and run-time arrays.
- Examine the statements used to process arrays.
- Read about various methods of sorting and searching arrays.
- Study how to use arrays of more than one dimension.

memory locations must be reserved for the failure times. For example, the specification statement

```
REAL, DIMENSION(50) :: FailureTime
```

instructs the compiler to establish an array named `FailureTime` consisting of 50 memory locations in which values of type `REAL` can be stored. In the program we can then refer to this entire array of real numbers by using the **array variable** `Failure-Time`, but we can also access each individual **element** of the array by using a **subscripted variable** formed by appending a **subscript** (or **index**) enclosed in parentheses to the array variable. This subscript specifies the position of an array element. Thus, `FailureTime(1)` refers to the first element of the array `FailureTime`, `FailureTime(2)` to the second element, and so on. The preceding specification statement thus not only reserves a block of memory locations in which to store the elements of the array `FailureTime`, but it also associates the subscripted variables `FailureTime(1)`, `FailureTime(2)`, `FailureTime(3)`,..., `Failure-Time(50)` with these locations.

Each of these subscripted variables names an individual memory location and hence can be used in much the same way as a simple variable. For example, the assignment statement

```
FailureTime(4) = 177.8
```

stores the value 177.8 in the fourth location of the array `FailureTime`, and the output statement

```
PRINT *, FailureTime(10)
```

displays the value stored in the tenth location of the array `FailureTime`.

An important feature of the notation used for arrays is that the subscript attached to the array name may be an integer variable or expression. For example, the statement

```
READ (10, *) FailureTime(N)
```

reads a value and stores it in the Nth location of the array `FailureTime`.

Using an array reference in which the subscript is a variable or an expression within a loop that changes the value of the subscript on each pass through the loop is a convenient way to process each item in the array. Thus, the DO loop

```
DO I = 1, 50
   READ (10, *) FailureTime(I)
END DO
```

is equivalent to the following sequence of 50 READ statements,

```
READ (10, *) FailureTime(1)
READ (10, *) FailureTime(2)
READ (10, *) FailureTime(3)
              ⋮
READ (10, *) FailureTime(50)
```

and thus reads 50 values and stores them in the array `FailureTime`. Since each execution of a READ statement requires a new line of input data, the 50 failure times must be on 50 separate lines, one value per line.

An alternative method of reading or displaying an array is to use an input or output statement containing the array name. The effect is the same as listing all of the array elements in the input/output statement. For example, the input statement

```
READ (10, *) FailureTime
```

is equivalent to

```
READ (10, *) FailureTime(1), FailureTime(2), . . .,
FailureTime(50)
```

Because the READ statement is executed only once, the values for FailureTime need not be read from separate lines.

The program in Figure 8.1 uses this method to read failure times from a file and store them in the array FailureTime. The mean of these failure times is then calculated using

```
Sum = 0.0
DO I = 1, NumTimes
    Sum = Sum + FailureTime(I)
END DO
Mean_Time_to_Failure = Sum / REAL(NumTimes)
```

where NumTimes is a named constant declared by

```
INTEGER, PARAMETER :: NumTimes = 50
```

Another DO loop containing array references with a variable subscript is then used to display a list of failure times greater than this mean:

```
DO I = 1, NumTimes
    IF (FailureTime(I) > Mean_Time_to_Failure) &
        PRINT '(1X, F9.1)', FailureTime(I)
END DO
```

Figure 8.1. Processing_Failing_Times_1

```
PROGRAM Processing_Failure_Times_1
!----------------------------------------------------------------------
! Program to read a list of failure times, calculate the mean time to
! failure, and then print a list of failure times that are greater
! than the mean.  Identifiers used are:
!    OpenStatus          : status variable for OPEN
!    InputStatus         : status variable for READ
!    FailureTime         : one-dimensional array of failure times
!    NumTimes            : size of the array (constant)
!    I                   : subscript
!    Sum                 : sum of failure times
!    Mean_Time_to_Failure : mean of the failure times
!
! Input (file):   A list of NumTimes failure times
! Output:         Information to user about the data file,
!                 Mean_Time_to_Failure, and a list of failure times
!                 greater than Mean_Time_to_Failure
!----------------------------------------------------------------------

  IMPLICIT NONE
  INTEGER, PARAMETER :: NumTimes = 50
  REAL, DIMENSION(NumTimes) :: FailureTime
  INTEGER :: OpenStatus, InputStatus, I
  REAL :: Sum, Mean_Time_to_Failure

  PRINT *, "Program reads", NumTimes, "failure times from fil8-1.dat."
  OPEN (UNIT = 10, FILE = "fil8-1.dat", STATUS = "OLD", IOSTAT = OpenStatus)
  IF (OpenStatus > 0) STOP "*** Cannot open the file ***"
```

```
! Read the failure times and store them in array FailureTime

READ (10, *, IOSTAT = InputStatus) FailureTime
IF (InputStatus > 0) STOP "*** Input error ***"
IF (InputStatus < 0) STOP "*** Not enough data ***"

! Calculate the mean time to failure

Sum = 0.0
DO I = 1, NumTimes
   Sum = Sum + FailureTime(I)
END DO
Mean_Time_to_Failure = Sum / REAL(NumTimes)
PRINT '(/ 1X, "Mean time to failure =", F6.1)', Mean_Time_to_Failure

! Print list of failure times greater than the mean

PRINT *
PRINT *, "List of failure times greater than the mean:"
DO I = 1, NumTimes
   IF (FailureTime(I) > Mean_Time_to_Failure) &
      PRINT '(1X, F9.1)', FailureTime(I)
END DO

END PROGRAM Processing_Failure_Times_1
```

Listing of fi18-1.dat *Used in Sample Run*

```
99.5, 133.8, 84.2, 217.5, 188.8, 103.1, 93.9, 165.0, 68.3, 111.4
88.8, 88.2, 90.1, 70.2, 150.5, 122.9, 138.8, 99.9, 111.6, 155.7
133.4, 122.2, 93.4, 101.5, 109.9, 103.3, 177.7, 188.1, 99.8, 144.4
87.5, 79.3, 190.2, 190.3, 170.1, 160.9, 121.1, 95.6, 140.5, 177.2
150.1, 140.3, 139.2, 113.8, 155.9, 144.4, 88.3, 83.5, 101.1, 112.8
```

Sample Run

```
Program reads 50 failure times from fi18-1.dat

Mean time to failure = 126.0

List of failure times greater than the mean:

133.8
217.5
188.8
165.0
150.5
138.8
155.7
133.4
177.7
188.1
144.4
190.2
190.3
```

Figure 8.1 (cont.)

```
170.1
160.9
140.5
177.2
150.1
140.3
139.2
155.9
144.4
```

Figure 8.1 (cont.)

Putting an **implied** DO **loop** in an input or output statement provides a third method of array input/output. Implied DO loops have the form

```
(list-of-variables, control-var = init-value, limit, step)
```

where the control variable control-var, initial value init-value, limit, and step size are the same as for a DO loop. The effect of an implied DO loop is exactly that of a DO loop—as if the left parenthesis were a DO, with indexing information immediately before the matching right parenthesis and the list-of-variables constituting the body of the DO loop. For example, the statement

```
READ (10, *) (FailureTime(I), I = 1, NumTimes)
```

which is equivalent to

```
READ (10, *) Failure(1), Failure(2), . . ., Failure(NumTimes)
```

could be used in the program in Figure 8.1 to read the failure times and store them in the array FailureTime. Since the READ statement is encountered only once, the input values need not be read from separate lines but may be on any number of lines. Implied DO loops can also be used to display the elements of an array. For example, the statement

```
PRINT *, (FailureTime(I), I = 1, NumTimes)
```

would have the same effect as

```
PRINT *, FailureTime(1), . . ., FailureTime(NumTimes)
```

PROFESSIONAL SUCCESS: ERROR HANDLING AND ROBUSTNESS

Robust software has the ability to recognize and handle certain data-induced errors without crashing or behaving unpredictably. These errors can occur for a variety of reasons. For instance, files which are smaller than expected could cause a program to try to read past the last piece of data, resulting in an error. Data which are not within the ranges expected by a program could cause an overflow, underflow, or division by zero error. Robustness is especially crucial in interactive software, where data are generated and input to the computer by individual users. Interactive applications such as voice-

mail and automated teller machine (ATM) programs are especially prone to input errors; unpredictable behavior by these systems could lead to serious consequences.

Robustness is built into software through the use of error handling modules. A number of fundamental approaches to implementing robustness are available. Passive error recovery allows a program to function normally until an error is detected. Instead of crashing, the program will generate an error message, and continue to run by either ignoring or trying to fix the faulty data. As the initial error may propagate, the program output must be checked for accuracy, to ensure that it has not been affected. Active error prevention is more robust, since it employs routines which prescreen all incoming data and files for problems. This approach is especially useful for interactive applications, as users can be immediately prompted to re-enter faulty data. Output will not be affected, since errors are avoided before they occur.

*All "Professional Success" boxed material contributed by Jack Leifer, University of South Carolina—Aiken.

8.2 COMPILE-TIME ARRAYS AND RUN-TIME ARRAYS

As we noted in the preceding section, memory for the array `FailureTime` was allocated at compile time. This means that the size of such *compile-time arrays* is fixed before execution begins. If the data set stored in the array is very small, a considerable waste of memory may result; if the data set is too large, it cannot be stored in the array and processed correctly. To deal with this problem, Fortran 90 provides *run-time* (or *allocatable*) *arrays* for which memory is allocated during execution, making it possible to allocate an array of appropriate size. In this section we will show how such arrays are declared and processed.

Compile-Time Arrays

The subscripts in our examples of arrays have been positive valued, ranging from 1 through some upper limit. Although this is the most common subscript range, Fortran does allow a subscript to be any integer value, positive, negative, or zero, provided that it does not fall outside the range specified in the array declaration. The general form of a declaration of a compile-time array is

```
type, DIMENSION(l:u) :: list-of-array-names
```

or

```
type :: list-of-array-specifiers
```

where an array specifier has the form

```
array-name(l:u)
```

and the pair `l:u` is a pair of integer constants. These statements declare that each of the identifiers in the `list` is an array for which memory is allocated at compile time and for which the range of values of the subscript will be from the lower limit `l` through the upper limit `u`. If the minimum value of the subscript for an array is 1, then only the maximum subscript need be specified.

For example, the array declarations

```
INTEGER, PARAMETER :: LowerLimit_1 = -1, UpperLimit_1 = 3, &
                      LowerLimit_2 = 0, UpperLimit_2 = 5

INTEGER, DIMENSION(LowerLimit_1 : UpperLimit_1) :: Gamma
REAL, DIMENSION(LowerLimit_2 : UpperLimit_2) :: Delta
```

establish two one-dimensional arrays. The integer array `Gamma` may have subscript values ranging from −1 through 3; thus, the following subscripted variables may be used: `Gamma(-1)`, `Gamma(0)`, `Gamma(1)`, `Gamma(2)`, `Gamma(3)`. The real array `Delta` has subscript values ranging from 0 through 5 so that any of the subscripted variables `Delta(0)`, `Delta(1)`,..., `Delta(5)` may be used.

Allocatable Arrays

A declaration of a compile-time array of the form

```
INTEGER, PARAMETER :: NumElements = 10
REAL, DIMENSION(NumElements) :: Array
```

causes the compiler to allocate a block of memory large enough to hold 10 real values. The size of this block cannot be altered, except by changing the value of the named constant NumElements and then recompiling the program. As we noted earlier, such fixed-size arrays suffer from two problems:

- If the size of the array exceeds the number of values to be stored in it, then memory is wasted by the unused elements.
- If the size of the array is smaller than the number of values to be stored in it, there is the problem of array overflow.

Both of these problems can be solved using **allocatable** or **run-time arrays**, for which memory is allocated during execution instead of during compilation. The declaration of an allocatable array must specify that it has the ALLOCATABLE **attribute**:

```
type, DIMENSION(:), ALLOCATABLE :: list-of-array-names
```

For example,

```
REAL, DIMENSION(:), ALLOCATABLE :: A, B
```

declares A and B to be one-dimensional allocatable arrays.

The actual bounds of an allocatable array are specified in an ALLOCATE statement:

```
ALLOCATE (list, STAT = status-variable)
```

where list is a list of array specifications of the form

```
array-name(l:u)
```

If the STAT = clause is present, the integer variable status-variable will be set to zero if allocation is successful but will be assigned some system-dependent error value if there is insufficient memory or if the array has already been allocated.

This statement allocates space for each array listed. The range of subscripts will be from the specified lower limit l through the upper limit u. If the minimum value of the subscript for an array is 1, then only the maximum subscript need be specified. For example, consider the statements

```
WRITE (*, '(1X, A)', ADVANCE = "NO") &
      "Enter size of arrays A and B:"
READ *, N
ALLOCATE(A(N), B(0:N+1), STAT = AllocateStatus)
IF (AllocateStatus /= 0) STOP "*** Not enough memory ***"
```

where N and AllocateStatus are integer variables. If memory is available, enough will be allocated for arrays A and B so that A can store N real values in A(1), A(2),..., A(N) and B can store N + 2 real values in B(0), B(1),..., B(N+1). Once this memory has been allocated, these arrays may be used in the same way as other (compile-time) arrays.

Memory that is no longer needed can be released so that it can be reallocated. This is accomplished by using a DEALLOCATE **statement**:

```
DEALLOCATE (list-of-arrays, STAT = status-variable)
```

If the STAT = clause is present, the integer variable status-variable will be set to zero if deallocation is successful but will be assigned some system-dependent error value if it is not successful, for example, if no memory was previously allocated to an array.

Example: Processing a List of Failure Times—Revisited

In the preceding section, we considered the problem of processing a list of failure times of components in a circuit, calculating their mean, and displaying a list of failure times greater than the mean. We assumed that there were 50 failure times, and we used a compile-time array of size 50 to store them.

Suppose, however, that the program in Figure 8.1 to do this processing is to be used with data sets of various sizes. If we use a compile-time array like FailureTime, we must change the definition of the named constant NumTimes for each data set.

A more attractive solution is to make FailureTime an allocatable array. The number of failure times can then be read during execution of the program, and an array of exactly the right size can be allocated at that time. The program in Figure 8.2 shows how the program in Figure 8.1 can be modified to use an allocatable array.

Figure 8.2. Processing a list of failure times

```
PROGRAM Processing_Failure_Times_2
!----------------------------------------------------------------------------
! Program to read a list of failure times, calculate the mean time to
! failure, and then print a list of failure times that are greater
! than the mean. An allocatable array is used to store the failure
! times.   Identifiers used are:
!     FileName        : name of data file
!     OpenStatus      : status variable for OPEN
!     InputStatus     : status variable for READ
!     AllocateStatus  : status variable for ALLOCATE
!     FailureTime     : one-dimensional array of failure times
!     NumTimes        : size of the array
!     I               : subscript
!     Sum             : sum of failure times
!     Mean_Time_to_Failure : mean of the failure times
!
! Input (keyboard): FileName
! Input (file):     NumTimes and a list of NumTimes failure times
! Output:           Mean_Time_to_Failure and a list of failure times greater
!                   than Mean_Time_to_Failure
! Note: First value in data file must be the number of failure times.
!----------------------------------------------------------------------------

IMPLICIT NONE
  CHARACTER(20) :: FileName
  REAL, DIMENSION(:), ALLOCATABLE :: FailureTime
  INTEGER :: OpenStatus, InputStatus, AllocateStatus, NumTimes, I
  REAL :: Sum, Mean_Time_to_Failure

  ! Get the name of the data file and open it for input

  WRITE (*, '(1X, A)', ADVANCE = "NO") "Enter name of data file: "
  READ *, FileName
  OPEN (UNIT = 10, FILE = FileName, STATUS = "OLD", IOSTAT = OpenStatus)
  IF (OpenStatus > 0) STOP "*** Cannot open the file ***"
```

```
! Get the number of failure times and allocate an array
! with that many elements to store the failure times

READ (10, *, IOSTAT = InputStatus) NumTimes
IF (InputStatus > 0) STOP "*** Input error ***"
IF (InputStatus < 0) STOP "*** Not enough data ***"
ALLOCATE(FailureTime(NumTimes), STAT = AllocateStatus)
IF (AllocateStatus /= 0) STOP "*** Not enough memory ***"

! Read the failure times and store them in array FailureTime

READ (10, *, IOSTAT = InputStatus) FailureTime
IF (InputStatus > 0) STOP "*** Input error ***"
IF (InputStatus < 0) STOP "*** Not enough data ***"

! Calculate the mean time to failure

Sum = 0.0
DO I = 1, NumTimes
   Sum = Sum + FailureTime(I)
END DO
Mean_Time_to_Failure = Sum / REAL(NumTimes)
PRINT '(/ 1X, "For the", I4, " failure times read, " / 1X, &
      &"the mean time to failure =", F6.1)', NumTimes, Mean_Time_to_Failure

! Print list of failure times greater than the mean

PRINT *
PRINT *, "List of failure times greater than the mean:"
DO I = 1, NumTimes
   IF (FailureTime(I) > Mean_Time_to_Failure) &
      PRINT '(1X, F9.1)', FailureTime(I)
END DO

! Deallocate the array of failure times
DEALLOCATE(FailureTime)

END PROGRAM Processing_Failure_Times_2
```

Figure 8.2 (cont.)

PRACTICE!

1. Each individual element of an array is accessed by using a(n) _____ variable.
2. In the array reference X(I), I is called a(n) _____.
3. (True or false) INTEGER, DIMENSION :: CODE(10) is a legal array declaration.
4. (True or false) The array declaration REAL, DIMENSION(5) :: X is equivalent to the array declaration REAL, DIMENSION(1:5) :: X.
5. (True or false) Given the declaration REAL, DIMENSION(10) :: X, the statement READ *, X is equivalent to the statement

    READ *, (X(I), I = 1, 10).

6. (True or false) Given the declaration REAL, DIMENSION(10)   ::   X, the statement PRINT *, X is equivalent to the DO loop

```
DO I = 1, 10
    PRINT *, X(I)
END DO
```

7. (True or false) For the statement READ *, X, the values to be stored in X must be entered one per line.

For Exercises 8–11, write declarations for the given arrays.

8. An array whose subscript values are integers from 0 through 10 and in which each element is a real value

9. An array whose subscript values are integers from –5 through 5 and in which each element is an integer

10. An array whose subscript values are integers from 1 through 20 and in which each element is a character string of length 10

11. An array whose subscript values are integers from 1 through 100 and in which each element is either .TRUE. or .FALSE.

For Exercises 12–14, write declarations and statements to construct the given array.

12. An array whose subscript values are integers from –5 through 5 and in which the elements are the subscripts in reverse order

13. An array whose subscript values are the integers from 1 through 20 and in which an array element is true if the corresponding subscript is even and is false otherwise

14. An array whose subscript values are the integers from 0 through 359 and whose elements are the values of the sine function at the angles $0°$, $1°$, . . . , $359°$

For Exercises 15–17, assume that the following declarations have been made:

```
INTEGER, DIMENSION(10) :: Number
INTEGER :: I
```

Tell what value (if any) is assigned to each array element, or explain why an error occurs:

15.
```
DO I = 1, 10
    Number(I) = I / 2
END DO
```

16.
```
DO I = 1, 6
    Number(I) = I * I
END DO
DO I = 7, 10
    Number(I) = Number(I - 5)
END DO
```

```
17. I = 1
    DO
        IF (I == 10) EXIT
        IF (MOD(I,3) == 0) THEN
            Number(I) = 0
        ELSE
            Number(I) = I
        END IF
        I = I + 1
    END DO
```

For Exercises 18–23, assume that the following declarations have been made:

```
    INTEGER, DIMENSION(10) :: Number
    REAL, DIMENSION(-4:5) :: Point
    CHARACTER(1), DIMENSION(10) :: Symbol
    INTEGER :: I
```

Assume also that the following format statements are given,

```
    100 FORMAT(10(1X, I1))
    110 FORMAT(10(1X, F1.0))
    120 FORMAT(5(A1, 1X))
    130 FORMAT(5A1)
    200 FORMAT(1X, 5I2)
    210 FORMAT(1X, 5F4.0)
    220 FORMAT(1X, 5A2)
```

and that the following data is entered:

```
    A1B2C3D4E5F6G7H8I9J0
```

Tell what output will be produced, or explain why an error occurs.

```
18. READ 100, Number
    DO I = 1, 10
        PRINT 200, Number(I)
    END DO
19. READ 100, (Number(I), I = 1, 10)
    PRINT 200, (Number(I), I = 1, 10)
20. READ 110, (Point(I), I = -4, 5)
    DO I = 1, 10
        PRINT 210, Point(I)
    END DO
21. READ 110, Point
    PRINT 210, (Point(I-4), I = 0, 9)
22. READ 120, Symbol
    PRINT 220, Symbol
23. READ 130, (Symbol(I), I = 1, 5)
    PRINT 220, (Symbol(I), I = 1, 5)
```

8.3 ARRAY PROCESSING

In the preceding sections, we considered array declarations, input/output of arrays, and some simple processing of lists using arrays. In this section we describe how other kinds of array processing are carried out in Fortran.

Array Constants

An **array constant** may be constructed as a *list of values* enclosed between (/ and /),

```
(/ value₁, value₂,..., valueₖ /)
```

where each `value`$_i$ is a constant expression. For example,

```
(/ 2, 4, 6, 8, 10, 12, 14, 16, 18, 20 /)
```

is a one-dimensional array constant of size 10 consisting of the first 10 positive even integers. A value in an array constant may also be an **implied**-DO **constructor** of the form

```
(value-list, implied-do-control)
```

For example,

```
(/ (2*I, I = 1, 10) /)
```

constructs the preceding array constant of size 10. Array constants may also be formed using a combination of these two methods; for example,

```
(/ 2, 4, (I, I = 6, 18, 2), 20 /)
```

constructs the same array constant.

Constants of any of these forms can be assigned to arrays of the same size and type. (Mixed-mode assignments are carried out as described in Section 2.4.) For example, if A is declared by

```
INTEGER, DIMENSION(10) :: A
```

it can be assigned the sequence 2, 4, 6, . . ., 20 by any of the following statements:

```
A = (/ 2, 4, 6, 8, 10, 12, 14, 16, 18, 20 /)
A = (/ (2*I, I = 1, 10) /)
A = (/ 2, 4, (I, I = 6, 18, 2), 20 /)
```

Each of these has the same effect as the elementwise assignment

```
DO I = 1, 10
   A(I) = 2*I
END DO
```

Array Expressions

Operators and functions normally applied to simple expressions may also be applied to arrays having the same number of elements and to arrays and simple expressions. In this case, operations applied to an array are carried out elementwise. To illustrate, consider the following declarations:

```
INTEGER, DIMENSION(4) :: A, B
INTEGER, DIMENSION(0:3) :: C
INTEGER, DIMENSION(6:9) :: D
LOGICAL, DIMENSION(4) :: P
```

If A and B are assigned values

```
A = (/ 1, 2, 3, 4 /)
B = (/ 5, 6, 7, 8 /)
```

then the assignment statement

```
A = A + B
```

assigns to A the sequence 6, 8, 10, 12. If C is assigned a value

```
C = (/ -1, 3, -5, 7 /)
```

the statement

```
D = 2 * ABS(C) + 1
```

assigns to D the sequence 3, 7, 11, 15. Logical operations are also allowed. For example, the statement

```
P = (C > 0).AND. (MOD(B, 3) == 0)
```

assigns to P the sequence of truth values `.FALSE.`, `.TRUE.`, `.FALSE.`, `.FALSE.`.

Array Assignment

As we know, a value can be assigned to a simple variable by an assignment statement of the form `variable = expression`. As we have seen, assignment statements may also be used for array variables:

```
array-variable = expression
```

The value of the expression assigned to an array variable must be either

1. An array of the same size as the array variable, or
2. A simple value

In the second case, the value is *broadcast to all the array elements,* with the result that each is assigned this value. For example, the assignment statement

```
A = 0
```

assigns 0 to each element of A.

Array Sections and Subarrays

Sometimes it is necessary to construct arrays by selecting elements from another array, called a **parent array**. These new arrays, called **array sections** or **subarrays**, are constructed by using expressions of the form

```
array-name(subscript-triplet)
```

or

```
array-name(vector-subscript)
```

A **subscript triplet** has the form

```
lower : upper : stride
```

and specifies the elements in positions `lower`, `lower + stride`, `lower + 2*stride`, ... going as far as possible without going beyond `upper` if `stride > 0`, or below `upper` if `stride < 0`. If `lower` is omitted, the lower bound in the array declaration is used; if `upper` is omitted, the upper bound in the array declaration is used; if `stride` is omitted, it is taken to be 1. For example, if A, B, and I are arrays declared by

```
INTEGER, DIMENSION(10) :: A
INTEGER, DIMENSION(5) :: B, I
INTEGER :: J
```

and A is assigned a value by

```
A = (/ 11, 22, 33, 44, 55, 66, 77, 88, 99, 110 /)
```

then

```
A(2:10:2)
```

is the section of array A consisting of the elements 22, 44, 66, 88, and 110.

A **vector subscript** is a sequence of subscripts of the parent array. For example, if A is the array considered earlier,

```
A = (/ 11, 22, 33, 44, 55, 66, 77, 88, 99, 110 /)
```

and I is the subscript vector

```
I = (/ 6, 5, 3, 9, 1 /)
```

then

```
B = A(I)
```

assigns to B the section of array A consisting of the elements 66, 55, 33, 99, and 11 that are in positions 6, 5, 3, 9, and 1 of A. The statement

```
B = A((/ 5, 3, 3, 4, 3/))
```

assigns B the sequence of elements 55, 33, 33, 44, and 33.

Subarrays may also appear on the left-hand side of an assignment statement. For example, suppose that A is the one-dimensional array considered earlier:

```
INTEGER, DIMENSION(10) :: A

A = (/ 11, 22, 33, 44, 55, 66, 77, 88, 99, 110 /)
```

The statement

```
A(1:10:2) = (/ I**2, (I = 1, 5) /)
```

changes the elements in the odd positions of A to 1, 4, 9, 16, 25.

Subarrays may also appear in input or output statements to read or display part of an array. For example, the statement

```
READ (10, *) FailureTime(1:NumTimes)
```

is an alternative to using an implied DO loop as described in Section 8.1 to read values into the first NumTimes locations of the array `FailureTime`:

```
READ (10, *) (FailureTime(I), I = 1, NumTimes)
```

Similarly,

```
PRINT *, FailureTime(1:NumTimes)
```

has the same effect as using an implied DO loop to display the first NumTimes elements of FailureTime:

```
PRINT *, (FailureTime(I), I = 1, NumTimes)
```

The WHERE Construct

A WHERE construct may be used to assign values to arrays depending on the value of a logical array expression. This construct has the form

```
WHERE (logical-array-expr) array-var₁ = array-expr₁
```

or

```
WHERE (logical-array-expr)
    array-var₁ = array-expr₁
        .
        .
    array-varₘ = array-exprₘ
ELSEWHERE
    array-varₘ₊₁ = array-exprₘ₊₁
        .
        .
    array-varₙ = array-exprₙ
END WHERE
```

where each array-var$_i$ has the same size as the value of logical-array-expr; in the second form, the ELSEWHERE part is optional.

The logical-array-expr is evaluated element by element, and whenever the expression is true (false), the value of the corresponding element of each array-expr$_i$ (in the ELSEWHERE part) is assigned to the corresponding element of array-var$_i$. In the first form, all other elements are left unchanged. For example, if arrays A and B are declared by

```
INTEGER, DIMENSION(5) :: A = (/ 0, 2, 5, 0, 10 /)
REAL, DIMENSION(5) :: B
```

the WHERE construct

```
WHERE (A > 0)
   B = 1.0 / REAL(A)
ELSEWHERE
   B = -1.0
END WHERE
```

assigns to B the sequence −1.0, 0.5, 0.2, −1.0, 0.1.

Arrays as Arguments

Intrinsic Array-Processing Subprograms   Fortran 90 provides several intrinsic functions whose arguments are arrays. Some of the more useful ones for one-dimensional arrays are

ALLOCATED(A)	Returns true if memory has been allocated to the allocatable array A and false otherwise
DOT_PRODUCT(A, B)	Returns the dot product of (numeric or logical) arrays A and V
MAXVAL(A)	Returns the maximum value in array A
MAXLOC(A)	Returns a one-dimensional array containing one element whose value is the position of the first occurrence of the maximum value in A
MINVAL(A)	Returns the minimum value in array A

MINLOC(A)	Returns a one-dimensional array containing one element whose value is the position of the first occurrence of the minimum value in A
PRODUCT(A)	Returns the product of the elements in A
SIZE(A)	Returns the number of elements in A
SUM(A)	Returns the sum of the elements in A

Other forms of these functions and other intrinsic array-processing subprograms are also available.[1]

Programmer-Defined Array-Processing Subprograms   For   programmer-defined subprograms, *an actual array argument must be declared in the calling program unit, and the corresponding formal array argument must be declared in the subprogram.* When the subprogram is referenced, the first element of the actual array argument is associated with the first element of the corresponding formal array argument. Successive actual array elements are then associated with the corresponding formal array elements.

To make it possible to design subprograms that can be used to process arrays of various sizes, Fortran allows both the array and its size or range of subscripts to be passed to the subprogram. The program in Figure 8.3 illustrates this. It is a simple *driver program* to test a function to calculate the mean of a list of numbers. Note that the formal argument NumElements is used to specify the dimension of the formal array argument X in this subprogram. The actual dimension NumItems = 10 and the actual array Item are passed to the subprogram from the main program when the function is referenced. Note also that function Mean uses the intrinsic function Sum to calculate the sum of the elements of array X.

Figure 8.3.   Calculating the mean of a list—version 1

```
PROGRAM Mean_Driver_1
!-------------------------------------------------------------------
! Driver program to test an internal function Mean that calculates the
! mean of an array of numbers. Identifiers used are:
!   Item     : one-dimensional array of numbers
!   NumItems : number of items (named constant)
!   Mean     : function that finds the mean of a set of numbers
!
! Input:  NumItems and a list of NumItems real numbers
! Output: The mean of the numbers
!-------------------------------------------------------------------

  IMPLICIT NONE
  INTEGER, PARAMETER :: NumItems = 10
  REAL, DIMENSION(NumItems) :: Item

  PRINT *, "Enter the", NumItems, "real numbers:"
  READ *, Item
  PRINT '(1X, "Mean of the ", I3, " Numbers is ", F6.2)', &
        NumItems, Mean(Item, NumItems)
```

---

[1] For a description of other array-processing functions, see Chapters 8 and 9 and Appendix D of our text *Fortran 90 for Engineers and Scientists.*

```
CONTAINS

!-Mean-------------------------------------------------------------
! Function to find the mean of the NumElements elements of the array
! X.  The size (NumElements) of X is passed as an argument.
!
! Accepts:  Array X and NumElements
! Returns:  The mean of the numbers stored in X
!------------------------------------------------------------------

FUNCTION Mean(X, NumElements)

  INTEGER, INTENT(IN) :: NumElements
  REAL, DIMENSION(NumElements), INTENT(IN) :: X
  REAL :: Mean

  Mean = SUM(X) / REAL(NumElements)

END FUNCTION Mean

END PROGRAM Mean_Driver_1
```

The actual array element `Item` in the program in Figure 8.3 is a compile-time array, but it could also be an allocatable array:

```
INTEGER :: NumItems, AllocateStatus
REAL, DIMENSION(:), ALLOCATABLE :: Item
REAL :: Mean

WRITE (*, '(1X, A)', ADVANCE = "NO") &
      "How many numbers are in the data set? "
READ *, NumItems
ALLOCATE(Item(NumItems), STAT = AllocateStatus)
IF (AllocateStatus /= 0) STOP "*** Not enough memory ***"

PRINT *, "Enter the", NumItems, " real numbers:"
READ *, Item
PRINT '(1X, "Mean of the ", I3, " Numbers is ", F6.2)', &
      NumItems, Mean(Item, NumItems)
```

Figure 8.3   (cont.)

However, *a formal array argument may not be an allocatable array.*

Assumed-Shape Arrays   An alternative to passing the size of a formal array argument to a subprogram is to use an **assumed-shape array** as the formal argument. In this case, the size of the formal array will assume the size of the corresponding actual array.

For an assumed-shape array, the DIMENSION specifier in its declaration has the form

DIMENSION(:)   or   DIMENSION(lower-bound:)

where in the second form, `lower-bound` specifies the lower bound on the subscripts for the formal array; in the first form, 1 will be used for the lower bound. For an external subprogram, an interface block must be used in the program unit that calls the subprogram. For example, function subprogram Mean in the program in Figure 8.4 declares the formal array X to be an assumed-shape array using

```
REAL, DIMENSION(:), INTENT(IN) :: X
```

and the main program uses the interface block

```
INTERFACE
  FUNCTION Mean(X)
    REAL :: Mean
    REAL, DIMENSION(:), INTENT(IN) :: X
  END FUNCTION Mean
END INTERFACE
```

for the function Mean. The size of X will be the size of the corresponding actual argument Item. The predefined function SIZE is used to determine what this size is.

Figure 8.4.   Calculating the mean of a list—version 2

```
PROGRAM Mean_Driver_2
!-----------------------------------------------------------------------
! Driver program to test an external function Mean that calculates the
! mean of an array of numbers.  Identifiers used are:
!   NumItems          : number of items
!   Allocate Status : status variable for ALLOCATE
!   Item              : one-dimensional array of items
!   Mean              : external function to find the mean
!
! Input:  NumItems and a list of NumItems real numbers
! Output: The mean of the numbers
!-----------------------------------------------------------------------

  IMPLICIT NONE
  REAL, DIMENSION(:), ALLOCATABLE :: Item
  INTEGER :: NumItems, AllocateStatus

  INTERFACE
    FUNCTION Mean(X)
      REAL :: Mean
      REAL, DIMENSION(:), INTENT(IN) :: X
    END FUNCTION Mean
  END INTERFACE

  WRITE (*, '(1X, A)', ADVANCE = "NO") &
        "How many numbers are in the data set? "
  READ *, NumItems
  ALLOCATE(Item(NumItems), STAT = AllocateStatus)
  IF (AllocateStatus /= 0) STOP "*** Not enough memory ***"

  PRINT *, "Enter the", NumItems, " real numbers:"
  READ *, Item

  PRINT '(1X, "Mean of the ", I3, " Numbers is ", F6.2)', &
        NumItems, Mean(Item)
  DEALLOCATE(Item)
```

```
END PROGRAM Mean_Driver_2

! Mean------------------------------------------------------------------
! External function to find the mean of the elements of the
! array X. Local variables used are:
!   Sum : sum of the numbers
!   I   : subscript
!
! Accepts:  Assumed-shape array X
! Returns:  The mean of the numbers stored in X
!-----------------------------------------------------------------------


FUNCTION Mean(X)

  IMPLICIT NONE
  REAL :: Mean
  REAL, DIMENSION(:), INTENT(IN) :: X

  Mean = SUM(X) / REAL(SIZE(X))

END FUNCTION Mean
```

Figure 8.4 (cont.)

Automatic Arrays   A subprogram that uses assumed-shape arrays may also need local array variables, called **automatic arrays**, whose sizes vary from one subprogram reference to the next. The SIZE function can be used to dimension such local arrays. For example, the following subroutine for interchanging two real arrays of the same size uses the automatic array Temp:

```
!-Swap-------------------------------------------------------
! Subroutine to swap two assumed-shape arrays A and B.
! Local array used is:
!    Temp : An automatic array used to interchange A and B
!
! Accepts:  A and B
! Returns:  A and B with elements interchanged
!-----------------------------------------------------------


SUBROUTINE Swap(A, B)

  REAL, DIMENSION(:), INTENT(INOUT) :: A, B
  REAL, DIMENSION(SIZE(A)) :: Temp

  Temp = A
  A = B
  B = Temp

END SUBROUTINE Swap
```

Array-Valued Functions   The value returned by some of the intrinsic functions such as MaxLoc and MinLoc is an array, and programmer-defined functions may also return arrays.

For example, a function like that described in Exercise 16 that constructs an array containing powers of 2 is an array-valued function.

Example: Vector Processing

Two-dimensional vectors can be represented algebraically as ordered pairs (a_1, a_2) of real numbers; a_1 and a_2 are called the *components* of the vector. Similarly, vectors in three-dimensional space can be represented algebraically by ordered triples (a_1, a_2, a_3). In general, *n-dimensional vectors* can be represented algebraically by ordered *n*-tuples $(a_1, a_2, \ldots, a_n)$. This algebraic representation is convenient for computation because the components of a vector can be stored in an array and the basic vector operations can be easily implemented using this array representation.

To illustrate, the norm of an *n*-dimensional vector $\mathbf{a} = (a_1, a_2, \ldots, a_n)$ is given by

$$|\mathbf{a}| = \sqrt{a_1^2 + a_2^2 + \cdots + a_n^2}$$

Writing a function subprogram to compute the norm of a vector using this formula is straightforward. Note that A * A computes the squares of the elements of A, and the Sum function adds them:

```
!Norm------------------------------------------------------------
! Function to calculate the norm of a vector.  Variables used:
!      A : array that stores the vector
!      N : number of components in the vector (its dimension)
!
! Accepts: A and N
! Returns: Norm of the N-dimensional vector stored in A
!----------------------------------------------------------------

FUNCTION Norm(A, N)

  REAL :: Norm
  REAL, INTENT(IN), DIMENSION(N) :: A
  INTEGER, INTENT(IN) :: N

  Norm = SQRT(SUM(A*A))

END FUNCTION Norm
```

The *sum* and *difference* of two vectors can be computed algebraically by simply adding and subtracting corresponding components. For example, if $\mathbf{a} = (3, 5)$ and $\mathbf{b} = (22, 7)$, then

$$\mathbf{a} + \mathbf{b} = (1, 12)$$
$$\mathbf{a} - \mathbf{b} = (5, -2)$$

In general, if $\mathbf{a} = (a_1, a_2, \ldots, a_n)$ and $\mathbf{b} = (b_1, b_2, \ldots, b_n)$, then

$$\mathbf{a} + \mathbf{b} = (a_1 + b_1, a_2 + b_2, \ldots, a_n + b_n)$$
$$\mathbf{a} - \mathbf{b} = (a_1 - b_1, a_2 - b_2, \ldots, a_n - b_n)$$

Since the basic arithmetic Fortran operations are performed elementwise on arrays, + and − can be used to compute the sum and difference of vectors stored in arrays.

Like addition and subtraction, *multiplication of a vector by a scalar* (i.e., a number) is performed componentwise:

$$c\mathbf{a} = (ca_1, ca_2, \ldots, ca_n)$$

For example, for the vector $\mathbf{a}$ given earlier,

$$2\mathbf{a} = (6, 10)$$

Since multiplication of an array by a scalar is carried out elementwise, implementing this vector operation in Fortran is trivial.

The *dot* (or *scalar*) *product* $\boldsymbol{a} \cdot \boldsymbol{b}$ of two vectors is the scalar obtained by adding the products of corresponding components:

$$\mathbf{a} \cdot \mathbf{b} = \sum_{i=1}^{n} a_i b_i = a_1 b_1 + a_2 b_2 + \cdots + a_n b_n$$

For example, for the vectors **a** and **b** given earlier,

$$\mathbf{a} \cdot \mathbf{b} = 29$$

In Fortran, if A and B are two one-dimensional arrays, the function reference DOT_ PRODUCT(A, B) returns the dot product of A and B and can thus be used to compute dot products of vectors stored in arrays.

Other vector operations are described in the exercises. Function subprograms to implement them are straightforward.

PRACTICE!

1. (True or false) If A and B are arrays declared by REAL, DIMENSION(5) :: A, B, the statement A = B can be used to copy the values stored in B into A.

Exercises 2–15 assume the following declarations have been made:

```
REAL, DIMENSION(10) :: &
    A = (/ 0.0, 1.1, 2.2, 3.3, 4.4, 5.5, 6.6, 7.7, 8.8,
        9.9 /), &
    B = (/ (32.0 / 2.0**I, I = 0, 9) /), C
INTEGER, DIMENSION(0:9) :: D = (/ (I + 5, I = 0, 5),
1, 2, 3, 4/)
INTEGER :: M = 3, N = 9
REAL, DIMENSION(0:9) :: E
REAL, DIMENSION(-3:6) :: F
REAL, DIMENSION(100:109) :: G
```

2. List the elements of A, or explain why the declaration is not legal.

3. List the elements of B, or explain why the declaration is not legal.

4. List the elements of D, or explain why the declaration is not legal.

5. List the elements of A(3:7), or explain why this expression is not legal.

6. List the elements of A(1:9:2), or explain why this expression is not legal.

7. List the elements of D(M:N:M), or explain why this expression is not legal.

8. List the elements of B(N:M), or explain why this expression is not legal.

9. List the elements of A(D), or explain why this expression is not legal.

10. List the elements of D(A), or explain why this expression is not legal.

11. For C = A + 2*B, list the elements of C, or explain why this statement is not legal.

12. For F = A + 2*B, list the elements of F, or explain why this statement is not legal.

13. For E = REAL(D) + 5, list the elements of E, or explain why this statement is not legal.

14. For G = B(1:10), list the elements of G, or explain why this statement is not legal.

15. For

```
WHERE (B > A)
    G = B - A
ELSEWHERE
    G = A - B
END WHERE
```

list the elements of G, or explain why this WHERE construct is not legal.

16. Write a function subprogram that accepts a positive integer and returns an array containing the first N powers of 2: $2^1, 2^2, \ldots, 2^N$.

17. Proceed as in Exercise 16 but write a subroutine subprogram.

18. Write a function subprogram that accepts two one-dimensional arrays A and B and returns another array in which each element is the maximum of the corresponding elements of A and B. Use assumed-shape arrays for the formal array arguments.

19. Proceed as in Exercise 18 but write a subroutine subprogram.

20. Write a function subprogram that accepts a one-dimensional array A and returns another array containing the elements of A but with all negative elements replaced by 0. Use an assumed-shape array for the formal array argument.

21. Proceed as in Exercise 20 but write a subroutine subprogram.

22. The *cross* (or *vector*) *product* $\mathbf{a} \times \mathbf{b}$ of two vectors is a vector. This product is defined only for three-dimensional vectors: if $\mathbf{a} = (a_1, a_2, a_3)$ and $\mathbf{b} = (b_1, b_2, b_3)$, then

$$\mathbf{a} \times \mathbf{b} = (a_2b_3 - a_3b_2, \, a_3b_1 - a_1b_3, \, a_1b_2 - a_2b_1)$$

Write a function subprogram that accepts a value for n and two n-dimensional vectors and that returns the cross product of the vectors if $n = 3$ or displays an error message otherwise. Write a program to test your subprogram.

23. Write a function subprogram that finds a unit vector having the same direction as a given vector.

24. A formula that can be used to find the angle between two vectors is

$$\cos\theta = \frac{\mathbf{a} \cdot \mathbf{b}}{|\mathbf{a}||\mathbf{b}|}$$

Write a function subprogram to compute the angle between two vectors.

8.4 SORTING AND SEARCHING

A common programming problem is **sorting**, that is, arranging the items in a list so that they are in either ascending or descending order. There are many sorting methods, and in this section we describe one of the simplest methods, simple selection sort, and one of the most efficient methods, quicksort. Other sorting schemes are described in the programming problems at the end of this chapter.

Another important problem is **searching** a collection of data for a specified item and retrieving some information associated with that item. For example, one searches a telephone directory for a specific name in order to retrieve the phone number listed with that name. We will describe two kinds of searches, linear search and binary search.

Sorting

Selection Sort   The basic idea of a selection sort of a list is to make a number of passes through the list or a part of the list, and on each pass to select one item to be correctly positioned. For example, on each pass through a sublist, the smallest item in the sublist might be found and moved to its proper position.

As an illustration, suppose that the following list is to be sorted into ascending order:

$$67, 33, 21, 84, 49, 50, 75$$

We locate the smallest item in position 3 and interchange it with the first item and thus properly position the smallest item at the beginning of the list:

$$21, 33, 67, 84, 49, 50, 75$$

We now scan the sublist consisting of the items from position 2 on to find the smallest item and exchange it with the second item (itself in this case) and thus properly position the next-to-smallest item in position 2:

$$21, 33, 67, 84, 49, 50, 75$$

We continue in this manner, locating the smallest item in the sublist of items from position 3 on and interchanging it with the third item, then properly positioning the smallest item in the sublist of items from position 4 on, and so on until we eventually do this for the sublist consisting of the last two items:

$$21, 33, 49, 84, 67, 50, 75$$

$$21, 33, 49, 50, 67, 84, 75$$

$$21, 33, 49, 50, 67, 84, 75$$

$$21, 33, 49, 50, 67, 75, 84$$

Positioning the smallest item in this last sublist obviously also positions the last item correctly and thus completes the sort.

An algorithm for this simple selection sort is as follows.

SIMPLE SELECTION SORT ALGORITHM

Algorithm to sort the list of items $X(1), X(2), \ldots, X(N)$ so they are in ascending order. To sort them into descending order, find the largest item rather than the smallest item on each pass.

Accepts: List $X(1), X(2), \ldots, X(N)$
Returns: Modified list $X(1), X(2), \ldots, X(N)$; elements are sorted into ascending order

For *I* ranging from 1 to *N* − 1, do the following:

1. On the *I*th pass, first find the *SmallestItem* in the sublist *X*(*I*), . . . , *X*(*N*) and its position *LocationSmallest*.

!Now interchange this smallest item with the item !at the beginning of this sublist.

2. Set *X*(*LocationSmallest*) equal to *X*(*I*).
3. Set *X*(*I*) equal to *SmallestItem*.

The following subroutine uses this algorithm to sort a list of integers.

Figure 8.5. Selection sort

```
!-SelectionSort-------------------------------------------------
! Subroutine to sort an array Item into ascending order using
! the simple selection sort algorithm. For descending order,
! change MINVAL to MAXVAL and MINLOC to MAXLOC. Local
! variables used are:
!   NumItems         : number of elements in array Item
!   SmallestItem     : smallest item in current sublist
!   MINLOC_array     : one-element array returned by MINLOC
!   LocationSmallest : location of SmallestItem
!   I                : subscript
!
! Accepts:  Array Item
! Returns:  Array Item (modified) with elements in ascending
!           order
!
! Note:   Item is an assumed-shape array, so a program unit that
!         calls this subroutine must
!           1. contain this subroutine as an internal subprogram,
!           2. import this subroutine from a module, or
!           3. contain an interface block for this subroutine.
!-------------------------------------------------------------

SUBROUTINE SelectionSort(Item)

  INTEGER, DIMENSION(:), INTENT(INOUT) :: Item
  INTEGER :: NumItems, SmallestItem, I
  INTEGER, DIMENSION(1) :: MINLOC_array

  NumItems = SIZE(Item)
  DO I = 1, NumItems - 1

     ! Find smallest item in the sublist
     ! Item(I), . . . . , Item(NumItems)

     SmallestItem = MINVAL(Item(I:NumItems))
     MINLOC_array = MINLOC(Item(I:NumItems))
     LocationSmallest = (I - 1) + MINLOC_array(1)

     ! Interchange smallest item with Item(I) at
     ! beginning of sublist

     Item(LocationSmallest) = Item(I)
     Item(I) = SmallestItem

  END DO

END SUBROUTINE SelectionSort
```

In this subroutine we have used the intrinsic functions MINVAL and MINLOC to locate the smallest value in each sublist and its position in that sublist. The function reference in the assignment statement

```
MINLOC_array = MINLOC(Item(I:N))
```

returns a one-element array whose value is the position, counting from 1, of the smallest value in the array section Item(I:N). The location of this smallest value in the entire list is thus given by

```
LocationSmallest = (I - 1) + MINLOC_array(1)
```

and the element in the list at this location is interchanged with the element at location I.

Quicksort   The **quicksort** method of sorting is more efficient than simple selection sort. It is in fact one of the fastest methods of sorting and is most often implemented by a recursive algorithm. The basic idea of quicksort is to choose some element called a **pivot** and then to perform a sequence of exchanges so that all elements that are less than this pivot are to its left and all elements that are greater than the pivot are to its right. This correctly positions the pivot and divides the (sub)list into two smaller sublists, each of which may then be sorted independently in the *same* way. This *divide-and-conquer* strategy leads naturally to a recursive sorting algorithm.

To illustrate this splitting of a list into two sublists, consider the following list of integers:

$$50, 30, 20, 80, 90, 70, 95, 85, 10, 15, 75, 25$$

If we select the first number as the pivot, we must rearrange the list so that 30, 20, 10, 15, and 25 are placed before 50, and 80, 90, 70, 95, 85, and 75 are placed after it. To carry out this rearrangement, we search from the right end of the list for an element less than 50 and from the left end for an item greater than 50:

$$50, 30, 20, 80, 90, 70, 95, 85, 10, 15, 75, 25$$

This locates the two numbers 25 and 80, which we now interchange to obtain

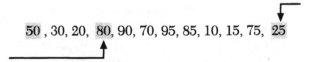

We then resume the search from the right for a number less than 50 and from the left for a number greater than 50:

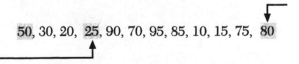

This locates the numbers 15 and 90, which are then interchanged:

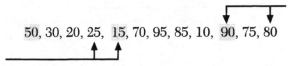

$$50, 30, 20, 25, \; 15, 70, 95, 85, 10, \; 90, 75, 80$$

A continuation of the searches locates 10 and 70:

$$50, 30, 20, 25, 15, \; 70, 95, 85, \; 10, 90, 75, 80$$

Interchanging these gives

$$50, 30, 20, 25, 15, \; 10, 95, 85, \; 70, 90, 75, 80$$

When we resume our search from the right for a number less than 50, we locate the value 10, which was found on the previous left-to-right search. This signals the end of the two searches, and we interchange 50 and 10, giving

$$10, 30, 20, 25, 15, \; 50, 95, 85, 70, 90, 75, 80$$

The two underlined sublists now have the required properties: all elements in the first sublist are less than 50, and all those in the right sublist are greater than 50. Consequently, 50 has been properly positioned.

Both the left sublist

$$10, 30, 20, 25, 15$$

and the right sublist

$$95, 85, 70, 90, 75, 80$$

can now be sorted independently. Each must be split by choosing and correctly positioning one pivot element (the first) in each of them. For this, a subroutine is needed to split a list of items in the array positions given by two parameters Low and High, denoting the beginning and end positions of the sublist, respectively. A recursive subroutine to sort a list is then easy to write. The anchor case occurs when the list being examined is empty or contains a single element; in this case the list is in order and nothing needs to be done. The inductive case occurs when the list contains multiple elements, in which case the list can be sorted by:

1. Splitting the list into two sublists
2. Recursively sorting the left sublist, and
3. Recursively sorting the right sublist

Figure 8.6. Quicksort

```
!--------------------------------------------------------------
! Note: In the following subroutines, Item is an assumed-shape
!       array so a program unit that calls these subroutines must:
!          1. contain this subroutine as an internal subprogram,
!          2. import this subroutine from a module, or
!          3. contain an interface block for this subroutine.
!--------------------------------------------------------------


!-Quicksort----------------------------------------------------
! Subroutine to sort a list using the quicksort method. Call
! it with First = the lower bound on the subscripts of the
! array and Last = the upper bound. Local variable used:
!    Mid : position of the split point
!
! Accepts:  Array Item
! Returns:  Array Item (modified) with elements in ascending
!              order
!--------------------------------------------------------------

RECURSIVE SUBROUTINE Quicksort(Item, First, Last)

   INTEGER, DIMENSION(:), INTENT(INOUT) :: Item
   INTEGER, INTENT(IN) :: First, Last
   INTEGER :: Mid
   IF (First < Last) THEN                !If list size >= 2
      CALL Split(Item, First, Last, Mid) ! split it
      CALL Quicksort(Item, First, Mid-1) ! sort left half
      CALL Quicksort(Item, Mid+1, Last)  ! sort right half
   END IF

END SUBROUTINE Quicksort

!-Split--------------------------------------------------------
! Subroutine to split a list into two sublists, using the
! first element as pivot, and return the position of the
! element about which the List was divided.  Local variables
! used are:
!    Left  : position of first element
!    Right : position of last element
!    Pivot : pivot element
!    Swap  : used to swap two elements
!
! Accepts: Array Item and positions Low and High of the first
!             and last elements
! Returns:  Array Item (modified) with elements in ascending
!              order
!
! Note:   Item is an assumed-shape array so a program unit that
!            calls this subroutine must:
!          1. contain this subroutine as an internal subprogram,
!          2. import this subroutine from a module, or
!          3. contain an interface block for this subroutine.
!--------------------------------------------------------------

SUBROUTINE Split(Item, Low, High, Mid)
```

```
      INTEGER, DIMENSION(:), INTENT(INOUT) :: Item
      INTEGER, INTENT(IN) :: Low, High
      INTEGER, INTENT(OUT) :: Mid
      INTEGER :: Left, Right, Swap

   Left = Low
   Right = High
   Pivot = Item(Low)

   ! Repeat the following while Left and Right haven't met
   DO
      IF (Left >= Right) EXIT

      ! Scan right to left to find element < Pivot
      DO
         IF (Left >= Right .OR. Item(Right) < Pivot) EXIT
         Right - Right - 1
      END DO

      ! Scan left to right to find element > Pivot
      DO
         IF (Item(Left) > Pivot) EXIT
         Left = Left + 1
      END DO

      ! If Left and Right haven't met, exchange the items
      IF (Left < Right) THEN
         Swap = Item(Left)
         Item(Left) = Item(Right)
         Item(Right) = Swap
      END IF
   END DO

   ! Switch element in split position with pivot
   Item(Low) = Item(Right)
   Item(Right) = Pivot
   Mid = Right

END SUBROUTINE Split
```

Figure 8.6 (cont.)

Searching

A **linear search** begins with the first item in a list and searches sequentially until either the desired item is found or the end of the list is reached. The following algorithm describes this method of searching.

LINEAR SEARCH ALGORITHM

Algorithm to linear search a list $X(1)$, $X(2)$, . . . , $X(N)$ for *ItemSought*. The logical variable *Found* is set to true and *Location* is set to the position of *ItemSought* if the search is successful; otherwise, *Found* is set to false.

Accepts:	List $X(1), X(2), \ldots, X(N)$ and *ItemSought*	1.	Initialize *Location* to 1 and *Found* to false.

Returns:	If *ItemSought* is found in the list:
	    Found = true and *Location* = position
	    of *ItemSought*
	If *ItemSought* is not found in the list:
	    Found = false (and *Location* = $N + 1$)
		2.	While *Location* $\leq N$ and not *Found*, do the following:
			    If *ItemSought* = $X(Location)$, then
			        Set *Found* to true.
			    Else
			        Increment *Location* by 1.

Implementing this algorithm as a subroutine is straightforward and is left as an exercise.

If a list has been sorted, **binary search** can be used to search for an item more efficiently than linear search. In this method, we first examine the middle element in the list, and if this is the desired element, the search is successful. Otherwise we determine whether the item being sought is in the first half or in the second half of the list and then repeat this process, using the middle element of that list.

To illustrate, suppose the list to be searched is

$$1279$$
$$1331$$
$$1373$$
$$1555$$
$$1824$$
$$1898$$
$$1995$$
$$2002$$
$$2335$$
$$2665$$
$$3103$$

and we are looking for 1995. We first examine the middle number 1898 in the sixth position. Because 1995 is greater than 1898, we can disregard the first half of the list and concentrate on the second half.

$$1995$$
$$2002$$
$$2335$$
$$2665$$
$$3103$$

The middle number in this sublist is 2335, and the desired item, 1995, is less than 2335, so we discard the second half of this sublist and concentrate on the first half.

$$1995$$
$$2002$$

Because there is no middle number in this sublist, we examine the number immediately preceding the middle position; that is, the number 1995.

The following subroutine uses this method to search a list of character strings.

Figure 8.7. Binary search

```
!-BinarySearch-------------------------------------------------
! Subroutine to search the list Item for ItemSought using
! binary search.  If ItemSought is found in the list, Found
! is returned as true and the Location of the item is
! returned; otherwise Found is false.  In this version of
! binary search, ItemSought and the elements of Item are
! character strings.  Local variables used are:
!   First   :  first item in (sub)list being searched
!   Last    :  last    "    "     "      "       "
!   Middle  :  middle  "    "     "      "       "
!
! Accepts:  Array Item and ItemSought in the list Item
! Returns:  If ItemSought is found:
!                 Found = true and
!                 Location = position of ItemSought

!           Otherwise:
!                 Found = false (and Location = last
!                 position examined)
!
! Note:   Item is an assumed-shape array so a program unit
!         that calls this subroutine must:
!         1. contain this subroutine as an internal subprogram,
!         2. import this subroutine from a module, or
!         3. contain an interface block for this subroutine.
!-------------------------------------------------------------

SUBROUTINE BinarySearch(Item, ItemSought, Found, Location)

  CHARACTER(*), DIMENSION(:), INTENT(IN) :: Item
  CHARACTER(*), INTENT(IN) :: ItemSought
  LOGICAL, INTENT(OUT) :: Found
  INTEGER, INTENT(OUT) :: Location
  INTEGER :: First, Last, Middle


  First = 1
  Last = SIZE(Item)
  Found = .FALSE.


! While First less than or equal to Last and not Found do

  DO
     IF ((First > Last).OR. Found) RETURN
     ! If empty list to be searched or item found, return

     ! Otherwise continue with the following

     Middle = (First + Last) / 2
     IF (ItemSought < Item(Middle)) THEN
        Last = Middle - 1
```

```
        ELSE IF (ItemSought > Item(Middle)) THEN
           First = Middle + 1
        ELSE
           Found =.TRUE.
           Location = Middle
        END IF
     END DO

  END SUBROUTINE BinarySearch
```

Figure 8.7 (cont.)

PROBLEM

A quality-control engineer monitors a machine by recording the number of defective parts the machine produces each hour. This information is to be summarized in a *frequency distribution* that shows the number of one-hour periods in which there were no defective parts, one defective part, two defective parts, . . . , five or more defective parts.

Solution

Specification The input/output specifications for this problem are clear:

Input: Integers representing counts of defective parts

Output: A frequency distribution

Design To solve this problem, we will use the following variables:

VARIABLES FOR QUALITY-CONTROL PROBLEM

NumDefects:	Number of defective parts counted in a one-hour period
FileName:	The name of a data file that contains these counts
Count:	An array: *Count (I)* is the number of one-hour periods during which *I* defective parts were produced, $I = 0, 1, \ldots, 5$

An appropriate algorithm is

ALGORITHM FOR QUALITY-CONTROL PROBLEM

Algorithm to read several values for *NumDefects*, the number of defective parts produced by a machine

Testing Motorola pagers (Photo courtesy of Hewlett-Packard)

in a given one-hour period, and to determine *Count* (*I*) = the number of periods in which there were *I* defective parts.

Input: Name of data file, and values stored in this file

Output: Values stored in array *Count*

1. Get the name of the data file and open it for input; if not successful, terminate execution.

2. Initialize array *Count* to all zeros.

3. Do the following:
   a. Attempt to read a value for *NumDefects*.

   b. If an input error occurs terminate execution.
   If the end of the file has been reached, terminate repetition.
   Otherwise continue with the following.
   c. If *NumDefects* > 5, set *NumDefects* to 5.
   d. Increase *Count* (*NumDefects*) by 1.

4. Display the values stored in array *Count*.

Coding, Testing, and Execution   The program in Figure 8.8 implements this algorithm. Also shown is a listing of a data file of test values and the frequency distribution produced by the program.

Figure 8.8.   Generating a frequency distribution

```
PROGRAM Frequency_Distribution
!-----------------------------------------------------------------------
! Program to generate a frequency distribution of the number of 1-hour
! periods in which there were 0, 1, 2,... defective parts produced by
! a machine. The data is read from a file. Identifiers used are:
!     FileName      : name of the data file
!     OpenStatus    : status variable for OPEN
!     InputStatus   : status variable for READ
!     MaxDefective  : constant representing maximum # of defective
!                     parts
!     Count         : Count(I) = # of 1-hour periods with I defective
!                     parts
!     NumDefects    : number of defective parts read from file
!     I             : subscript
!
! Input (keyboard): FileName
! Input (file):     Number of defects per hour
! Output:           Frequency distribution -- elements of array Count
!-----------------------------------------------------------------------

  IMPLICIT NONE
  INTEGER, PARAMETER :: MaxDefective = 5
  INTEGER, DIMENSION(0:MaxDefective) :: Count = 0
  INTEGER :: OpenStatus, InputStatus, NumDefects, I
  CHARACTER(20) :: FileName

  ! Get file name, open the file as unit 10

  WRITE (*, '(1X, A)', ADVANCE = "NO") "Enter name of data file: "
  READ *, FileName
  OPEN (UNIT = 10, FILE = FileName, STATUS = "OLD", IOSTAT = OpenStatus)
  IF (OpenStatus > 0) STOP "*** Cannot open the file ***"

  ! While there is more data, read # of defective parts and
  ! increment appropriate counter
```

```
      DO
         READ (10, *, IOSTAT = InputStatus) NumDefects
         IF (InputStatus > 0) STOP "*** Input error ***"
         IF (InputStatus < 0) EXIT ! end of data

         NumDefects = MIN(NumDefects, MaxDefective)
         Count(NumDefects) = Count(NumDefects) + 1
      END DO

      ! Print the frequency distribution

      PRINT *
      PRINT *, "# of defectives # of hours"
      PRINT *, "=============== =========="
      DO I = 0, MaxDefective
         PRINT '(1X, I8, I15)', I, Count(I)
      END DO

      CLOSE (10)

   END PROGRAM Frequency_Distribution
```

Listing of `fi18-8.dat` **Used in Sample Run**

```
0
1
0
2
2
0
1
6
3
0
3
1
2
0
1
2
0
```

Sample Run

```
Enter name of data file: fi18-8.dat

# of defectives   # of hours
===============   ==========
       0                6
       1                4
       2                4
       3                2
       4                0
       5                1
```

Figure 8.8 (cont.)

A Graphical Solution

A **bar graph** or **histogram** is often used to display frequency distributions graphically. Each of the categories is represented by a bar whose length corresponds to the number of items in that category. Thus, the frequency distribution produced by the sample run in Figure 8.8 could be represented by the following bar graph:

The subroutine in Figure 8.9 can be used to display a similar bar graph. Calling it in the program in Figure 8.8 with the statement

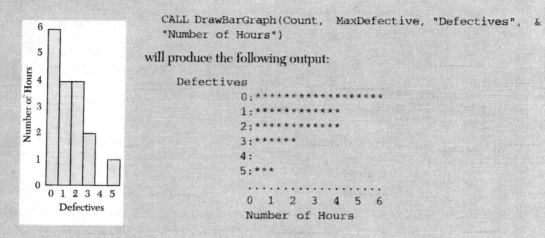

```
CALL DrawBarGraph(Count, MaxDefective, "Defectives", &
     "Number of Hours")
```

will produce the following output:

```
Defectives
0:*******************
1:************
2:************
3:******
4:
5:***

 .................
 0  1  2  3  4  5  6
Number of Hours
```

Figure 8.9. Subroutine to generate a bar graph

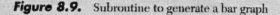

```
!-DrawBarGraph-----------------------------------------------------
! Subroutine to plot a bar graph representation of a frequency
! distribution.  Identifiers used are:
!   Frequency            : array of frequencies
!   NumFrequencies       : number of frequencies
!   MaxFrequency         : largest frequency
!   Vertical_Axis_Label  : label for vertical axis
!   Horizontal_Axis_Label : label for horizontal axis
!   I, J                 : subscript and loop control variable
!
! Accepts:  Array Frequency, integer NumFrequencies, and character
!           strings Vertical_Axis_Label and Horizontal_Axis_Label
! Output:   A bar graph of the elements of Frequency
!------------------------------------------------------------------

SUBROUTINE DrawBarGraph(Frequency, NumFrequencies, &
         Vertical_Axis_Label, Horizontal_Axis_Label)

  INTEGER, INTENT(IN) :: NumFrequencies
  INTEGER, DIMENSION (0:NumFrequencies), INTENT(IN) :: Frequency
  CHARACTER(*) :: Vertical_Axis_Label, Horizontal_Axis_Label
  INTEGER :: I, J, MaxFrequency
  CHARACTER(3) :: Stars = "***"

  PRINT '(//1X, A)', Vertical_Axis_Label
  MaxFrequency = MAXVAL(Frequency)
```

```
    DO I = 0, NumFrequencies
        PRINT '(1X, I10, ":", 20A)', I, (Stars, J = 1, Frequency(I))
    END DO

    PRINT '(11X, 80A)', (".", I = 0, 3 * MaxFrequency)
    PRINT '(9X, 20I3)', (I, I = 0, MaxFrequency)
    PRINT '(11X, A)', Horizontal_Axis_Label

END SUBROUTINE DrawBarGraph
```

Figure 8.9 (cont.)

8.5 INTRODUCTION TO MULTIDIMENSIONAL ARRAYS AND MULTIPLY SUBSCRIPTED VARIABLES

There are many problems in which the data being processed can be naturally organized as a table. For example, suppose that water temperatures are recorded four times each day at each of three locations near the discharge outlet of a nuclear power plant's cooling system. These temperature readings can be arranged in a table having four rows and three columns:

	LOCATION		
TIME	**1**	**2**	**3**
1	65.5	68.7	62.0
2	68.8	68.9	64.5
3	70.4	69.4	66.3
4	68.5	69.1	65.8

In this table, the three temperature readings at time 1 are in the first row, the three temperatures at time 2 are in the second row, and so on.

These 12 data items can be conveniently stored in a two-dimensional array. The array declaration

```
REAL, DIMENSION(4, 3) :: Temperature
```

or

```
REAL, DIMENSION(1:4, 1:3) :: Temperature
```

reserves 12 memory locations for these data items. The doubly subscripted variable

```
Temperature(2,3)
```

then refers to the entry in the second row and third column of the table, that is, to the temperature 64.5 recorded at time 2 at location 3. In general

```
Temperature(I,J)
```

refers to the entry in the Ith row and Jth column, that is, to the temperature recorded at time I at location J.

To illustrate the use of an array with more than two dimensions, suppose that the temperature readings are made for one week, so that seven temperature tables are collected:

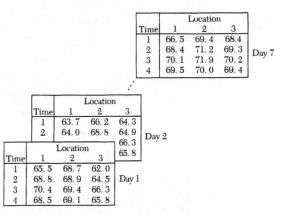

A three-dimensional array `TemperatureArray` declared by

    REAL, DIMENSION(4, 3, 7) :: TemperatureArray

or

    REAL, DIMENSION(1:4, 1:3, 1:7) :: TemperatureArray

can be used to store these 84 temperature readings. The value of the triply subscripted variable

    TemperatureArray(1,3,2)

is the temperature recorded at time 1 at location 3 on day 2, that is, the value 64.3 in the first row and third column of the second table. In general,

    TemperatureArray(Time,Location,Day)

is the temperature recorded at time `Time` at location `Location` on day `Day`.

The general form of a **compile-time array declaration** is

    type, DIMENSION(l₁:u₁, l₂:u₂,..., lₖ:uₖ)) :: &
        list-of-array-names

or

    type :: list-of-array-specifiers

where each array specifier has the form

    array-name(l₁:u₁, l₂:u₂, ..., lₖ:uₖ)

The number `k` of dimensions, called the **rank** of the array, is at most seven. Each pair $l_i : u_i$ must be a pair of integer constants specifying the range of values for the `i`th subscript to be from l_i through u_i; l_i may be omitted if its value is 1.

For example, consider the declarations

    REAL, DIMENSION(1:2, 21:3) :: Gamma
    REAL, DIMENSION(0:2, 0:3, 1:2) :: Beta

Gamma is a two-dimensional 2×5 real array, with the first subscript either 1 or 2 and the second subscript ranging from −1 through 3. Thus, the doubly subscripted variables `Gamma(1,-1)`, `Gamma(1,0)`, `Gamma(1,1)`, `Gamma(1,2)`, `Gamma(1,3)`, `Gamma(2,-1)`, `Gamma(2,0)`, `Gamma(2,1)`, `Gamma(2,2)`, and `Gamma(2,3)` may be used. The first subscript in the three-dimensional $3 \times 4 \times 2$ real array `Beta` is equal to 0, 1, or 2; the second subscript ranges from 0 through 3; and the third subscript is equal to 1 or 2.

The general form of an **allocatable** (or **run-time**) **array declaration** is

```
type, DIMENSION(:, :, ..., :), ALLOCATABLE :: list
```

It declares that each of the identifiers in the list is a k-dimensional array, where k is the number of colons (:) in the DIMENSION specifier. The number of subscripts in each dimension, called the **extent** of the array, will be specified during execution. For example,

```
REAL, DIMENSION(:, :, :), ALLOCATABLE :: Beta
REAL, DIMENSION(:, :), ALLOCATABLE :: Gamma
```

declares that Beta is a three-dimensional run-time array and that Gamma is a two-dimensional run-time array.

Memory is allocated and the actual ranges of subscripts are specified for a run-time array by an ALLOCATE statement. For example, for the run-time arrays Beta and Gamma declared above, the statement

```
ALLOCATE(Beta(0:2, 0:3, 1:2), Gamma(1:2, -1:3), &
         STAT = AllocateStatus)
```

allocates memory for Beta and Gamma, provided sufficient memory is available; if it is not, the integer status variable AllocateStatus will be assigned a positive value. It also specifies that the first subscript of the three-dimensional $3 \times 4 \times 2$ real array Beta will be 0, 1, or 2, that the second subscript ranges from 0 through 3, and that the third subscript is equal to 1 or 2; and that for the two-dimensional array Gamma, the first subscript will be either 1 or 2 and the second subscript ranges from −1 through 3. The DEALLOCATE statement used to release memory allocated to multidimensional allocatable arrays has the same form as for one-dimensional arrays.

Example: Temperature Table

Figure 8.10 gives a simple program that illustrates input and output of two-dimensional arrays. It reads the number of times NumTimes at which temperatures are recorded and the number of locations NumLocations at which these readings are made; allocates memory for an allocatable array Temperature having NumTimes rows and NumLocations columns; reads NumTimes × NumLocations values into this array; and displays these temperatures in tabular format. Note the use of nested implied DO loops to input the temperatures into the array and an implied DO loop within a DO loop to display them.

Figure 8.10. Two-dimensional arrays

```
PROGRAM Table_of_Temperatures
!-------------------------------------------------------------------
! Program illustrating i/o of a two-dimensional array. Variables
! used are:
!     Temperature    : two-dimensional array of temperatures
!     NumTimes       : number of times temperatures are recorded
!     NumLocs        : number of locations at which temperatures
!                      are recorded
!     AllocateStatus : status variable for ALLOCATE
!     Time           : row subscript for the table
!     Location       : column subscript for the table
!
! Input:  NumTimes, NumLocs, and elements of Temperature
! Output: The array Temperature in table format
!-------------------------------------------------------------------
```

```
IMPLICIT NONE
REAL, DIMENSION(:, :), ALLOCATABLE :: Temperature
INTEGER :: NumTimes, NumLocs, AllocateStatus, Time, Location

PRINT *, "Enter number of times temperatures are recorded"
PRINT *, "and number of locations where recorded:"
READ *, NumTimes, NumLocs

ALLOCATE (Temperature(NumTimes, NumLocs), STAT = AllocateStatus)
IF (AllocateStatus /= 0) STOP "*** Not enough memory ***"

PRINT *, "Enter the temperatures at the first location,"
PRINT *, "then those at the second location, and so on:"

READ *, ((Temperature(Time, Location), &
         Location = 1, NumLocs), Time = 1, NumTimes)

PRINT *
PRINT 10, (Location, Location = 1, NumLocs)
10 FORMAT(1X, T13, "Location" / 1X, "Time", 10I6)

DO Time = 1, NumTimes
   PRINT '(/1X, I3, 2X, 10F6.1/)', Time, &
         (Temperature(Time, Location), Location = 1, NumLocs)
END DO

DEALLOCATE (Temperature)

END PROGRAM Table_of_Temperatures
```

Sample Run

```
Enter number of times temperatures are recorded
and number of locations where recorded:
4, 3
Enter the temperatures at the first location,
then those at the second location, and so on:
65.5, 68.7, 62.0
68.8, 68.9, 64.5
70.4, 69.4, 66.3
68.5, 69.1, 65.8

          Location
Time    1     2     3

  1    65.5  68.7  62.0

  2    68.8  68.9  64.5

  3    70.4  69.4  66.3

  4    68.5  69.1  65.8
```

Figure 8.10   (cont.)

In Section 8.3, we considered array constants, array sections and subarrays, array expressions and assignment, and several intrinsic functions for processing one-dimensional arrays. Similar features are also provided in Fortran for processing multidimensional arrays.[2]

[2] For a description of the features provided in Fortran for processing multidimensional arrays, see Chapter 9 of our text *Fortran 90 for Engineers and Scientists*.

PRACTICE!

1. Write a declaration for a two-dimensional array whose rows are numbered from 1 through 5, whose columns are numbered from 1 through 10, and in which each element is a real value.

2. Write a declaration for a two-dimensional array whose rows are numbered from 0 through 4, whose columns are numbered from 1900 through 1910, and in which each element is a character string of length 5.

3. Write statements to set each element in the array of Exercise 1 to the sum of the row number and the column number in which that element appears.

4. Write statements to set each element in the array of Exercise 2 to a string of blanks.

For Exercises 5–16, assume that the following declarations have been made:

```
INTEGER, DIMENSION(3, 3) :: Array
INTEGER, DIMENSION(6) :: Number
INTEGER :: I, J
```

and that the following data is entered for those statements that involve input:

```
1, 2, 3, 4, 5, 6, 7, 8, 9
```

Tell what value (if any) is assigned to each array element, or explain why an error results.

5.
```
DO I = 1, 3
   DO J = 1, 3
      Array(I,J) = I + J
   END DO
END DO
```

6.
```
DO I = 1, 3
   DO J = 3, 1, -1
      IF (I == J) THEN
         Array(I,J) = 0
      ELSE
         Array(I,J) = 1
      END IF
   END DO
END DO
```

7.
```
DO I = 1, 3
   DO J = 1, 3
      IF (I < J) THEN
         Array(I,J) = -1
      ELSE IF (I == J) THEN
         Array(I,J) = 0
      ELSE
         Array(I,J) = 1
      END IF
   END DO
END DO
```

8.
```
DO I = 1, 3
   DO J = 1, I
      Array(I,J) = 0
   END DO
```

```
        DO J = I + 1, 3
            Array(I,J) = 2
        END DO
    END DO
 9. DO I = 1, 3
        DO J = 1, 3
            READ *, Array(I,J)
        END DO
    END DO
10. READ *, Array
11. READ *, ((Array(I,J), J = 1, 3), I = 1, 3)
12. READ *, ((Array(J,I), I = 1, 3), J = 1, 3)
13. READ *, ((Array(I,J), I = 1, 3), J = 1, 3)
14. DO I = 1, 3
        READ *, (Array(I,J), J = 1, 3)
    END DO
15. READ *, Number
    DO I = 1, 3
        DO J = 1, 3
            Array(I,J) = Number(I) + Number(J)
        END DO
    END DO
16. READ *, Number, (Array(1,J), J = 1, 3)
    DO I = 1, 2
        DO J = 1, 3
            Array(Number(I + 1), Number(J)) = Number(I + J)
        END DO
    END DO
```

APPLICATION: ELECTRICAL NETWORKS

PROBLEM

Consider the following electrical network containing six resistors and a battery:

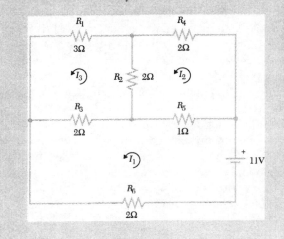

We wish to find the currents I_1, I_2, and I_3 in the three loops (where current is considered positive when the flow is in the direction indicated by the arrows).

Solution

Specification.   The input information for this problem is the circuit pictured in the diagram; in particular, the six resistances R_1, R_2, . . . , R_6 will be needed to solve the problem. The output consists of the currents I_1, I_2, and I_3 in the three loops.

Design.   The current through resistor R_1 is I_3, the current through resistor R_2 is $I_2 - I_3$, and so on. Ohm's law states that the voltage drop across a resistor is $R \cdot I$, where R is the resistance in ohms and I is the current in amperes. One of Kirchhoff's laws states that the algebraic sum of the voltage drops around any loop is equal to the applied voltage. This gives rise to the following system of linear equations for the loop currents I_1, I_2, and I_3:

$$5I_1 - 1I_2 - 2I_3 = 11$$
$$-1I_1 + 5I_2 - 2I_3 = 0$$
$$-2I_1 - 2I_2 + 7I_3 = 0$$

To find the loop currents, we must solve this *linear system*; that is, we must find the values for I_1, I_2, and I_3 that satisfy these equations simultaneously.

Linear systems arise in many areas of mathematics, science, and engineering, such as solving differential equations, electrical circuit problems, statical systems, and dynamical systems. Several methods for solving them have been developed, including the method called *Gaussian elimination*.

The computations required to solve a linear system can be carried out most conveniently if the coefficients and constants of the linear system are stored in a matrix. For the preceding linear system, this gives the following 3×4 matrix:

$$LinSys = \begin{bmatrix} 5 & -1 & -2 & 11 \\ -1 & 5 & -2 & 0 \\ -2 & -2 & 7 & 0 \end{bmatrix}$$

The first step in Gaussian elimination is to eliminate I_1 from the second and third equations by adding multiples of the first equation to these equatios. This corresponds to adding multiples of the first row of the matrix $LinSys$ to the second and third rows so that all entries in the first column except $LinSys(1, 1)$ are zero.Thus, we add $-LinSys(2, 1)/LinSys(1, 1) = 1/5$ times the first row of $LinSys$ to the second row and $-LinSys(3, 1)/LinSys(1, 1) = 2/5$ times the first row of the $LinSys$ to the third row to obtain the new matrix:

$$LinSys = \begin{bmatrix} 5 & -1 & -2 & 11 \\ 0 & 4.8 & -2.4 & 2.2 \\ 0 & -2.4 & 6.2 & 4.4 \end{bmatrix}$$

The variable I_2 is then eliminated from the third equation. The corresponding operation on the rows of the preceding matrix is to add $-LinSys(3,2)/LinSys(2,2) = 1/2$ times the second row to the third row. The resulting matrix thus is

$$LinSys = \begin{bmatrix} 5 & -1 & -2 & 11 \\ 0 & 4.8 & -2.4 & 2.2 \\ 0 & 0 & 5 & 5.5 \end{bmatrix}$$

which corresponds to the linear system

$$5I_1 - 1I_2 - 2I_3 = 11$$
$$4.8I_2 - 2.4I_3 = 2.2$$
$$5I_3 = 5.5$$

Once the original system has been reduced to such a *triangular* form, it is easy to find the solution. It is clear from the last equation that the value of I_3 is

$$I_3 = \frac{5.5}{5} = 1.100$$

Substituting this value for I_3 in the second equation and solving for I_2 gives

$$I_2 = \frac{2.2 + 2.4(1.1)}{4.8} = 1.008$$

and substituting these values for I_2 and I_3 in the first equation gives

$$I_1 = \frac{11 + 1.008 + 2(1.100)}{5} = 2.842$$

From this example, we see that the basic row operation performed at the ith step of the reduction process is

For $j = i + 1, i + 2, \ldots, n$

$$\text{Replace row}_j \text{ by row}_j - \frac{LinSys(j, i)}{LinSys(i, i)} \times \text{row}_i$$

Clearly, for this to be possible, the element $LinSys(i, i)$, called a **pivot element**, must be nonzero. If it is not, we must interchange the ith row with a later row to produce a nonzero pivot. In fact, to minimize the effect of roundoff error in the computations, it is best to rearrange the rows to obtain a pivot element that is largest in absolute value.

The following algorithm, which summarizes the Gaussian elimination method for solving a linear system, uses this pivoting strategy. Note that if it is not possible to find a nonzero pivot element at some stage, the linear system is said to be a *singular* system and does not have a unique solution.

GAUSSIAN ELIMINATION ALGORITHM

Algorithm to solve a linear system of N equations with N unknowns using Gaussian elimination. *LinSys* is the $N \times (N + 1)$ matrix that stores the coefficients and constants of the linear system.

Input: Coefficients and constants of the linear system

Output: Solution of the linear system or a message indicating that the system is singular

1. Enter the coefficients and constants of the linear system and store them in the matrix *LinSys*.

2. For I ranging from 1 to N, do the following:
   a. Find the entry *LinSys(K, I)*, $K = I, I + 1, \ldots, N$ that has the largest absolute value to use as a pivot.
   b. If the pivot is zero, display a message that the system is singular, and terminate the algorithm. Otherwise proceed.
   c. Interchange row I and row K.

d. For J ranging from $I + 1$ to N, do the following:

   Add $\dfrac{-LinSys(J, I)}{LinSys(I, I)}$ times the Ith row

   of *LinSys* to the Jth row of *LinSys* to eliminate $X(I)$ from the Jth equation.

3. Set $X(N)$ equal to $\dfrac{LinSys(N, N + 1)}{LinSys(N, N)}$.

4. For J ranging from $N - 1$ to 1 in steps of -1, do the following:

   Substitute the values of $X(J + 1), \ldots, X(N)$ in the Jth equation and solve for $X(J)$.

Coding and Execution. The program in Figure 8.11 implements this algorithm for Gaussian elimination. Because real numbers cannot be stored exactly, the statement implementing step 2b checks if ABS (LinSys(I,I)) is less than some small positive number Epsilon rather than if LinSys(I,I) is exactly 0.

Figure 8.11. Gaussian elimination

```
PROGRAM Linear_Systems
!-----------------------------------------------------------------
! Program to solve a linear system using Gaussian elimination.
! Variables used are:
!     N              : number of equations and unknowns
!     LinSys         : matrix for the linear system
!     X              : solution
!     AllocateStatus : status variable for ALLOCATE
!     I, J           : subscripts
!     Singular       : indicates if system is (nearly) singular
!
! Input:   The number of equations, the coefficients, and the
!          constants of the linear system
! Output:  The solution of the linear system or a message indicating
!          that the system is (nearly) singular
!-----------------------------------------------------------------

   IMPLICIT NONE
   REAL, DIMENSION(:, :), ALLOCATABLE :: LinSys
   REAL, DIMENSION(:), ALLOCATABLE :: X
   INTEGER :: N, AllocateStatus, I, J
   LOGICAL :: Singular


   ! Read N and allocate N x (N + 1) matrix LinSys
   ! and one-dimensional array X of size N
```

```
      WRITE (*, '(1X, A)', ADVANCE = "NO") "Enter number of equations: "
      READ *, N
      ALLOCATE(LinSys(N, N+1), X(N), STAT = AllocateStatus)
      IF (AllocateStatus /= 0) STOP "*** Not enough memory ***"

      ! Read coefficients and constants

      DO I = 1, N
         PRINT *, "Enter coefficients and constant of equation", I, ":"
         READ *, (LinSys(I,J), J = 1, N + 1)
      END DO

      ! Use subroutine Gaussian_Elimination to find the solution,
      ! and then display the solution

      CALL Gaussian_Elimination(LinSys, N, X, Singular)
      IF (.NOT. Singular) THEN
         PRINT *, "Solution is:"
         DO I = 1, N
            PRINT '(1X, "X(", I2, ") =", F8.3)', I, X(I)
         END DO
      ELSE
         PRINT *, "Matrix is (nearly) singular"
      END IF

      DEALLOCATE(LinSys, X)

CONTAINS

   !-Gaussian_Elimination-----------------------------------------------
   ! Subroutine to find solution of a linear system of N equations in N
   ! unknowns using Gaussian elimination, provided a unique solution
   ! exists. The coefficients and constants of the linear system are
   ! stored in the matrix LinSys. If the system is singular, Singular
   ! is returned as true, and the solution X is undefined. Local
   ! variables used are:
   !   I, J       : subscripts
   !   Multiplier : multiplier used to eliminate an unknown
   !   AbsPivot   : absolute value of pivot element
   !   PivotRow   : row containing pivot element
   !   Epsilon    : a small positive real value ("almost zero")
   !   Temp       : used to interchange rows of matrix
   !
   ! Accepts: Two-dimensional array LinSys and integer N
   ! Returns: One-dimensional array X and logical value Singular
   !--------------------------------------------------------------------

   SUBROUTINE Gaussian_Elimination(LinSys, N, X, Singular)

   INTEGER, INTENT(IN) :: N
   REAL, DIMENSION(N, N+1), INTENT(IN) :: LinSys
   REAL, DIMENSION(N), INTENT(OUT) :: X
```

Figure 8.11 (cont.)

```fortran
LOGICAL, INTENT(OUT) :: Singular
REAL, DIMENSION(N+1) :: Temp
REAL :: AbsPivot, Multiplier
REAL, PARAMETER :: Epsilon = 1E-7
INTEGER :: PivotRow

Singular = .FALSE.
DO I = 1, N

   ! Locate pivot element

   AbsPivot = ABS(LinSys(I, I))
   PivotRow = I
   DO J = I + 1, N
      IF (ABS(LinSys(J,I)) > AbsPivot) THEN
          AbsPivot = ABS(LinSys(J,I))
          PivotRow = J
      END IF
   END DO

   ! Check if matrix is (nearly) singular

   IF (AbsPivot < Epsilon) THEN
      Singular = .TRUE.
      RETURN
   END IF

   ! It isn't, so interchange rows PivotRow and I if necessary

   IF (PivotRow /= I) THEN
      Temp(I:N+1) = LinSys(I, I:N+1)
      LinSys(I, I:N+1) = LinSys(PivotRow, I:N+1)
      LinSys(PivotRow, I:N+1) = Temp(I:N+1)
   END IF

   ! Eliminate Ith unknown from equations I + 1, ..., N

   DO J = I + 1, N
      Multiplier = -LinSys(J,I) / LinSys(I,I)
      LinSys(J, I:N+1) = LinSys(J, I:N+1) &
                         + Multiplier * LinSys(I, I:N+1)
   END DO

END DO

! Find the solutions by back substitution

X(N) = LinSys(N, N + 1) / LinSys(N,N)
DO J = N - 1, 1, -1
   X(J) = (LinSys(J, N + 1) - &
          SUM(LinSys(J, J+1:N) * X(J+1:N))) / LinSys(J,J)
END DO
```

Figure 8.11 (cont.)

```
      END SUBROUTINE Gaussian_Elimination

   END PROGRAM Linear_Systems
```

Sample Runs

```
Enter number of equations: 3
Enter coefficients and constant of equation 1:
5 -1 -2 11
Enter coefficients and constant of equation 2:
-1 5 -2 0
Enter coefficients and constant of equation 3:
-2 -2 7 0
Solution is:
X( 1) = 2.842
X( 2) = 1.008
X( 3) = 1.100

Enter number of equations: 3
Enter coefficients and constant of equation 1:
1 1 1 1
Enter coefficients and constant of equation 2:
2 3 4 2
Enter coefficients and constant of equation 3:
3 4 5 3
Matrix is (nearly) singular
```

Figure 8.11 (cont.)

PROFESSIONAL SUCCESS: PROGRAM TESTING AND DEBUGGING

Run-time and logic errors refer to programming errors which are not detected by the computer during the compilation process. Both typically occur due to problems with either the design or coding of the program algorithm, and are indicated by incorrect output. Algorithm design errors, once found, are corrected in the software by rewriting the appropriate lines of code. After the algorithm has been verified, the program should be checked for typographical or branching errors which affect the output. This process, known as debugging, is done most efficiently through the use of diagnostic PRINT or WRITE statements, which allow the data-flow through the program to be monitored. In Fortran 90, PRINT statements direct output to the screen, while WRITE statements send output to an external file. Including a PRINT or WRITE statement after each line in a multi-step formula causes intermediate values to be output as they are calculated by the program. This technique allows the location of the initial error to be exactly pinpointed. PRINT or WRITE statements distributed throughout the program also ensure that each part is being executed the correct number of times. It is not uncommon to find cases where sections of the code are passed over entirely, due to incorrect branching or looping errors! Once a program is functioning correctly, the diagnostic PRINT or WRITE statements should either be removed or *commented out* so that none of the intermediate calculations are shown in the final version of the output.

*All "Professional Success" boxed material contributed by Jack Leifer, University of South Carolina—Aiken.

KEY TERMS

Allocatable (run-time) array
ALLOCATABLE attribute
Array constant
Array section
Array variable
Assumed-shape array
Automatic array
Bar graph
Binary search
Compile-time array
Data structure
DEALLOCATE statement

DIMENSION statement
Element
ELSEWHERE part
Extent (array)
Gaussian elimination
Histogram
Implied DO constructor
Implied DO loop
Linear search
Linear systems
One-dimensional array
Parent array

Pivot element
Quicksort
Rank
Searching
Selection sort
Sorting
Subarray
Subscript (index)
Subscripted variable
Subscript triplet
Vector subscript
WHERE construct

PROGRAMMING POINTERS

Program Style and Design

1. *One-dimensional arrays can be used to store lists of values.* If the data values must be processed more than once in a program, it is appropriate to store them in an array. Otherwise, it is usually better to use simple variables.

2. *Use named constants to dimension compile-time arrays.* If it is necessary to change the size of an array, only the named constants need to be changed.

3. *Use allocatable arrays in programs that must process arrays whose sizes vary from one execution of the program to the next.* Unlike programs that use compile-time arrays, no changes in declarations are required to process arrays of different sizes.

4. *Specify reasonable sizes for arrays.* The size of an array is determined by the number of data values to be stored. Specifying too large an array wastes memory.

5. *Use broadcasting rather than a loop to construct an array whose elements are all the same.* For example, using the assignment statement

```
A = 0
```

to zero out the array A is simpler than using the DO loop

```
DO I = 1, SIZE(A)
   A(I) = 0
END DO
```

6. *The basic arithmetic operations and instrinsic functions can be applied to arrays and are performed elementwise.* For example, two arrays A and B of the same size can be added to give array C by a simple assignment statement:

```
C = A + B
```

7. *Assumed-shape arrays can be used to design general subprograms for processing arrays.* For example, the subroutines for sorting and searching arrays-see Section 8.4—can be used with arrays of any size.

Potential Problems

1. *Declarations of array variables must include dimension information.* If, for example, Alpha has been declared by REAL :: Alpha with no DIMENSION specified, the compiler may interpret a reference to an element of

Alpha, as in X = Alpha(1), as a reference to a function named Alpha, which is an error.

2. *Subscripts must be integer valued and must stay within the range specified in the array declarations.* Very subtle errors can result from an array getting "out of bounds."

3. *In an assignment of one array to another, the arrays must be the same size.* For example, consider arrays A, B, and C declared by

```
INTEGER, DIMENSION(6) :: A = (/ 11, 22, 33, 44, 55, 66 /)
INTEGER, DIMENSION(10) :: B
INTEGER, DIMENSION(0:5) :: C
```

Array A cannot be assigned to array B since these arrays have different sizes. However, array A can be assigned to array C; even though they have different subscript ranges, they do have the same size.

4. *Subprograms that use assumed-shape arrays and array-valued functions must be internal subprograms or module subprograms, or there must be an interface block in each program unit that references them.*

5. *Allocatable arrays may not be formal arguments.*

Programming Problems

SECTION 8.2

1. The Cawker City Candy Company maintains two warehouses, one in Chicago and one in Detroit, each of which stocks at most 25 different items. Write a program that first reads the product numbers of the items stored in the Chicago warehouse and stores them in an array and then repeats this for the items stored in the Detroit warehouse, storing these product numbers in another array. The program should then find and display the *intersection* of these two lists of numbers, that is, the collection of product numbers common to both lists. Do not assume that the lists have the same number of elements.

2. Repeat Problem 1, but find and display the *union* of the two lists, that is, the collection of product numbers that are elements of at least one of the lists.

3. Suppose that a row of mailboxes are numbered 1 through 150 and that beginning with mailbox 2, we open the doors of all the even-numbered mailboxes. Next, beginning with mailbox 3, we go to every third mailbox, opening its door if it is closed and closing it if it is open. We repeat this procedure with every fourth mailbox, then every fifth mailbox, and so on. Write a program to determine which mailboxes will be closed when this procedure is completed.

4. Write a program to investigate the *birthday problem:* if there are *n* persons in a room, what is the probability that two or more of them have the same birthday? You might consider values of *n*, say from 10 through 40, and for each value of *n*, generate *n* random birthdays, and then scan the list to see whether two of them are the same. To obtain some approximate probabilities, you might do this 100 times for each value of *n*.

SECTIONS 8.3 AND 8.4

5. Write a program to test the subprogram in Exercise 16 or 17 of Section 8.3.

6. Write a program to test the subprogram in Exercise 18 or 19 of Section 8.3.

7. Write a program to test the subprogram in Exercise 20 or 21 of Section 8.3.

8. Write a program that calls subprograms to read and count a list of numbers and to calculate their mean, variance, and standard deviation. Print how many numbers there are and their mean, variance, and standard deviation with appropriate labels. If $\bar{x}$ denotes the mean of the numbers $x_1, \ldots, x_n$, the *variance* is the average of the squares of the deviations of the numbers from the mean:

$$\text{variance} = \frac{1}{n} \sum_{i=1}^{n} (x_i - \bar{x})^2$$

and the *standard deviation* is the square root of the variance.

9. Write a subprogram to evaluate a polynomial $a_0 + a_1 x + a_2 x^2 + \cdots + a_n x^n$ for any degree n, coefficients $a_0, a_1, \ldots, a_n$, and values of x that are supplied to it as arguments. Then write a program that reads a value of n, the coefficients, and various values of x and then uses this subprogram to evaluate the polynomial at these values.

10. A more efficient way of evaluating polynomials is *Horner's method* (also known as *nested multiplication*) in which a polynomial $a_0 + a_1 x + a_2 x^2 + \cdots + a_n x^n$ is rewritten as

$$a_0 + (a_1 + (a_2 + \cdots + (a_{n-1} + a_n x)x) \cdots x)x$$

For example:

$$7 + 6x + 5x^2 + 4x^3 + 3x^4 = 7 + (6 + (5 + (4 + 3x)x)x)x$$

Proceed as in Problem 9, but use Horner's method to evaluate the polynomial.

11. Write a subroutine to add two large integers of any length, say up to 300 digits. A suggested approach is as follows: treat each number as a list, each of whose elements is a block of digits of that number. For example, the integer 179,534,672,198 might be stored with $N(1) = 198$, $N(2) = 672$, $N(3) = 534$, $N(4) = 179$. Then add the two integers (lists) element by element, carrying from one element to the next when necessary. Test your subroutine with a program that reads two large integers and calls the subroutine to find their sum.

12. Proceed as in Problem 11, but write a subroutine to multiply two large integers, say of length up to 300 digits.

13. Write a program to test the selection sort and quicksort subroutines.

14. *Insertion sort* is an efficient sorting method for small data sets. It consists of beginning with the first item $X(1)$, then inserting $X(2)$ into this one-item list in the correct position to form a sorted two-element list, then inserting $X(3)$ into this two-element list in the correct position, and so on. For example, to sort the list 7, 1, 5, 2, 3, 4, 6, 0, the steps are as follows (the element being inserted is highlighted):

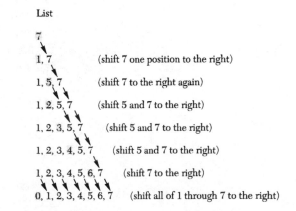

List

7

1, 7   (shift 7 one position to the right)

1, 5, 7   (shift 7 to the right again)

1, 2, 5, 7   (shift 5 and 7 to the right)

1, 2, 3, 5, 7   (shift 5 and 7 to the right)

1, 2, 3, 4, 5, 7   (shift 5 and 7 to the right)

1, 2, 3, 4, 5, 6, 7   (shift 7 to the right)

0, 1, 2, 3, 4, 5, 6, 7   (shift all of 1 through 7 to the right)

Write a subroutine to sort a list of items using this insertion sort method, and then write a main program that reads a set of values and calls this subroutine to sort them.

15. Insertion sort (see Problem 14) performs best for small lists and for partially sorted lists. *Shell sort* (named after Donald Shell) uses insertion sort to sort small sublists to produce larger, partially ordered sublists. Specifically, one begins with a "gap" of a certain size g and then uses insertion sort to sort sublists of elements that are g positions apart: first, $X(1)$, $X(1 + g)$, $X(1 + 2g)$, . . . , then the sublist $X(2)$, $X(2 + g)$, $X(2 + 2g)$, . . . , then $X(3)$, $X(3 + g)$, $X(3 + 2g)$, . . . , and so on. Next, the size of the gap g is reduced, and the process is repeated. This continues until the gap g is 1 and the final insertion sort results in the sorted list.

    Write a subroutine to sort a list of items using this Shell sort method, beginning with a gap g of the form $(3^k - 1) / 2$ for some integer k, and dividing it by 3 at each stage. Then write a main program that reads a set of values and calls this subroutine to sort them.

16. The Cawker City Candy Company manufactures different kinds of candy, each identified by a product number. Write a program that reads two arrays, `Number` and `Price`, in which `Number(1)` and `Price(1)` are the product number and the unit price for the first item, `Number(2)` and `Price(2)` are the product number and the unit price for the second item, and so on. The program should then allow the user to select one of the following options:

    a. Retrieve and display the price of a product whose number is entered by the user.

    b. Print a table displaying the product number and the price of each item.

    Make the program modular by using subprograms to perform the various tasks.

17. The following data was collected by a company and represents discrete values of a function for which an explicit formula is not known:

x	f(x)
1.123400	167.5600
2.246800	137.6441
3.370200	110.2523
4.493600	85.38444
5.617000	63.04068
6.740400	43.22099
7.863800	25.92535
8.987200	11.15376
10.11060	−1.093781
11.23400	−10.81726
12.35740	−18.01665
13.48080	−22.69202
14.60420	−24.84334
15.72760	−24.47060
16.85100	−21.57379
17.97440	−16.15295
19.09780	−8.208008
20.22120	2.260895
21.34460	15.25394
22.46800	30.77100
23.59140	48.81213
24.71480	69.37738
25.83820	92.46655
26.96160	118.0799
28.08500	146.2172

One can, however, use *linear interpolation* to approximate the $f(x)$-value for any given x-value between the smallest and the largest x-values. First, find the two x-values x_i and x_{i+1} in the list that bracket the given x-value, and then interpolate to find the corresponding $f(x)$-value:

$$f(x) = f(x_i) + \frac{f(x_{i+1}) - f(x_i)}{x_{i+1} - x_i}(x - x_i)$$

(If the x-value is out of range, print a message.) Test your program with the following x-values: −7.8, 1.1234, 13.65, 22.5, 23.5914, 25, 25.085, and 33.8.

18. Write a program to test the function subprogram for calculating cross products in Exercise 22 of Section 8.3.

19. Write a program to test the function subprogram for finding unit vectors in Exercise 23 of Section 8.3.

20. Write a program to test the function subprogram for finding the angle between two vectors in Exercise 24 of Section 8.3.

SECTION 8.5

21. A car manufacturer has collected data on the noise level (measured in decibels) produced by six different models of cars at seven different speeds. This data is summarized in the following table:

CAR	SPEED (MPH)						
	20	**30**	**40**	**50**	**60**	**70**	**80**
1	88	90	94	102	111	122	134
2	75	77	80	86	94	103	113
3	80	83	85	94	100	111	121
4	68	71	76	85	96	110	125
5	77	84	91	98	105	112	119
6	81	85	90	96	102	109	120

Write a program that will display this table in a nice format and that will calculate and display the average noise level for each car model, the average noise level at each speed, and the overall average noise level.

22. An electronics firm manufactures four types of radios. The number of capacitors, resistors, and transistors (denoted by C, R, and T, respectively) in each of these is given in the following table:

RADIO TYPE	C	R	T
1	2	6	3
2	6	11	5
3	13	29	10
4	8	14	7

Each capacitor costs $0.35, a resistor costs $0.25, and a transistor costs $1.40. Write a program to find the total cost of the components for each of the types of radios.

23. Suppose that each of the four edges of a thin square metal plate is maintained at a constant temperature and that we wish to determine the steady-state temperature at each interior point of the plate. To do this, we divide the plate into squares (the corners of which are called *nodes*) and find the temperature at each interior node by averaging the four neighboring temperatures; that is, if T_{ij} denotes the old temperature at the node in row i and column j, then

$$\frac{T_{i-1,j} + T_{i,j-1} + T_{i,j+1} + T_{i+1,j}}{4}$$

will be the new temperature.

To model the plate, we can use a two-dimensional array, with each array element representing the temperature at one of the nodes. Write a program that first reads the four constant temperatures (possibly different) along the edges of the plate, and some estimate of the temperature at the interior points, and uses these values to initialize the elements of the array. Then determine the steady-state temperature at each interior node by repeatedly averaging the temperatures at its four neighbors, as just described. Repeat this procedure until the new temperature at each interior node differs from the old temperature by no more than some specified small amount. Then print the array and the number of iterations used to produce the final result. (It may also be of interest to print the array at each stage of the iteration.)

APPLICATION

24. Write the system of linear equations for the loop currents I_1, I_2, and I_3 in the following simple resistor and battery circuit. Then use Gaussian elimination to find these currents.

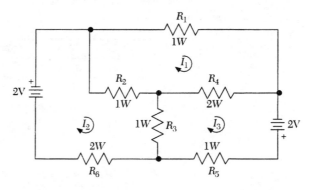

25. Consider the following electrical network:

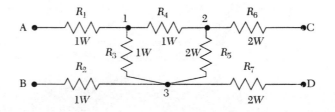

If the voltages at the endpoints are $V_A = V_B = V_C = V_D = 1V$, then applying Kirchoff's law of currents at the nodes 1, 2, and 3 yields (after some simplification) the following system of linear equations for the voltages V_1, V_2, and V_3 at these nodes:

$$\frac{5}{2}V_1 - \frac{1}{2}V_2 - V_3 = 1$$

$$-\frac{1}{2}V_1 + \frac{3}{2}V_2 - \frac{1}{2}V_3 = \frac{1}{2}$$

$$-V_1 - \frac{1}{2}V_2 + 3V_3 = \frac{3}{2}$$

Use Gaussian elimination to find these voltages.

9

Other Data Types

9.1 PARAMETERIZED DATA TYPES

The internal representation of data varies from one machine to another. For example, 32 bits are typically used to store integers, which provides values in the range -2147483648 through 2147483647; 32 bits are also commonly used for real values, also called *single-precision* values, which provides approximately seven digits of precision and a range of values from approximately -10^{38} to 10^{38}. For computations in which more precision is needed than is available using the default real data type, Fortran provides parameterized real types.

A parameterized type declaration has the form

```
type-specifier(KIND = kind-number),
attributes :: list
```

or

```
type-specifier(kind-number), attributes
:: list
```

where `kind-number` is an integer constant or a constant integer expression whose value is positive. The kind numbers, called **kind type parameters**, for the various types are machine dependent. There must be at least two kinds of real types, one for single-precision values and another for **double-precision** values, which provides approximately

OBJECTIVES

In this chapter, you will

- See how to declare and use parameterized data types and complex data types.
- Read about derived data types and structures.
- Apply the concepts learned to an A-C circuit design problem.

twice as many significant digits as single precision. The kind numbers for these two types typically are 1 and 2:

TYPE	KIND NUMBER	DESCRIPTION
REAL	1	Single-precision values with approximately 7 significant digits; usually stored in 32 bits (normally the default real type)
REAL	2	Double-precision values with approximately 14 significant digits; usually stored in 64 bits

For example,

```
REAL (KIND = 2) :: Z
REAL (KIND = 2), DIMENSION(5,5) :: Beta
```

declares the variable Z and the 5×5 array Beta to be real of kind 2 (commonly, double precision).

The number of kinds of integer types varies from one Fortran compiler to another, but most compilers provide at least three and some provide four kinds:

TYPE	KIND NUMBER	DESCRIPTION
INTEGER	1	8-bit integers: -2^7 through $2^7 - 1$
INTEGER	2	16-bit integers: -2^{15} through $2^{15} - 1$
INTEGER	3	32-bit integers: -2^{31} through $2^{31} - 1$
INTEGER	4	64-bit integers: -2^{63} through $2^{63} - 1$

Because the number of integer and real kinds and their meaning differ from one compiler to another, Fortran provides several intrinsic functions for use with parameterized types. Two of the most useful functions are SELECTED_REAL_KIND and SELECTED_INT_KIND because they facilitate writing programs that are portable from one machine to another.

A reference to SELECTED_REAL_KIND has the form

```
SELECTED_REAL_KIND(p,r)
```

where p and r are integers, with r optional. It returns a kind type parameter that will provide at least p decimal digits of precision and a range of at least -10^r to 10^r, provided such a kind is available. It returns -1 if there is no kind with the requested range, -2 if there is no kind with the requested precision, and -3 if no kind with either the range or precision is available. For example, the statement

```
REAL(KIND = SELECTED_REAL_KIND(20, 50)) :: X
```

declares that X is to be a real variable whose values are to have at least 20 decimal digits of precision and may be in the range -10^{50} to 10^{50}. If no such kind is available, the specified kind number is negative and the declaration causes a compilation error. The statements

```
INTEGER, PARAMETER :: Prec10 = SELECTED_REAL_KIND(10)
REAL(KIND = Prec10) :: A, B
```

declare that A and B are real variables whose values are to have at least 10 decimal digits of precision. This declaration cannot fail because, as we have noted, a real kind that provides approximately 14 digits of precision must be supported.

A reference to `SELECTED_INT_KIND` has the form

```
SELECTED_INT_KIND(r)
```

where r is an integer. It returns a kind type parameter that will provide a range of at least -10^r to 10^r, if such a kind is available; otherwise it returns -1. For example, the statements

```
INTEGER, PARAMETER :: Range20 = SELECTED_INT_KIND(20)
INTEGER(KIND = Range20) :: M, N
```

declare that M and N are integer variables whose values may have up to 20 digits. If no such integer kind is available, a compiler error will result.

To specify the kind of a constant, an underscore followed by a kind number is appended to the constant (except for characters[1]). For example,

```
123456789_3
```

is an integer constant whose kind number is 3, and

```
12345678901234567890_Range20
```

is an integer constant whose kind number is `Range20`, where `Range20` is the named constant defined earlier by

```
INTEGER, PARAMETER :: Range20 = SELECTED_INT_KIND(20)
```

Similarly,

```
1.23456789123_2
```

is a real constant whose kind number is 2, and

```
0.1234554321_Prec10
```

is a real constant whose kind number is `Prec10`, where the named constant `Prec10` was defined earlier by

```
INTEGER, PARAMETER :: Prec10 = SELECTED_REAL_KIND(10)
```

When a value is assigned to a parameterized real variable in a program, it is important that the kind of the value being assigned is the same as the kind of the variable. For example, consider the following program:

```
PROGRAM Demo_2

   IMPLICIT NONE
   REAL :: X
   INTEGER, PARAMETER :: DP = SELECTED_REAL_KIND(14)
   REAL(KIND = DP) :: A, B

   X = 0.1
   B = 0.1_DP
   A = X
   PRINT *, A
   A = B
   PRINT *, A

END PROGRAM Demo_2
```

---

[1] See Chapter 11 of our text *Fortran 90 for Engineers and Scientists*.

On some systems the values displayed for A by the first two PRINT statements resemble the following:

```
0.1000000014901161
0.100000000000000
```

The value 0.1_DP of the real variable B of kind DP is stored with more precision than the value 0.1 of the single-precision variable X. This accounts for the discrepancy between the two values displayed for A.

It is important to ensure that all variables, arrays, and functions that are to have values of a particular kind are declared to be of that kind. For example, if R is a real variable of kind DP and Area is an ordinary (single-precision) real variable, the computation in the statement

```
Area = 3.1415926535898_DP * R ** 2
```

will be carried out in extended precision, but the resulting value will then be assigned to the single-precision variable Area, thus losing approximately half of the significant digits.

As these examples illustrate, although mixed-kind expressions are permitted, accuracy may be lost because of the use of lower-precision constants or variables. For example, if the assignment statement

```
A = (B + 3.7) ** 2
```

were used in the program Demo_2, the value for A would be limited to single-precision accuracy because of the single-precision constant 3.7. To ensure that the expression has the same kind as A, the assignment statement

```
A = (B + 3.7_DP) ** 2
```

should be used.

9.2 THE COMPLEX DATA TYPE

A **complex number** is a number of the form

$$a + bi$$

where a and b are real numbers and

$$i^2 = -1$$

The first real number, a, is called the **real part** of the complex number, and the second real number, b, is called the **imaginary part**.[2]

In Fortran, a complex constant is represented as a pair of real constants

```
(a, b)
```

where a and b represent the real part and the imaginary part of the complex number, respectively. For example,

```
(1.0, 1.0)
(-6.0, 7.2)
(-5.432, -1.4142)
```

---

[2] It is customary in electrical engineering to use j instead of i to denote the complex number $\sqrt{-1}$. This helps to avoid confusion with I or i used to denote current.

are complex constants equivalent to

$$1.0 + 1.0i$$
$$-6.0 + 7.2i$$
$$-5.432 - 1.4142i$$

respectively.

The names of variables, arrays, or functions that are complex may be any legal Fortran names, but their types must be declared using the COMPLEX **type statement**. For example, the statements

```
COMPLEX :: A, B
COMPLEX, DIMENSION(10,10) :: Rho
```

declare A, B, and the 10 × 10 array Rho to be complex variables. The statements

```
INTEGER, PARAMETER :: DP = SELECTED_REAL_KIND(14)
COMPLEX(KIND = DP) :: Gamma
```

or

```
INTEGER, PARAMETER :: DP = SELECTED_REAL_KIND(14)
COMPLEX(DP) :: Gamma
```

declare the variable Gamma whose type is complex of kind DP. For a complex value, this means that both the real part and the imaginary part are real values of kind DP (that is, both are double-precision values).

The basic arithmetic operations for complex numbers are denoted in Fortran by the usual operators +, −, *, /, and **. The only relational operators that may be used with complex values are == and /=.

Some of the mathematical functions commonly used with complex numbers are the absolute value, conjugate, and complex exponential functions. For the complex number $z = a + bi$, these functions are defined as follows:

Absolute value: $|z| = \sqrt{a^2 + b^2}$

Conjugate: $\bar{z} = a - bi$

Complex exponential: $e^z = e^a(\cos b + i \sin b)$

These three functions are implemented in Fortran by the intrinsic functions ABS, CONJG, and EXP, respectively. Several of the other functions listed in Table 2.2, such as SIN, COS, and LOG, may also be used with complex arguments. Three intrinsic functions that are useful in converting from real type to complex type, and vice versa, are

AIMAG(z)	Gives the imaginary part of the complex argument z as a real value whose kind is the same as the kind of z
CMPLX(x, y, KIND = k) or CMPLX(x, KIND = k)	Converts the two integer, real, or double-precision arguments x and y into a complex number. The first argument x becomes the real part of the complex number, and the second argument y becomes the imaginary part. The second form is equivalent to CMPLX(x, 0, KIND = k). The KIND = specifier is optional.
REAL(z, KIND = k)	Gives the real part of the complex argument z. The KIND = specifier is optional.

Complex values may be read using a list-directed READ statement, with the complex numbers entered as a pair of real numbers enclosed in parentheses. They may also be read using a formatted READ statement. In this case, a pair of F, E, EN, ES, or G descriptors may be used for each complex value to be read, and parentheses are not used to enclose the parts of the complex number when it is entered. Complex values displayed using a list-directed output statement appear as a pair of real values separated by a comma and enclosed within parentheses. For formatted output of complex values, a pair of F, E, EN, ES, or G descriptors is used for each complex value.

APPLICATION: A-C CIRCUITS

PROBLEM

An a-c circuit contains a capacitor, an inductor, and a resistor in series:

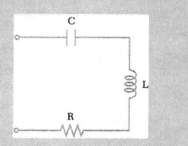

A program must be written to calculate the current in this circuit for several frequencies and voltages.

Solution

Specification The input to the problem will be the resistance, the inductance, the capacitance, the frequency of the a-c source, and the voltage. The output will be the current in the circuit. Thus, a specification for the problem is as follows:

Input:	Resistance (ohms)
	Inductance (henrys)
	Capacitance (farads)
	Frequency (radians/second)
	Voltage (volts)
Output:	Current (amperes)

Design The impedance Z_R for a resistor is simply the resistance R, but for inductors and capacitors, it is a function of the frequency. The impedance Z_L of an inductor is the complex value given by

$$Z_L = \omega L i$$

where ω is the frequency (in radians per second) of the a-c source and L is the self-inductance (in henrys). For a capacitor, the impedance is

$$Z_C = \frac{-i}{\omega C}$$

where C is the capacitance (in farads). The total impedance Z is then given by

$$Z = Z_R + Z_L + Z_C$$

and the current I by

$$I = \frac{V}{Z}$$

An algorithm for this problem is straightforward:

ALGORITHM FOR A-C CIRCUIT PROBLEM

Algorithm to compute the current in an a-c circuit containing a capacitor, an inductor, and a resistor in series.

Input:	Resistance (R), inductance (L), capacitance (C), frequency (*Omega*)
Output:	Current (I)

1. Enter R, L, C.
2. Enter *Omega*.
3. Enter the voltage V as a complex number.
4. Compute the impedance Z.
5. Compute the current I.
6. Display I.

Coding, Execution, and Testing The program in Figure 9.1 implements this algorithm. A sample run is also shown.

Figure 9.1. A-C circuit

```
PROGRAM AC_Circuit
!-------------------------------------------------------------------
! Program to compute the current in an a-c circuit containing a
! capacitor, an inductor, and a resistor in series.   Variables
! used are:
!    R     : resistance (ohms)
!    L     : inductance (henrys)
!    C     : capacitance (farads)
!   Omega : frequency (radians/second)
!    V     : voltage (volts)
!    Z     : total impedance
!    I     : current (amperes)
!
! Input:  R, L, C, Omega, and V
! Output: I
!-------------------------------------------------------------------

   IMPLICIT NONE
   REAL :: R, L, C, Omega
   COMPLEX :: V, Z, I

   WRITE (*, '(1X, A)', ADVANCE = "NO") &
        "Enter resistance (ohms), inductance (henrys), ", &
        "and capacitance (farads): "
   READ *, R, L, C
   WRITE (*, '(1X, A)', ADVANCE = "NO") "Enter frequency (radians/second): "
   READ *, Omega
   WRITE (*, '(1X, A)', ADVANCE = "NO") &
        "Enter voltage as a complex number in the form (x, y): "
   READ *, V

   ! Calculate resistance using complex arithmetic
   Z = R +  Omega * L * (0.0, 1.0)  - (0.0, 1.0) / (Omega * C)

   ! Calculate and display current using complex arithmetic
   I = V / Z
   PRINT *
   PRINT 10, I, ABS(I)
   10 FORMAT(1X, "Current = ", F10.4, " + ", &
           F10.4, "I" / 1X, "with magnitude = ", F10.4)

END PROGRAM AC_Circuit
```

Sample Run

```
Enter resistance (ohms), inductance (henrys),
and capacitance (farads): 5000, .03, .02
Enter frequency (radians/second): 377
Enter voltage as a complex number in the form (x, y): (60000, 134)

Current =     12.0000 +      0.0000I
with magnitude =     12.0000
```

PRACTICE!

1. (True or false) Parameterized real data types make it possible to store the exact representation of a real number.

2. The declaration `INTEGER(KIND = _____) :: Number` declares that `Number` is an integer variable whose value may contain up to 15 digits.

3. (True or false) Every Fortran 90 compiler must provide at least two kinds of reals.

4. The declaration `REAL(KIND = _____) :: X` declares that `X` is a real variable whose values have at least 12 digits of precision and for which the range is from -10^{40} to 10^{40}.

5. (True or false) In the complex number $a + bi$, a and b are called the real parts and i the imaginary part.

6. (True or false) If `Z` is a complex variable, then the statement `Z = (2.0, 3.0)` is a valid assignment statement.

7. (True or false) If `Z` is a complex variable and `X` and `Y` are real variables, then the statement `Z = (X, Y)` is a valid assignment statement.

8. If `Z` is a complex variable, the statement `Z = (2, 3) * (1, 4)` assigns the value _____ to `Z`.

9. (True or false) The formatted output of a complex value is accomplished using a `Cw.d` format descriptor.

10. (True or false) Real values may be assigned to complex variables.

11. (True or false) If `Z` is a complex variable, `Z > (0, 0)` is a valid logical expression.

For Exercises 12–23, assume the declarations

```
INTEGER :: N1, N2
REAL :: R1, R2
INTEGER, PARAMETER :: DP = SELECTED_REAL_KIND(14)
REAL(KIND = DP) :: D1, D2
COMPLEX :: C1, C2
```

and the assignment statements

```
N1 = 2
R1 = 0.5
D1 = 0.1_DP
C1 = (6.0,8.0)
```

Find the value assigned to the specified variable by the given assignment statement, or indicate why there is an error.

12. `D2 = 1.23456_DP * D1`

13. `C2 = C1 ** N1`

14. `R2 = C1`

15. `R2 = REAL(C1)`

16. `R2 = AIMAG(C1)`

17. `C2 = C1 * (0,1)`

18. `C2 = 1 / C1`

19. `R2 = ABS(C1)`

20. `C2 = CONJG(C1)`

21. `C2 = CMPLX(N1, R1)`

22. `C2 = REAL(C1) + AIMAG(C1)`

23. `C2 = EXP((0,0))`

24. Write declarations for integer variables `Num_1` and `Num_2` whose values will be between −1,000,000 and 1,000,000.

25. Write declarations for a real variable `Alpha` whose values will have at least 12 digits of precision.

26. Write declarations for real variables `X` and `Y` whose values will have at least 9 digits of precision and will be between $-1,000,000$ and $1,000,000$.

27. For `Alpha` as in Exercise 25, write a statement to assign `Alpha` the first 10 digits of $\pi (\pi = 3.1415926535897932\overline{38} \ldots)$.

28. Write declarations for a complex variable `Beta` whose values will have real and imaginary parts with at least 9 digits of precision and which will be between $-1,000,000$ and $1,000,000$.

PROFESSIONAL SUCCESS: USE OF EXTERNAL LIBRARIES

Besides the intrinsic functions and procedures described in Appendix A, many implementations of Fortran 90 allow access to additional sets of external routines. IMSL (International Mathematics and Statistics Library) and NAG (Numerical Algorithms Group) are external libraries which each contain about one thousand different program modules; they cover matrix and vector operations, statistical analysis and various specialized functions. Like programmer-defined modules, both IMSL and NAG routines are declared at the beginning of the main program unit via USE statements. Before they can be referenced, however, some implementations of Fortran 90 require that the external libraries be explicitly *linked* to the program during the compilation process. Once the appropriate declarations and links have been made, the external functions may be called as subroutines from the main program when necessary. Use of these external routines (as well those intrinsic functions provided as part of Fortran 90) in place of programmer-generated code is preferable for a number of reasons. For instance, the amount of debugging and testing necessary is generally reduced when library routines are used, since they replace newly written code which is prone to error. In addition, library functions are written using the most up-to-date and efficient mathematical algorithms available; hence, they will tend to compile and run more quickly than programmer-generated code. Computer lists of external modules, and their associated functions may be accessed through the internet: *www.nag.co. uk/numeric/FBFN/fl90plus.html* (NAG) and *www.vni. com/products/imsl* (IMSL).

*All "Professional Success" boxed material contributed by Jack Leifer, University of South Carolina—Aiken.

9.3 INTRODUCTION TO DERIVED DATA TYPES AND STRUCTURES

Arrays are used to store elements of the same type, but in many situations we need to process items that are related in some way but that are not all of the same type. For example, a date consists of a month name (of character type), a day (of integer type), and a year (of integer type); a record of computer usage might contain, among other items, a user's name and password (character strings), identification number (integer), resource limit (integer), and resources used to date (real). In Fortran 90, a **derived data type** can be used to declare a **structure**, which can be used to store such related data items of possibly different types. The positions in the structure in which these data items are stored are called the **components** of the structure. Thus, a structure for storing computer usage information might contain a name component, a password component, an identification number component, a resource limit, and a resources used component.

A simple form of a derived type definition is

```
TYPE type-name
    declaration₁
    declaration₂
        ⋮
    declarationₖ
END TYPE type-name
```

where `type-name` is a valid Fortran identifier that names the derived type and each `declaration`ᵢ declares one or more components in a structure of this type. For example, the type definition

```
TYPE Computer_Usage_Info
    CHARACTER(15):: LastName, FirstName
    INTEGER :: IdNumber
    CHARACTER(6) :: Password
    INTEGER :: ResourceLimit
    REAL :: ResourcesUsed
END TYPE Computer_Usage_Info
```

defines the derived type `Computer_Usage_Info`. A structure of this type will have six components: `LastName` and `FirstName`, which are of character type with values of length 15; `IdNumber` of integer type; `Password` of character type with values of length 6; `ResourceLimit` of integer type; and `ResourcesUsed` of real type. A typical value of type `Computer_Usage_Info` might be pictured as follows:

LastName	FirstName	IdNumber	Password	ResourceLimit	ResourcesUsed
Babbage	Charles	10101	ADA	750	380.81

The components of a structure need not be of different types. For example, the type definition

```
TYPE Point
    REAL :: X, Y
END TYPE Point
```

defines the derived type `Point`, and a structure of type `Point` will have two components named `X` and `Y`, each of which is of real type:

X	Y
2.5	3.2

The type identifiers in such definitions can then be used to declare the types of structures in declarations of the form

```
TYPE(type-name) :: list-of-identifiers
```

For example,

```
TYPE(Point) :: P, Q
```

declares structures `P` and `Q` of type `Point`;

```
TYPE(Computer_Usage_Info) :: User
```

declares a structure `User` of type `Computer_Usage_Info`; and

```
TYPE(Computer_Usage_Info), DIMENSION(50) :: UserList
```

or

```
TYPE(Computer_Usage_Info) :: UserList(50)
```

declares a one-dimensional array `UserList`, each of whose elements is a structure of type `Computer_Usage_Info`.

Values of a derived type are sequences of values for the components of that derived type. Their form is

```
type-name(list of component values)
```

For example,

```
Point(2.5, 3.2)
```

is a value of type `Point` and can be assigned to variable `P` of type `Point`,

```
P = Point(2.5, 3.2)
```

or associated with a named constant `Center` of type `Point`,

```
TYPE(Point), PARAMETER :: Center = Point(2.5, 3.2)
```

Similarly,

```
Computer_Usage_Info("Babbage", "Charles", &
                    10101, "ADA", 750, 380.81)
```

is a value of type `Computer_Usage_Info` and can be assigned to the variable `User` or to a component of the array `UserList`:

```
User = Computer_Usage_Info("Babbage", "Charles", &
                           10101, "ADA", 750, 380.81)
UserList(1) = User
```

The components in such *derived-type constructors* may also be variables or expressions. For example, if `A` is a real variable with value 1.1, the assignment statement

```
P = Point(A, 2*A)
```

assigns the structure having real components 1.1 and 2.2 to the variable `P`.

Individual components of a structure are accessed using **qualified variables** formed by joining the structure name to the component name with the **component selector** character (%):

```
structure-name%component-name
```

For example, `P%X` is the first component of the structure `P` of type `Point`, and `P%Y` is the second component; `UserList(1)%LastName`, `UserList(1)%First-Name`, `UserList(1)%IdNumber`, `UserList(1)%Password`, `UserList(1)-%ResourceLimit`, and `UserList(1)%ResourcesUsed` refer to the six components of the structure `UserList(1)`.

Each component of a structure has a specified type and may be used in the same way as any item of that type. For example, since `User%LastName` is of character type, it may be assigned a value in an assignment statement

```
User%LastName = "Babbage"
```

or by an input statement

```
READ *, User%LastName
```

Its value can be displayed by an output statement

```
PRINT *, User%LastName
```

and its value can be modified by a substring reference:

```
User%LastName(1:1) = "C"
```

Input and output of a structure must be done componentwise, that is, by reading or displaying the value of each component in the structure individually. For example, to input a value for User, we must read values for each component of User separately:

```
READ *, User%LastName, User%FirstName, User%IdNumber, &
        User%Password, User%ResouceLimit, User%ResourcesUsed
```

Similarly, to display the value of User, we must display each component individually, as in

```
PRINT '(1X, "Name:            ", 2A)', User%FirstName,
                                        User%LastName
PRINT '(1X, "Id Number:       ", I5)', User%IdNumber
PRINT '(1X, "Resource Limit: ", I5)', User%ResouceLimit
PRINT '(1X, "Used to date:    ", F6.2)', User%ResourcesUsed
```

Sometimes it is necessary to copy the components of one structure into another structure. This can be done with series of assignment statements that copy the individual components of one structure to the components of the other structure. For example, if User_1 and User_2 are structure variables of type Computer_Usage_Info and we wish to copy the components of User_1 into User_2, we could use

```
User_2%LastName = User_1%LastName
User_2%FirstName = User_1%FirstName
User_2%IdNumber = User_1%IdNumber
User_2%Password = User_1%Password
User_2%ResourceLimit = User_1%ResourceLimit
User_2%ResourcesUsed = User_1%ResourcesUsed
```

If the structures have the same type, this can be done more conveniently with a single assignment statement of the form

```
structure-variable = structure-expression
```

For example, the six assignment statements above could be replaced by the single assignment statement

```
User_2 = User_1
```

Structures may also be used as arguments of subprograms. In this case, the corresponding actual and formal structure arguments must have the same type. The value returned by a function may also be a structure.

Example: Retrieving Computer Usage Records

To illustrate processing of structures, suppose that a data file contains information about computer users like that we have been considering: the user's last name, first name, id number, and login password, amount of resources allocated to the user, and the amount of computer resources used to date:

```
Babbage         Charles         10101ADA    75038081
Newton          Isaac           10102APPLE  65059884
Leibniz         Gottfried       10103CALC   25019374
Fahrenheit      Freda           10104FRZ32  25017793
Celsius         Christine       10105FRZ0   85019191
Tower           Lean            10106PISA   35022395
Vander          VanHenry        10107VAN    75016859
Freeloader      Freddie         10108RED    450 7661
    :               :               :           :
Yale            Harvard         20125IVY    15012770
```

Each line of the file consists of a user's last name, first name, five-digit id number, password with up to six characters, resource limit (in dollars) with at most four digits, and resources used to date, which appears with no decimal point but is to be processed as a number with three digits before the decimal point and two following it. A program is to be written to search this file for a specified user and, if it is found, display the user's id number, name, and percentage of resources remaining.

Since each line of information in this file consists of a user's last name, first name, id number, password, resource limit, and resources used to date, it is natural to organize this information in structures of type `Computer_Usage_Info`, as in the program in Figure 9.2. This program repeatedly reads a person's id number from the keyboard and reads id numbers from the file until a match is found or an input error occurs or the end of the file is reached. If the id number is found, the program then reads values for the remaining components of the structure User and displays the required information.

Figure 9.2. Retrieving computer usage records

```
PROGRAM Computer_Usage_Records
!-------------------------------------------------------------------
! Program to read id numbers from the keyboard, search a file of
! computer usage records to determine if this is the number of a
! computer user, and if so, retrieve and display information about
! that user.  Identifiers used are:
!   Computer_Usage_Info : name of a derived type
!   FileName            : name of computer usage file
!   OpenStatus          : status variable for OPEN
!   InputStatus         : status variable for READ
!   User                : structure of type Computer_Usage_Info
!   InputNumber         : an id number entered from the keyboard
!   UserNumber          : an id number in the computer usage file
!   Found               : indicates if InputNumber matches some
!                         user's id number in the file
!
! Input (keyboard): InputNumber
! Input (file) :    UserNumber and computer usage record assigned
!                   to User
! Output (screen) : User's id number, name, and percentage of computer
!                   resources remaining or a message that the id number
!                   was not found in the file
!-------------------------------------------------------------------

IMPLICIT NONE
```

```
TYPE Computer_Usage_Info
   CHARACTER(15):: LastName, FirstName
   INTEGER :: IdNumber
   CHARACTER(6) :: Password
   INTEGER :: ResourceLimit
   REAL :: ResourcesUsed
END TYPE Computer_Usage_Info

CHARACTER(20) :: FileName
TYPE(Computer_Usage_Info) :: User
INTEGER :: OpenStatus, InputStatus, InputNumber, UserNumber
LOGICAL :: Found

! Get name of file and open it for input
WRITE (*, '(1X, A)', ADVANCE = "NO") "Enter name of computer usage file: "
READ *, FileName
OPEN (UNIT = 10, FILE = FileName, STATUS = "OLD", IOSTAT = OpenStatus)
IF (OpenStatus > 0) STOP "*** Cannot open file ***"

! Read id numbers and search file for matches
DO
   PRINT *
   WRITE (*, '(1X, A)', ADVANCE = "NO") "Enter id number (0 to stop): "
   READ *, InputNumber
   IF (InputNumber == 0) EXIT
   ! If no more id numbers to process, terminate repetition

   ! Otherwise search file for id number
   DO
      READ (10, '(T31, I5)', IOSTAT = InputStatus) UserNumber
      IF (InputStatus > 0) STOP "*** Input error ***"
      IF (InputStatus < 0) EXIT ! end of file
      ! If end of file reached, stop searching

      ! Else check if ids match
      Found = (InputNumber == UserNumber)
      IF (Found) EXIT
   END DO

   ! Id found -- back up in the file, read the user info
   ! and display the required information

   IF (Found) THEN
      BACKSPACE 10
      READ (10, '(2A15, 10X, I4, F5.2)') &
         User%LastName, User%FirstName, &
         User%ResourceLimit, User%ResourcesUsed
      PRINT &
         '(1X, I5, 1X, 2A / 1X, "has used", F5.1, "% of resources")',&
         UserNumber, User%FirstName, User%LastName, &
         100.0 * (User%ResourceLimit - User%ResourcesUsed) &
         / User%ResourceLimit
   ELSE
      PRINT *, InputNumber, " not found"
   END IF
```

Figure 9.2 (cont.)

```
        ! Rewind file and get new id number
      REWIND 10
   END DO

END PROGRAM Computer_Usage_Records
```

Sample Run

```
Enter name of computer usage file: USERS.DAT

Enter id number (0 to stop): 10101
10101 Charles         Babbage
has used 49.2% of resources

Enter id number (0 to stop): 10108
10108 Freddie         Freeloader
has used 83.0% of resources

Enter id number (0 to stop): 20125
20125 Harvard         Yale
has used 14.9% of resources

Enter id number (0 to stop): 10199
10199 not found

Enter id number (0 to stop): 0
```

Figure 9.2 (cont.)

PRACTICE!

1. Programmer-defined types in Fortran are called _____ types, and an item of such a type is called a(n) _____.

2. (True or false) All components of a structure must have the same type.

3. Each component of a structure can be accessed using _____.

4. (True or false) One structure may be assigned to another provided they are of the same type.

Exercises 5–16 assume the following declarations have been made:

```
TYPE PersonalComputer
    CHARACTER(10) :: Manufacturer
    INTEGER :: DiskSpace, RAM, ClockSpeed
    LOGICAL :: CDROM
END TYPE PersonalComputer

TYPE InventoryRecord
    INTEGER :: StockNumber
    TYPE(PersonalComputer) :: PC
    REAL, DIMENSION(6) :: ListPrice
END TYPE InventoryRecord

TYPE(PersonalComputer) :: MyPC
TYPE(PersonalComputer), DIMENSION(10) :: PCArray
TYPE(InventoryRecord) :: Item
```

Write statements to do what is asked for.

5. Assign the character string "IBM" to the appropriate component of MyPC.

6. Read a clock speed (in megahertz) and store it in the appropriate field of MyPC.

7. Display the disk space of MyPC.

8. Read an amount of RAM for PCArray(5).

9. Display the manufacturer, disk space, amount of RAM, clock speed of PCArray(3), and whether or not it contains a CD ROM.

10. Read values for the disk space, amount of RAM, and clock speed of each structure in the array PCArray.

11. Assign 11782 to the stock number in Item.

12. Read values for the disk space, amount of RAM, and clock speed for the personal computer stored in Item.

13. Display a message indicating whether the manufacturer of the personal computer stored in Item is Apple.

14. Assign a price of $1999.99 to the third list price in Item.

15. Display all of the prices in Item.

16. Define a derived type for processing data consisting of a month name, number of the day, and year.

17. For a structure variable Day whose type is defined in Exercise 16, write a single assignment statement that assigns a value to Day, which represents the date July 4, 1776.

18. Write statements to input a value for a structure variable Day whose type is defined in Exercise 16.

19. Define a derived type for processing inventory information, including a 20-character name of an item, its stock number, and date received, which is a structure containing the month name, number of the day, and year.

20. For a structure variable Item whose type is defined in Exercise 19, write a single assignment statement that assigns a value to Item, which represents a camera with stock number 12384 that was received on December 10, 1995.

21. Write statements to input a value for a structure variable Item whose type is defined in Exercise 19.

KEY TERMS

Complex number	Double-precision value	Parameterized type
COMPLEX type statement	Imaginary part	Qualified variable
Component	Kind-clause	Real part
Component selector	Kind type parameter	Structure
Derived data type		

PROGRAMMING POINTERS

Program Style and Design

1. *A derived type is an appropriate data type to use for nonhomogeneous data collections, that is, those in which the items of information to be processed are of different types.*

2. *In a definition of a derived type, it is good style to indent and align the component declarations:*

```
type-name
  declaration₁
  declaration₂
     ⋮
  declarationₖ
END TYPE type-name
```

Potential Problems

1. *A component of a structure is accessed with a qualified variable of the form* `structure-name%component-name`. *Using a component name without qualifying it with the name of the structure to which it belongs (by attaching the structure name to it) will in fact process a different item that has the same name as the component.*

2. *The scope of each component identifier is the structure in which it appears. This means that*
    - *The same identifier may not be used to name two different components within the same structure.*
    - *An identifier that names a component within a structure may be used for some other purpose outside that structure.*

3. *Structures cannot be read or written as units; instead, individual components must be read or written.*

4. *In an assignment of one structure to another, the structures must have the same type.*

5. *Structures may be used as arguments in subprograms, but each actual argument must have the same type as the corresponding formal argument. The value of a function may be a structure.*

Programming Problems

SECTION 9.1

1. For the sequence of numbers $a_0, a_1, a_2, \ldots$ defined by

    $$a_0 = e^1 - 1$$

    and

    $$a_{n+1} = (n+1)a_n - 1 \qquad \text{for } n = 0, 1, 2, \ldots$$

    it can be shown that for each n,

    $$a_n = n!\left[e^1 - \left(1 + 1 + \frac{1}{2!} + \cdots + \frac{1}{n!}\right)\right]$$

    so that this sequence converges to 0. Write a program that prints a table of values of a_n for $n = 0, 1, 2, \ldots, 15$, calculated first in single precision and then in double precision.

2. Write a program to find a double-precision approximation to an integral using the trapezoidal method (see Section 6.3).

SECTIONS 9.2 AND APPLICATION

3. Write a program that reads three complex numbers P, Q, and R and then determines whether the triangle whose vertices are the points corresponding to P, Q, and R in the complex plane is a right triangle.

4. In a circuit containing a circuit with a resistor and an inductor in series, the voltage is given by

$$V = (R + i\omega L)I$$

where V is the voltage in volts, R is the resistance in ohms, L is the inductance in henrys, and ω is the angular velocity in radians per second. Write a program that can be used to compute the voltage (complex) given the current (complex), or to find the current given the voltage. Use $R = 1.3\Omega$, $L = 0.55$ mH, and $\omega = 365.0$ rad/sec.

SECTION 9.3

5. Write a program that accepts a time of day in military format and finds the corresponding standard representation in hours, minutes, and A.M./P.M. or accepts the time in the usual format and finds the corresponding military representation. For example, the input 0100 should produce 1:00 A.M. as output, and the input 3:45 P.M. should give 1545. Use a structure to store the time in the two formats.

6. Define derived types to store information about four geometric figures: circle, square, rectangle, and triangle. For a circle, the structure should store its radius and its center; for a square, the length of a side; for a rectangle, the lengths of two adjacent sides; and for a triangle, the lengths of the three sides. Then write a program that reads one of the letters C (circle), S (square), R (rectangle), T (triangle), and the appropriate numeric quantity or quantities for a figure of that type and then calculates its area. For example, the input R 7.2 3.5 represents a rectangle with length 7.2 and width 3.5; and T 3 4 6.1 represents a triangle having sides of lengths 3, 4, and 6.1. (For a triangle, the area can be found by using **Hero's formula**:

$$\text{area} = \sqrt{s(s-a)(s-b)(s-c)}$$

where a, b, and c are the lengths of the sides and s is one-half of the perimeter.)

7. Write a program to read the records in the file INVENTOR.DAT (see Appendix B) and store them in an array of structures, read a stock number entered by the user, and then search this array for the item having that stock number. If a match is found, the item name and number currently in stock should be displayed; otherwise, a message indicating that it was not found should be displayed.

8. Define a derived type for cards in a standard deck of 52 cards consisting of 4 suits (hearts, diamonds, spades, clubs) and 13 cards per suit. Then write a program to deal two 10-card hands from such a deck. (See Section 7.2 regarding random number generation.) Be sure that the same card is not dealt more than once.

10

Pointers and Linked Structures

10.1 POINTERS

Dynamic data structures are data structures that expand or contract as required during program execution. Such data structures are especially useful for storing and processing data sets whose sizes change during program execution; for example, the collection of jobs that have been entered into a computer system and are awaiting execution or the collection of passenger names and seat assignments on an airplane flight. Dynamic data structures are constructed using special variables called **pointer variables** (or simply **pointers**). In this section we describe pointers in Fortran, and in the next section we will show how they can be used to implement a dynamic data structure known as a linked list.

Pointer Variables

A variable is declared to be a pointer variable by including the POINTER attribute in the attribute list of its declaration:

```
type, attribute-list, POINTER :: pointer-
variable
```

This declares that pointer-variable can be used to access a memory location where a value of the specified type and attributes can be stored. For example, if the data values are strings, then a pointer to a memory location that can be used to store a string can be declared by

```
CHARACTER(8), POINTER :: StringPtr
```

This pointer variable StringPtr may be used only to access memory locations in which character strings of length 8 can be stored. Similarly,

OBJECTIVES

In this chapter, you will

- Study how pointers are provided in Fortran.
- See how linked lists can be created and used.
- Apply the concepts learned to an Internet address example.

```
TYPE Inventory_Info
   INTEGER :: Number
   REAL :: Price
END TYPE Inventory_Info

TYPE(Inventory_Info), POINTER :: InvPtr
```

declares that `InvPtr` is a pointer variable that may be used to access locations where structures of type `Inventory_Info` are stored.

The ALLOCATE Statement

The ALLOCATE statement has the form

```
ALLOCATE (list)
```

or

```
ALLOCATE (list, STAT = status-variable)
```

It was used in Chapter 8 to allocate memory for run-time arrays, but it is also used to acquire memory locations to associate with pointer variables during program execution. For example, the statement

```
ALLOCATE(StringPtr)
```

associates with `StringPtr` a memory location where a string such as `"Computer"` can be stored. We say that `StringPtr` "points" to this memory location, called a **target**, and we picture this with a diagram like the following:

StringPtr ----------▸ | Computer |

Each execution of an ALLOCATE statement acquires a new memory location and associates it with the specified pointer. Thus, if `TempPtr` is also a pointer declared by

```
CHARACTER(8), POINTER :: TempPtr
```

the statement

```
ALLOCATE(TempPtr)
```

acquires a new memory location pointed to by `TempPtr`:

StringPtr ------▸ | Computer |

TempPtr ------▸ | ? |

Pointer Association Status

Pointer variables may be in one of three states: undefined, associated, or disassociated. Like all variables, each pointer variable is initially **undefined**. When a pointer points to a target, its status changes to **associated**:

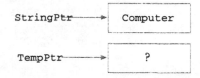

If this association is broken without associating the pointer variable with a new target, the pointer is said to be **null** or **disassociated**. A null pointer is commonly pictured using the ground symbol:

pointer ──||

Fortran provides the intrinsic function ASSOCIATED to test whether a pointer variable is associated with a target. A reference of the form

```
ASSOCIATED(pointer)
```

returns .TRUE. if pointer is associated with a target and .FALSE. otherwise. The association status of pointer must not be undefined.

The NULLIFY statement can be used to change a pointer variable's status to null. This statement has the form

```
NULLIFY(list-of-pointers)
```

Any associations of memory locations with these pointer variables are broken, and these memory locations can no longer be accessed unless pointed to by some other pointer variables. If there are no such pointers, these memory locations are *marooned* and cannot be reused.

When execution of a program begins, the program has a "pool" of available memory locations, called the **free store**. The effect of an ALLOCATE statement is to

1. Remove a block of memory from the free store.
2. Allocate that block to the executing program.

Since the size of the free store is limited, each ALLOCATE statement causes the pool of available memory to shrink. If more memory is needed than is available, program execution is halted unless a STAT = clause is included in the ALLOCATE statement. In this case, the integer variable in the STAT = clause will be assigned 0 if allocation is successful and a positive value otherwise.

Memory that is no longer needed can be returned to the free store by using a DEALLOCATE statement of the form

```
DEALLOCATE(list)
```

or

```
DEALLOCATE(list, STAT = status-variable)
```

In the second form, the integer variable will be assigned 0 if deallocation is successful and a positive value otherwise, for example, if some of the pointer variables in the list are null. If the STAT = clause is omitted, unsuccessful deallocation will terminate program execution.

Memory returned to the free store can be reallocated by subsequent ALLOCATE statements. The ALLOCATE and DEALLOCATE operations are thus complementary.

Pointer Assignment

If $pointer_1$ and $pointer_2$ have the same type, an assignment statement of the form

```
pointer₁ => pointer₂
```

causes $pointer_1$ to have the same association status as $pointer_2$, and if $pointer_2$ is associated, $pointer_1$ will point to the same target as $pointer_2$. The previous target (if any) pointed to by $pointer_1$ can no longer be accessed unless it is pointed to by some other pointer. The following diagrams illustrate:

Before assignment:

After assignment $pointer_1 \Rightarrow pointer_2$:

As an illustration, suppose that both `StringPtr` and `TempPtr` are pointer variables declared by

```
CHARACTER(8), POINTER :: StringPtr, TempPtr
```

and point to memory locations containing the strings `Computer` and `Software`, respectively:

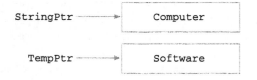

The assignment statement

```
TempPtr => StringPtr
```

causes `TempPtr` to point to the same memory location as `StringPtr`:

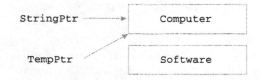

The string `Software` stored in the first location can no longer be accessed (unless it is pointed to by some other pointer).

A pointer assignment statement may also have the form

```
pointer-variable => target-variable
```

where `target-variable` has the same type as `pointer-variable` but has the TARGET attribute (and not the POINTER attribute). The declaration of such a variable has the form

```
type, attribute-list, TARGET :: pointer-variable
```

This assignment statement causes `pointer-variable` to point to `target-variable`, that is, to the memory location allocated to `target-variable`.

To illustrate, consider the declarations:

```
CHARACTER(8), POINTER :: StringPtr
CHARACTER(8), TARGET :: Name = "John Doe"
```

The statement

```
StringPtr => Name
```

causes `StringPtr` to point to the memory location allocated to Name (at compile time):

Name | John Doe | ◄------- StringPtr

A reference to the ASSOCIATED function of the form

```
ASSOCIATED(pointer, target)
```

can be used to determine if `pointer` points to `target`. Thus, after the preceding pointer assignment statement is executed,

```
ASSOCIATED(StringPtr, Name)
```

will return `.TRUE.`. A reference of the form

```
ASSOCIATED(pointer₁, pointer₂)
```

can be used to determine if $pointer_1$ and $pointer_2$ point to the same target.

Pointers in Expressions

One important rule governs the use of pointers in expressions:

When an associated pointer appears in an expression, it is automatically **dereferenced;** that is, the value stored in its target is used. If an associated pointer appears in an input list, an input value will be stored in its target.

To illustrate, consider the declarations

```
CHARACTER(8), POINTER :: StringPtr, NamePtr_1, NamePtr_2
CHARACTER(8), TARGET :: Name_1 = "Mary Doe", Name_2
CHARACTER(8) :: Product = "Computer"
```

and suppose that a memory location has been associated with `StringPtr` by

```
ALLOCATE(StringPtr)
```

StringPtr ────────► [   ]

The statements

```
StringPtr = "Computer"
```

and

```
StringPtr = Product
```

are ordinary assignment statements and store the string `"Computer"` in the memory location pointed to by `StringPtr`:

```
StringPtr ──────▶  Computer
```

The output statement

```
PRINT *, StringPtr
```

will display

```
Computer
```

as will

```
IF StringPtr(4:6) = "put" THEN
    PRINT *, StringPtr
END {IF}
```

A string that is input in response to the READ statement

```
READ '(A)', StringPtr
```

will be stored in the memory location pointed to by `StringPtr`.

Dereferencing also occurs for pointer variables that point to target variables. For example, suppose that `NamePtr1` and `NamePtr2` point to the variables `Name_1` and `Name_2`, respectively:

```
NamePtr_1 => Name_1
NamePtr_2 => Name_2
```

The output statement

```
PRINT *, NamePtr_1
```

will then display the value stored in `Name_1`:

```
Mary Doe
```

The assignment statement

```
NamePtr_2 = NamePtr_1
```

assigns the string `Mary Doe` stored in `Name_1` to `Name_2` and is therefore equivalent to the assignment statement

```
Name_2 = Name_1
```

As this example illustrates, there is a fundamental difference between the pointer assignment operator (=>) and the ordinary assignment operator (=). If both `TempPtr` and `StringPtr` are associated,

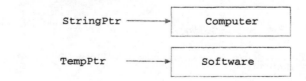

the statement

```
TempPtr = StringPtr
```

copies the contents of the memory location pointed to by `StringPtr` into the location pointed to by `TempPtr`:

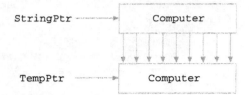

This result is quite different from that produced by the pointer assignment

```
TempPtr => StringPtr
```

which causes `TempPtr` to point to the same memory location pointed to by `StringPtr`:

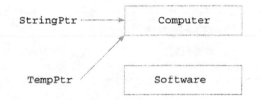

Pointers and Subprograms

Pointers (and targets) may be used as arguments of subprograms, provided they satisfy the following conditions:

1. If a formal argument is a pointer variable, the corresponding actual argument must also be a pointer variable of the same type.
2. A pointer formal argument cannot have an `INTENT` attribute.
3. If a formal argument is a pointer (or target) variable, the subprogram must have an explicit interface.

When the subprogram is invoked, the association status of each actual argument that is a pointer is passed to the corresponding formal argument.

The value returned by a function may also be a pointer. In this case, the value must be returned by using a `RESULT` clause (see Section 6.7) to return the value assigned within the function to a local pointer variable.

PRACTICE!

1. Write a declaration for a variable `P1` to be a pointer to a memory location in which an integer can be stored.
2. Write a declaration for a variable `P2` to be a pointer to a memory location that can store structures having two components of type real, `XCoord` and `YCoord`.
3. Write statements that associate a memory location with `P1` of Exercise 1 and stores the value −1234 in this location.
4. Write statements that associate a memory location with `P2` of Exercise 2 and stores the values 3.15 and 12.9 in the `XCoord` and `YCoord` components associated with this location.
5. Name and describe three kinds of pointer association status.

6. Write a statement that displays the message `"Not associated"` if the variable `P1` is not associated with a memory location.

For Exercises 7–13, assume that the following declarations have been made,

```
TYPE NumberNode
   INTEGER :: Data
   TYPE(NumberNode), POINTER :: Next
END TYPE NumberNode

TYPE(NumberNode), POINTER :: P1, P2
INTEGER, POINTER :: P3
```

and that the following three statements have already been executed:

```
ALLOCATE(P1)
ALLOCATE(P2)
ALLOCATE(P3)
```

Tell what will now be displayed by each of the following program segments, or explain why an error occurs:

7.
```
P1%Data = 123
P2%Data = 456
P1%Next => P2
PRINT *, P1%Data
PRINT *, P1%Next%Data
```

8.
```
P1%Data = 12
P2%Data = 34
P1 => P2
PRINT *, P1%Data
PRINT *, P2%Data
```

9.
```
P1%Data = 12
P2%Data = 34
P1 = P2
PRINT *, P1%Data
PRINT *, P2%Data
```

10.
```
P1%Data = 123
P2%Data = 456
P1%Next => P2
PRINT *, P2%Data
PRINT *, P2%Next%Data
```

11.
```
P1%Data = 12
P2%Data = 34
P3%Data = 34
P1%Next => P2
P2%Next => P3
PRINT *, P1%Data
PRINT *, P2%Data
PRINT *, P3%Data
```

12.
```
P1%Data = 111
P2%Data = 222
P1%Next => P2
P2%Next => P1
PRINT *, P1%Data, P2%Data
PRINT *, P1%Next%Data
PRINT *, P1%Next%Next%Data
```

13.
```
P1%Data = 12
P2%Data = 34
P1 => P2
P2%Next => P1
PRINT *, P1%Data
PRINT *, P2%Data
PRINT *, P1%Next%Data
PRINT *, P2%Next%Data
```

10.2 IMPLEMENTING LINKED LISTS

Pointer variables are important because they are used to construct dynamic structures. In this section we show how linked lists can be implemented using structures and pointers.

A **linked list** consists of a collection of elements called **nodes**, each of which stores two items of information: (1) an element of the list and (2) a **link**, which is a pointer, that indicates the location of the node containing the successor of this list element. The nodes are represented in Fortran as structures having two kinds of components, **data components** and **link components**. The data components have types that are appropriate for storing the necessary information, and the link components are pointers. For example, the type of the nodes in the linked list

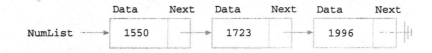

can be defined by

```
TYPE List_Node
    INTEGER :: Data
    TYPE (List_Node), POINTER :: Next
END TYPE List_Node
```

Each node in this list is a structure of type `List_Node`, consisting of two components. The first component `Data` is of integer type and is used to store the data. The second component Next is a pointer and points to the next node in the list.

In addition to the nodes of the list in which to store the data items, a pointer to the first node is needed. Thus we declare a pointer variable `NumList` by

```
TYPE(List_Node), POINTER :: NumList
```

for the linked list of integers.

Constructing a Linked List

To illustrate the basic steps in the construction of a linked list, suppose that the integers 1723 and 1996 have already been stored in a linked list:

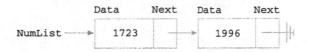

and suppose that we wish to add 1550 to this list. In the construction, we use two pointers, `NumList` to point to the first node in the list and `TempPtr` as a temporary pointer:

```
TYPE (List_Node), POINTER :: NumList, TempPtr
```

We first acquire a new node temporarily pointed to by `TempPtr`,

```
ALLOCATE(TempPtr)
```

and store 1550 in the data component of this structure:

```
TempPtr%Data = 1550
```

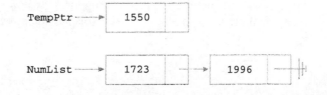

This node can then be joined to the list by setting its link component so that it points to the first node:

```
TempPtr%Next => NumList
```

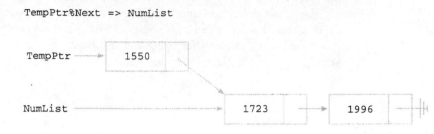

The pointer `NumList` is then updated to point to this new node:

```
NumList => TempPtr
```

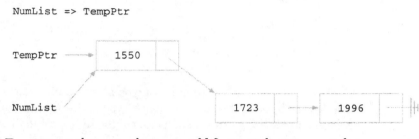

To construct the entire list, we could first initialize an empty list:

```
NULLIFY(NumList)
```

and then repeat the preceding four statements three times, replacing 1550 by 1996 in the second assignment statement, then by 1723, and finally again using the value 1550. In practice, however, such linked lists are usually constructed by reading the data values rather than by assigning them with assignment statements. In this example, the linked list could be constructed by using the following program segment, where `Item` and `AllocateStatus` are integer variables.

```
! Initially the list is empty
NULLIFY(NumList)

! Read the data values and construct the list
DO
   READ *, Item
   IF (Item == End_Data_Flag) EXIT
   ALLOCATE(TempPtr, STAT = AllocateStatus)
   IF (AllocateStatus /= 0) STOP "*** Not enough memory ***"
   TempPtr%Data = Item
   TempPtr%Next => NumList
   NumList => TempPtr
END DO
```

Traversing a Linked List

Once a linked list has been constructed, we may want to **traverse** it from beginning to end, displaying each element in the list. To traverse a linked list, we move through the list by varying a pointer variable in a repetition structure.

To illustrate, suppose we wish to display the integers stored in the linked list:

NumList ⟶ 1550 ⟶ 1723 ⟶ 1996

We begin by initializing a pointer variable `CurrPtr` to point to the first node:

```
CurrPtr => NumList
```

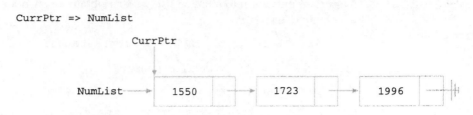

and display the integer stored in this node:

```
PRINT *, CurrPtr%Data
```

To move to the next node, we follow the link from the current node:

```
CurrPtr => CurrPtr%Next
```

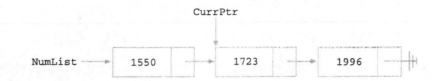

After displaying the integer in this node, we move to the next node:

```
CurrPtr => CurrPtr%Next
```

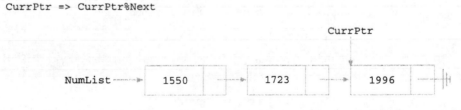

and display its data. Since we have now reached the last node, we need some way to signal this condition. But this is easy, for if we attempt to move to the next node, `CurrPtr` becomes null:

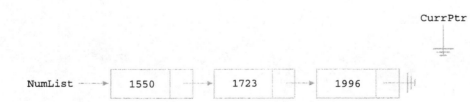

The function `ASSOCIATED` can be used to determine when this occurs:

```
CurrPtr => NumList
DO

   IF (.NOT. ASSOCIATED(CurrPtr)) EXIT ! end of list
   PRINT *, CurrPtr%Data
   CurrPtr => CurrPtr%Next
END DO
```

Insertion and Deletion in Linked Lists

To insert an element into a linked list, we first obtain a new node temporarily accessed via a pointer `TempPtr`,

```
ALLOCATE(TempPtr, STAT = AllocateStatus)
```

and store the element in its data component:

```
TempPtr%Data = Element
```

There are now two cases to consider: (1) inserting the element at the beginning of the list, and (2) inserting it after some specified element in the list. The first case has already been illustrated. For the second case, suppose that the new node is to be inserted between the nodes pointed to by `PredPtr` and `CurrPtr`:

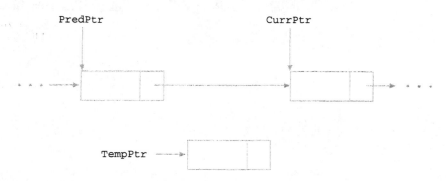

The node is inserted by setting the pointer in the link component of the new node to point to the node pointed to by `CurrPtr`,

```
TempPtr%Next => CurrPtr
```

and then resetting the pointer in the link component of the node pointed to by `PredPtr` to point to the new node:

```
PredPtr%Next => TempPtr
```

The following diagram illustrates:

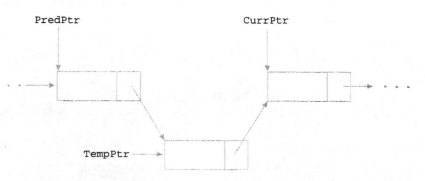

For deletion, there also are two cases to consider: (1) deleting the first element in the list, and (2) deleting an element that has a predecessor. The first case is easy and consists of the following steps:

1. Set `CurrPtr` to point to the first node in the list:

    ```
    CurrPtr => List
    ```

2. Set `List` to point to the second node in the list:

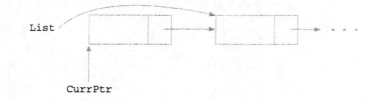

3. Release the node pointed to by `CurrPtr`:

```
DEALLOCATE (CurrPtr)
```

For the second case, suppose that the predecessor of the node to be deleted is pointed to by `PredPtr`:

```
List => CurrPtr%Next
```

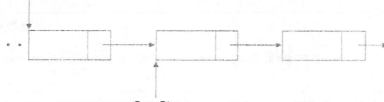

The node is deleted by setting the link component of the node pointed to by Pred-Ptr so that it points to the successor of the node to be deleted,

```
PredPtr%Next => CurrPtr%Next
```

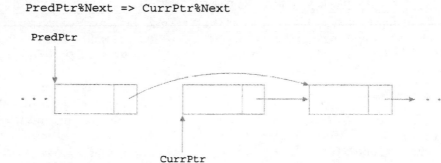

and then releasing the node pointed to by `CurrPtr`:

```
DEALLOCATE(CurrPtr)
```

PRACTICE!

For Exercises 1–10, use the following linked list and pointers P1, P2, P3, and P4:

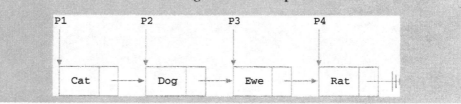

Draw a similar diagram for each of the following to show how this configuration changes when the given program segment is executed, or explain why an error occurs.

1. `P1 => P2%Next`   2. `P4 => P1`

3. `P4%Data = P1%Data`   4. `P4%Next%Data = P1%Data`

5. `P2%Next => P3%Next`   6. `P4%Next => P1`

7. `P1%Next => P3%Next`   8. `P1 => P3`
   `P1 => P3`   `P1%Next => P3%Next`

9. `P4%Next => P3%Next`   10. `P4%Next => P3`
   `P3%Next => P2%Next`   `P4%Next%Next => P2`
   `P2%Next => P1%Next`   `P4%Next%Next%Next => P1`
   `P2%Next => P1%Next`   `NULLIFY(P1)`

11. Write a nonrecursive function to count the nodes in a linked list.

12. Proceed as in Exercise 11 but write a recursive function.

13. Write a function to find the average of a linked list of real numbers.

14. Write a subprogram to append a node at the end of a linked list.

15. Write a logical-valued function to determine whether the data items in a linked list are arranged in ascending order.

16. Write a subprogram to merge two linked lists that are in ascending order.

APPLICATION: INTERNET ADDRESSES

TCP (Transmission Control Protocol) and *IP* (Internet Protocol) are communication protocols that specify rules computers use in exchanging messages in networks. TCP/IP addresses are used to uniquely identify computers in the Internet; for example,

        titan.ksc.nasa.gov

is the address of a site at the NASA Kennedy Space Center. These addresses are made up of four fields that represent specific parts of the Internet:

        host.subdomain.subdomain.rootdomain

which the computer will translate into a unique TCP/IP address. This address is a 32-bit value, but it is usually represented in a dotted-decimal notation by separating the 32 bits into four 8-bit fields, expressing each field as a decimal integer, and separating the fields with a period; for example,

        128.159.4.20

is the TCP/IP address for the above site at the NASA Kennedy Space Center.

PROBLEM

A **gateway** is a device used to interconnect two different computer networks. Suppose that a gateway connects a university to the Internet and that the university's network administrator needs to monitor connections through this gateway. Each time a connection is made (for example, a student using the World Wide Web), the TCP/IP address of the student's computer is stored in a data file. The administrator wants to check periodically who has used the gateway and how many times they have used it.

Solution

Specification   The input and output for this problem are clear:

Input:	The name of the data file containing the TCP/IP addresses TCP/IP addresses from the file
Output:	A list of distinct TCP/IP addresses and the number of times they appear in the file

Design   The data file contains TCP/IP addresses, and these addresses must be read from the file and stored in a list. Since there are 2^{32} possible addresses and the number of distinct addresses is not known in advance, a static data structure such as an array cannot be used efficiently. The flexibility provided by a dynamic structure such as a linked list makes it a more appropriate storage structure. Each node will store an address and the number of times that address appeared in the data file.

The variables we will use are

IDENTIFIERS FOR TCP/IP-ADDRESS PROBLEM

FileName	The name of the data file containing the addresses
Address	A TCP/IP address
AddressList	Linked list of addresses and counts

As each address is read from the file, we must determine if it has already been added to the list, and if so, increment its count by 1. If it is not in the list, we will simply insert each new address at the beginning of the list because the order in which the addresses occur is not important. After all the addresses in the file have been read, the list is traversed and the addresses and their counts displayed. The following algorithm summarizes this approach:

ALGORITHM FOR TCP/IP-ADDRESS PROBLEM

Algorithm to find the distinct TCP/IP addresses stored in a file and the number of times each address appears.

Input: *FileName*
           Addresses from the file
Output: A list of addresses and their counts

1. Get the name (*FileName*) of the data file containing the TCP/IP addresses and open it for input. If it cannot be opened, terminate execution.
2. Initialize *AddressList* as an empty linked list.
3. Repeat the following:
   a. Read an *Address* from the file.
   b. If an input error occurs, terminate execution.

   If there were no more addresses, terminate repetition.

   Otherwise continue with the following.
   c. Search *AddressList* to determine if *Address* already appears in the list.
   d. If *Address* is found

   Increment the count in the node containing the address by 1.

   Otherwise

   Insert a node containing *Address* and a count of 1 at the beginning of *AddressList*.
4. Traverse *AddressList*, displaying each TCP/IP address and its count.

Coding and Execution   The program in Figure 10.1 implements this algorithm. It uses the methods described in the preceding sections for inserting items into a linked list and for traversing a linked list.

Figure 10.1.   Internet addresses

```
PROGRAM Internet_Addresses
!-------------------------------------------------------------------------
! Program to read TCP/IP addresses from a file and produce a list of distinct
! addresses and a count of how many times each appeared in the file.  The
! addresses and counts are stored in a linked list.
! Variables used are:
!   FileName    : name of data file containing addresses
!   OpenStatus  : status variable for OPEN statement
!   InputStatus : status variable for READ statement
!   Address     : an address read from the file
!   AddressList : pointer to first node in the linked list of addresses
! Subroutines used to process linked list:
!   Add_To_List, Search, Output_Addresses
```

```
!
! Input (keyboard): FileName
! Input (file):     Addresses
! Output:           A list of distinct addresses and their counts
!------------------------------------------------------------------------

  IMPLICIT NONE

  ! Define an address node type
  TYPE List_Node
    CHARACTER(15) :: TCP_IP_Address      ! Address data
    INTEGER :: Count                     ! Counter for this address
    TYPE(List_Node), POINTER :: Next     ! Pointer to next node
  END TYPE List_Node

  CHARACTER(15) :: Address, FileName*20
  INTEGER :: OpenStatus, InputStatus
  TYPE(List_Node), POINTER :: AddressList

  ! Get name of data file and open it for reading
  WRITE (*, '(1X, A)', ADVANCE = "NO") "Enter name of file of addresses: "
  READ *, FileName
  OPEN (UNIT = 10, FILE = FileName, STATUS = "OLD", IOSTAT = OpenStatus)
  IF (OpenStatus > 0) STOP "*** Cannot open address file ***"

  ! Create empty linked list
  NULLIFY(AddressList)

  ! Read addresses from the file and store them in the list,
  ! until end of file reached
  DO
    READ(10, '(A)', IOSTAT = InputStatus) Address
    IF (InputStatus > 0) STOP "*** Input error ***"
    IF (InputStatus < 0) EXIT ! end of file

    CALL Add_To_List(AddressList, Address)
  ENDDO

  CALL Output_Addresses(AddressList)

CONTAINS

  !------------------------------------------------------------------------
  ! This subroutine determines if Address is already in the linked list
  ! AddressList (using Search).  If it is not, it is added at the beginning
  ! of the list; if it is, its count is incremented by 1.  Local variables:
  !   AllocateStatus : status variable for OPEN statement
  !   LocPtr         : pointer to a node containing Address or null if
  !                    not found
  !   In_the_List    : indicates if Address is already in AddressList
  ! Accepts:  AddressList and Address
  ! Returns:  Modified AddressList
  !------------------------------------------------------------------------
```

Figure 10.1 (cont.)

```fortran
      SUBROUTINE Add_To_List(AddressList, Address)

        TYPE(List_Node), POINTER :: AddressList
        CHARACTER(*), INTENT(IN) :: Address
        TYPE(List_Node), POINTER :: LocPtr
        INTEGER :: AllocateStatus
        LOGICAL :: In_the_List

        IF (.NOT. ASSOCIATED(AddressList)) THEN  ! List is empty

          ALLOCATE(AddressList, STAT = AllocateStatus)
          IF (AllocateStatus /= 0) STOP "*** Out of memory *** "

          AddressList%TCP_IP_Address = Address
          AddressList%Count = 1
          NULLIFY(AddressList%Next)

        ELSE  ! List not empty -- determine if Address is already in the list

          CALL Search(AddressList, Address, LocPtr, In_the_List)

          IF (In_the_List) THEN    ! Increment its count by 1
            LocPtr%Count = LocPtr%Count + 1

          ELSE                     ! Create a new node and insert it at the front
            ALLOCATE(LocPtr, STAT = AllocateStatus)
            IF (AllocateStatus /= 0) STOP "*** Out of memory *** "

            LocPtr%TCP_IP_Address = Address
            LocPtr%Count = 1
            LocPtr%Next => AddressList
            AddressList => LocPtr
          END IF
        END IF

      END SUBROUTINE Add_To_List
      !-----------------------------------------------------------------------
      ! This subroutine searches AddressList for a node containing Address.
      ! If it is found, LocPtr points to the node and In_the_List is set to
      ! true; otherwise LocPtr is NULL and In_the_List is false.
      !
      ! Accepts: AddressList, Address
      ! Returns: LocPtr, In_the_List
      !-----------------------------------------------------------------------

      SUBROUTINE Search(AddressList, Address, LocPtr, In_the_List)

        TYPE(List_Node), POINTER :: AddressList, LocPtr
        CHARACTER(*), INTENT(IN) :: Address
        LOGICAL, INTENT(OUT) :: In_the_List

        LocPtr => AddressList
        In_the_List = .FALSE.
```

Figure 10.1 (cont.)

```
             ! Traverse the list until the address is found
             ! or the end of list is encountered
             DO
                IF( In_the_List .OR..NOT. ASSOCIATED(LocPtr)) EXIT
                ! Address found or end of list -- terminate repetition

                IF(LocPtr%TCP_IP_Address == Address) THEN  ! Address found
                   In_the_List = .TRUE.
                ELSE                                    ! Move to next node
                   LocPtr => LocPtr%Next
                END IF
             END DO


     END SUBROUTINE Search
     !-----------------------------------------------------------------------
     ! This subroutine prints the contents of the linked list pointed to by
     ! AddressList.  For each node, it prints the address and count.  Local
     ! variable used:
     !    Ptr : pointer that runs through the list
     !
     ! Accepts: AddressList
     ! Output:  Addresses and counts stored in nodes of AddressList
     !-----------------------------------------------------------------------


     SUBROUTINE Output_Addresses(AddressList)

        TYPE(List_Node), POINTER :: AddressList, Ptr

        Ptr => AddressList


        PRINT *, "Summary of Internet address data"
        PRINT *
        PRINT *, "   Address Count "
        PRINT *, "---------------------------- "
        ! Print node information until end of list reached
        DO
           IF (.NOT. ASSOCIATED(Ptr)) EXIT ! End of list reached

           ! Otherwise display contents of node pointed to by Ptr
           PRINT '(1X, A, 4X, I4)', Ptr%TCP_IP_Address, Ptr%Count

           ! Move to next node
           Ptr => Ptr%Next
        END DO

     END SUBROUTINE Output_Addresses


  END PROGRAM Internet_Addresses
```

Figure 10.1 (cont.)

Listing of `fil10-1.dat` **Used in Sample Run**

```
128.159.4.20
123.111.222.33
100.1.4.31
34.56.78.90
120.120.120.120
128.159.4.20
123.111.222.33
123.111.222.33
77.66.55.44
100.1.4.31
123.111.222.33
128.159.4.20
```

Sample Run

```
Enter name of file of addresses: fil10-1.dat
Summary of Internet address data

   Address          Count
----------------------------------
77.66.55.44           1
120.120.120.120       1
34.56.78.90           1
100.1.4.31            2
123.111.222.33        4
128.159.4.20          3
```

Figure 10.1   (cont.)

KEY TERMS

ALLOCATE statement	Dynamic data structure	Null (disassociated) status
ASSOCIATED function	Free store	POINTER attribute
Associated status	Link	Pointer (variable)
Data component	Link component	Target
DEALLOCATE statement	Linked list	Traversing
Dereferencing	Node	Undefined status

PROGRAMMING POINTERS

Program Style and Design

1. *Linked structures are appropriate for storing dynamic data sets, which grow and shrink during processing due to repeated insertions and deletions.*

2. *Memory locations allocated to pointer variables should be returned to the free store when they are no longer needed.*

Potential Problems

1. *Each pointer variable is declared to have a specific type; a pointer points to a memory location in which only a value of that type can be stored. For example, if* P *and* Q *are pointer variables declared by*

```
INTEGER, POINTER :: P
CHARACTER(20), POINTER :: Q
```

then memory locations pointed to by P can store only integers, whereas those to which Q points can store only strings of length 20.

2. *Only limited operations can be performed on pointers.* In particular:
   - *A pointer* P *can be associated with a memory location in only the following ways:*
     a. `ALLOCATE(P)` or `ALLOCATE(P, STAT = integer-variable)`
     b. `P => Q,` *where* Q *is a pointer variable or a target variable with the same type as* P.
   - *A pointer* P *can be disassociated from a memory location by*

     `DEALLOCATE(P)` or `DEALLOCATE(P, STAT = integer-variable)`

   - *A function reference of the form* `ALLOCATED(P, Q)` *can be used to determine if two pointers* P *and* Q *of the same type point to the same memory location.*
   - *A function reference of the form* `ALLOCATED(P, T)` *can be used to determine if a pointer* P *points to a target* T *of the same type.*
   - *Pointers may be used as arguments in subprograms, but corresponding actual and formal arguments must have the same type, the formal argument cannot have an* `INTENT` *attribute, and the subprogram must have an explicit interface.*

3. *When a pointer* P *appears in an expression, it is automatically dereferenced.* For example, if P points to a memory location containing the integer 17, the statement `PRINT *, P + 1` will display the value 18. Similarly, the value input for the statement `READ *, P` will be stored in the memory location pointed to by P.

4. *If* P *is a pointer that is undefined or null, then an attempt to use* P *in an expression is an error because* P *does not point to a memory location and thus cannot be dereferenced.*

5. *Don't confuse pointer assignment with ordinary assignment.* For example, suppose that P points to a memory location containing the integer 17 and Q points to a memory location containing the integer 900:

$$P \longrightarrow \boxed{17}$$

$$Q \longrightarrow \boxed{900}$$

Then in the statement

    P = Q

P and Q are dereferenced and the value 900 is copied into the memory location pointed to P:

$$P \longrightarrow \boxed{900}$$

$$Q \longrightarrow \boxed{900}$$

The statement

    P => Q

however, causes P to point to the same memory location as Q:

6. *Null $\neq$ undefined.* A pointer becomes defined when it is associated with a memory location or is nullified using the function NULLIFY. Nullifying a pointer is analogous to "blanking out" a character variable or "zeroing out" a numeric variable.

7. *Memory locations that were once associated with a pointer variable and that are no longer needed should be returned to the "storage pool" of available locations by using the* DEALLOCATE *statement.* Special care is required so that inaccessible memory locations are avoided. For example, as shown in Potential Problem 5, if P and Q are pointer variables of the same type, the assignment statement

```
P => Q
```

causes P to point to the same memory location as that pointed to by Q. Any memory location previously pointed to by P becomes inaccessible and cannot be disposed of properly unless it is pointed to by some other pointer. Temporary pointers should be used to maintain access, as the following statements demonstrate:

```
TempPtr => P
P => Q;
DEALLOCATE(TempPtr)
```

8. *Pay attention to special cases in processing linked lists, and be careful not to lose access to nodes.* In particular, remember the following "programming proverbs":

   • *Don't take a long walk off a short linked list.* It is an error to attempt to process elements beyond the end of the list.

   • *You can't get water from an empty well.* Don't try to access elements in an empty list; this case usually requires special consideration. For example, if List is null, then initializing CurrPtr to List and attempting to access CurrPtr%Data or CurrPtr%Next is an error.

   • *Don't burn bridges before you cross them.* Be careful that you change links in the correct order, or you may lose access to a node or to many nodes! For example, in the following attempt to insert a new node at the beginning of a linked list,

```
List => NewNodePtr
NewNodePtr%Next = List
```

   the statements are not in correct order. As soon as the first statement is executed, List points to the new node, and access to the remaining nodes in the list (those formerly pointed to by List) is lost. The second statement then simply sets the link field of the new node to point to itself:

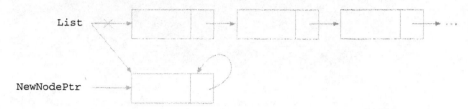

List

NewNodePtr

The correct sequence is first to connect the new node to the list and then to reset `List`:

```
NewNodePtr%Next => List
List => NewNodePtr
```

Programming Problems

1. Write a program to test the function in Exercise 11 of Section 10.2.
2. Write a program to test the function in Exercise 12 of Section 10.2.
3. Write a program to test the function in Exercise 13 of Section 10.2.
4. Write a program to test the subprogram in Exercise 14 of Section 10.2.
5. Write a program to test the function in Exercise 15 of Section 10.2.
6. Write a program to test the subprogram in Exercise 16 of Section 10.2.
7. Declarations like those for linked lists can be used to define a *linked stack:*

```
TYPE StackNode
   type :: Data
   TYPE(StackType), POINTER :: Next
END TYPE StackNode

TYPE (StackNode), POINTER :: Stack
```

The value of `Stack` will be a pointer to the top of the stack. For example, a linked stack of integers might be pictured as

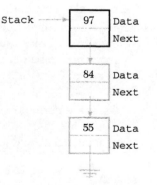

a. Describe how an element would be popped from this linked stack. Include a picture of the modified stack.
b. Assuming that this linked stack has been modified as in part (a), describe how the integer 77 would be pushed onto the linked stack. Include a picture of the modified stack.

8. A limited number of complimentary copies of new CAD/CAM software will be released tomorrow, and requests are to be filled in the order in which they are received. Write a program that reads the names and addresses of the persons requesting this software together with the number of copies requested and stores these in a linked list. The program should then produce a list of names, addresses, and number of requests that can be filled.

9. Modify the program in Problem 8 so that multiple requests from the same person are not allowed.

10. The Cawker City Computer Company maintains two warehouses, one in Chicago and one in Detroit, each of which stocks a large number of different items. Write a program that first reads the product numbers of items stored in the Chicago warehouse and stores them in a linked list `Chicago` and then repeats this for the items stored in the Detroit warehouse, storing these product numbers in a linked list `Detroit`. The program should then find and display the *intersection* of these two lists of numbers, that is, the collection of product numbers common to both lists. Do not assume that the lists have the same number of elements.

11. Repeat Problem 10, but find and display the *union* of the two lists, that is, the collection of product numbers that are elements of at least one of the lists.

A

Intrinsic Procedures

The following are descriptions of all the standard intrinsic functions and subroutines in Fortran 90. The generic forms are given first, with optional arguments indicated by an underline. Specific names (if any) are given next in the form *specific-name* $(X \rightarrow Y)$, where X is the argument type and Y is the result type (DP = double precision, I = integer, R = real, C = complex and Char = character). An asterisk on a specific name indicates that the function may not be passed as an argument to a subprogram. Complete descriptions of these procedures can be found in Appendix D our text *Fortran 90 for Engineers and Scientists*.

```
ABS(A) {ABS (R → R),
CABS (C → R), DABS (DP → DP), IABS (I → I)}
```

Absolute value of A; result type is same type as A, but real if A is complex.

```
ACHAR(I)
```

The character in position I of the ASCII collating sequence.

```
ACOS(X) {ACOS (R → R),
DACOS (DP → DP)}
```

Angle in $[0, \pi]$ (in radians) whose cosine is X.

```
ADJUSTL(STRING)
```

String obtained by adjusting STRING to the left, removing leading blanks and adding trailing blanks.

```
ADJUSTR(STRING)
```

String obtained by adjusting STRING to the right, removing trailing blanks and adding leading blanks.

```
AIMAG(Z) {AIMAG (C → R)}
```

Imaginary part of Z.

```
AINT(A, KIND) {AINT (R → R),
DINT (DP → DP)}
```

Real value obtained by truncating the fractional part of A.

```
ALL(MASK, DIM)
```

Returns true if all values in logical array MASK along dimension DIM are true and false otherwise.

```
ALLOCATED(ARRAY)
```

Returns true if allocatable ARRAY is currently allocated, false if not.

```
ANINT(A, KIND) {ANINT (R → R),
DNINT (DP → DP)}
```

Real value of the integer nearest to A—AINT(A + 0.5) if A > 0, and AINT(A - 0.5) otherwise.

```
ANY(MASK, DIM)
```

Like ALL(MASK, DIM) but determines whether any value in MASK along dimension DIM is true.

```
ASIN(X) {ASIN (R → R), DASIN (DP → DP)}
```

Angle in $[-\pi/2, \pi/2]$ (in radians) whose sine is X.

```
ASSOCIATED(POINTER, TARGET)
```

Returns true if POINTER is associated with TARGET.

```
ATAN(X) {ATAN (R → R), DATAN (DP → DP)}
```

Angle in $(-\pi/2, \pi/2)$ (in radians) whose tangent is X, which is real.

```
ATAN2(Y, X) {ATAN2 (R → R), DATAN2 (DP → DP)}
```

The angle in $(-\pi, \pi]$ (in radians) whose tangent is Y/X if X ≠ 0, positive if Y > 0, negative if Y < 0. ATAN2(0,X) is 0.0 if X > 0, π if X < 0; ATAN2(Y,0) is $-\pi/2$ if Y < 0, $\pi/2$ if Y > 0.

```
BIT_SIZE(I)
```

Returns number of bits in an integer type; argument is any integer.

```
BTEST(I, POS)
```

Returns true if bit in position POS of I is 1, false if it is 0; 0 ≤ POS < BITSIZE(I).

```
CEILING(A)
```

Least integer ≥ A.

```
CHAR(I, KIND) {CHAR (I → Char)}
```

Character in position I of the collating sequence associated with the specified kind.

```
CMPLX(X, Y, KIND)
```

A complex value with real part REAL(X, KIND) and imaginary part REAL(Y, KIND).

```
CONJG(Z) {CONJG (C → C)}
```
Conjugate of Z.

```
COS(X) {COS (R → R), CCOS (C → C), DCOS (DP → DP)}
```

Returns the cosine of X (radians); is real or complex.

COSH(X) {COSH (R → R), DCOSH (DP → DP)}

Hyperbolic cosine of X.

COUNT(MASK, DIM)

The number of true values in MASK along dimension DIM.

CSHIFT(ARRAY, SHIFT, DIM)

The array obtained by shifting the elements of all vectors along dimension DIM of ARRAY by the amounts specified in SHIFT (toward the beginning of the vector if SHIFT > 0, and toward the end of the vector if SHIFT < 0). The shift is circular so that elements shifted out at one end of a vector are shifted in at the other end.

DATE_AND_TIME(DATE, TIME, ZONE, VALUES)

Subroutine that returns the current date and time. The values assigned to the arguments will be

DATE: CCYYMMDD (century, year, month, day)

TIME: hhmmss.sss (hours, minutes, seconds)

ZONE: ±hhmm (hours and minutes in the time difference with respect to Coordinate Universal Time (UTC); also called Greenwich Mean Time)

VALUES: an array of 8 integers: year; month number (1 to 12); day of the month; time difference with respect to UTC in minutes; hour (0 to 23); minute (0 to 59); second (0 to 60); milliseconds (0 to 999)

DBLE(A)

Value obtained by converting A (integer, real, or complex) to double-precision real type.

DIGITS(X)

Number of significant digits for numbers having the same type and kind as X when X is represented using the mathematical model for integer data $X = \pm(f_1 f_2 \cdots f_p)_{\text{base } b}$, or the mathematical model for real data $X = \pm b^e \times (0.f_1 f_2 \cdots f_p)_{\text{base } b}$.

DIM(X, Y) {IDIM (I → I), DIM (R → R), DDIM (DP → DP)}

X − Y if X > Y and 0 otherwise; X and Y may be integer or real.

DOT_PRODUCT(VECTOR_A, VECTOR_B)

Dot product of VECTOR_A and VECTOR_B, which are one-dimensional arrays with integer, real, complex, or logical elements.

DPROD(X, Y) {DPROD (R → D)}

Double-precision product of real X and Y.

EOSHIFT(ARRAY, SHIFT, BOUNDARY, DIM)

Like CSHIFT(ARRAY, SHIFT, DIM), but uses an end-off shift—elements shifted off at one end are lost—and copies of BOUNDARY's elements are shifted in at the other end.

EPSILON(X)

A positive number that is almost negligible compared to 1.0 for numbers of the same type and kind as X.

EXP(X) {EXP (R → R), CEXP (C → C), DEXP (DP → DP)}

Returns e^X; X is real or complex.

EXPONENT(X)

Returns the exponent e when X is represented using the model for real data.

FLOOR(A)

Greatest integer ≤ A; A is real.

FRACTION(X)

Fractional part of the model representation of X, which is real.

HUGE(X)

Largest number for numbers having the same type and kind as X, which is integer or real.

IACHAR(C)

Position of character C in the ASCII collating sequence.

IAND(I, J)

Value obtained by performing a bitwise AND on integers I and J.

IBCLR(I, POS)

Value obtained by clearing the bit in position POS of integer I to zero; bits are numbered 0 to **BIT_SIZE**(I) − 1, from right to left.

IBITS(I, POS, LEN)

Returns the value obtained by extracting LEN consecutive bits from I, beginning at position POS, and setting leftmost bits to 0; bits are numbered 0 to BIT_SIZE(I) − 1, from right to left.

IBSET(I, POS)

Like IBCLR(I, POS), but sets the bit in position POS of I to one.

ICHAR(C) {*ICHAR (Char → I)}

Position of character C in the machine's collating sequence.

IEOR(I, J)

Value obtained by performing a bitwise exclusive OR on integers I and J.

INDEX(STRING, SUBSTRING, BACK)

Starting position of the first occurrence of SUBSTRING in STRING if BACK is omitted or has the value .FALSE., the starting position of the last occurrence of SUBSTRING in STRING if BACK has the value .TRUE., and 0 if SUBSTRING is not found in STRING.

INT(A, KIND) {*INT (R → I), *DINT (DP → I), *IFIX (R → I)}

Integer value obtained by truncating the fractional part of real A; KIND (optional) is integer.

IOR(I, J)

Like IEOR(I, J), but performs an inclusive OR on I and J

ISHFT(I, SHIFT)

Value obtained by shifting I by SHIFT positions, to the left if SHIFT < 0, to the right if SHIFT > 0. Bits shifted out are lost and vacated bits are filled with 0s; I and SHIFT are integers with |SHIFT| ≤ BIT_SIZE(I).

ISHFTC(I, SHIFT, SIZE)

Like ISHFT(I, SHIFT) but with circular shifting of the rightmost SIZE bits; bits shifted off one end are inserted at the other end.

KIND(X)

The kind value of X.

LBOUND(ARRAY, DIM)

The lower bound (a scalar) for subscript DIM of ARRAY, or if DIM is omitted, an array containing the lower bound of each dimension of ARRAY.

LEN(STRING) {*LEN (Char → I)}

Length of STRING.

LEN_TRIM(STRING)

Length of STRING, not counting trailing blanks.

LGE(STRING_A, STRING_B) {*LGE (Char → L)}

True if STRING_A is lexically greater than or equal to STRING_B, false otherwise.

LGT(STRING_A, STRING_B)

True if STRING_A is lexically greater than STRING_B, false otherwise.

LLE(STRING_A, STRING_B) {*LLE (Char → L)}

True if STRING_A is lexically less than or equal to STRING_B, false otherwise.

LLT(STRING_A, STRING_B) {*LLT (Char → L)}

True if STRING_A is lexically less than STRING_B, false otherwise.

LOG(X) {ALOG (R → R), CLOG (C → C), DLOG (DP → DP)}

Natural logarithm of X, which is real and positive or complex and nonzero with imaginary part in $(-\pi, \pi]$.

LOG10(X) {ALOG10 (R → R), DLOG10 (DP → DP)}

Common (base-10) logarithm of X, which is real and positive.

LOGICAL(L, KIND)

Convert logical argument L to the specified KIND, which is integer.

MATMUL(MATRIX_A, MATRIX_B)

Matrix product MATRIX_A x MATRIX_B of numerical or logical matrices, which are one- or two-dimensional arrays.

MAX(A1, A2, A3, ...)
    {*AMAX0 (I → R), *AMAX1 (R → R), *DMAX1 (DP → DP),
    *MAX0 (I → I), *MAX1 (R → I)}

Maximum value of A1, A2, A3, ..., which are all integer or all real.

MAXEXPONENT(X)

Maximum exponent for numbers have the same type and kind as X, when X is represented using the standard model for real data (see DIGITS(X)).

MAXLOC(ARRAY, MASK)

A one-dimensional integer array whose entries are the locations of the first element of integer or real ARRAY having the maximum value of all elements determined by the logical array MASK, or in the entire array if MASK is omitted.

MAXVAL(ARRAY, DIM, MASK)

Array of elements of integer or real ARRAY whose values are the maximum values of all elements in ARRAY along each vector specified by integer DIM that correspond to true elements of the logical array MASK. If MASK is omitted, the entire array is examined; if DIM is omitted, the entire array is examined and a scalar is returned.

MERGE(TSOURCE, FSOURCE, MASK)

The scalar or array formed by selecting from TSOURCE when MASK is true and from FSOURCE when MASK is false; TSOURCE and FSOURCE may be of any type.

MIN(A1, A2, A3, ...)
{*AMIN0 (I → R), *AMIN1 (R → R), *DMIN1 (DP → DP),
*MIN0 (I → I), *MIN1 (R → I)}

Minimum value of A1, A2, A3, ... , which are all integer or all real.

MINEXPONENT(X)

Like MAXEXPONENT(X), but returns the minimum exponent.

MINLOC(ARRAY, MASK)

Like MAXLOC(ARRAY, MASK), but locates a minimum element.

MINVAL(ARRAY, DIM, MASK)

Like MAXVAL(ARRAY, DIM, MASK), but finds minimum values.

MOD(A, P) {MOD (I → I), AMOD (R → R), DMOD (DP → DP)}

Remainder when A is divided by P: A - INT(A/P) * P; arguments are integer or real.

MODULO(A, P)

A modulo P. For A an integer, returns value R such that A = P*Q + R, with Q an integer, P and R of the same sign, and $0 \le |R| < |P|$. For A real, returns A - FLOOR(A/P)*P.

MVBITS(FROM, FROMPOS, LEN, TO, TOPOS)

Subroutine that copies LEN bits from FROM beginning at bit FROMPOS to position TOPOS of TO; no other bits of TO are changed. The bits of an integer I are numbered 0 to BIT_SIZE(I) - 1, from right to left; arguments are all integer type.

NEAREST(X, S)

Nearest machine-representable number different from X in the direction indicated by the sign of S (toward $+\infty$ or toward $-\infty$); X and S are real with $S \ne 0$.

NINT(A, KIND) {NINT (R → I), IDNINT (DP → I)}

Integer of the specified kind (if any) nearest to real A.

NOT(I)

Value obtained by complementing each bit of integer I ($0 \to 1$, $1 \to 0$).

PACK(ARRAY, MASK, <u>VECTOR</u>)

A one-dimensional array containing the elements of ARRAY for which the corresponding element of logical array or scalar MASK is true, padding with elements of one-dimensional array VECTOR (if any) if there are not enough elements selected by MASK.

PRECISION(X)

The decimal precision of real numbers having the same kind as X, which is real or complex.

PRESENT(A)

Returns true if an actual argument was passed to the optional formal argument A of the procedure containing this reference to function PRESENT, and false otherwise.

PRODUCT(ARRAY, <u>DIM</u>, <u>MASK</u>)

Product of all elements of ARRAY along dimension DIM (if present—else all array elements) that correspond to true elements of logical array MASK; if MASK is omitted, all array elements along dimension DIM are multiplied. If DIM is omitted or ARRAY is one-dimensional, value returned is a scalar.

RADIX(X)

Base of the mathematical model for values of the same type and kind as integer or real X (see DIGITS(X)).

RANDOM_NUMBER(HARVEST)

Subroutine that returns values for HARVEST that are pseudorandom numbers selected from the uniform distribution over the interval [0, 1); argument is real and may be either a scalar or an array variable.

RANDOM_SEED(<u>SIZE</u>, <u>PUT</u>, <u>GET</u>)

Subroutine that restarts the pseudorandom number generator if no arguments are present or queries it if there is exactly one argument. If integer SIZE is present, it is set to the number of integers used to hold the value of the seed; if PUT is present, it is used for the seed; if GET is present, it is set to the current value of the seed; PUT and GET are one-dimensional integer arrays of size = SIZE.

RANGE(X)

The decimal exponent range in the model for integer or real numbers having the same kind as real or complex X (see DIGITS(X)).

REAL(A, <u>KIND</u>) {*REAL (I $\to$ R), *FLOAT (I $\to$ R), *SNGL (DP $\to$ R)}

The real value of the specified kind obtained by converting integer, real, or complex A to this type.

REPEAT(STRING, NCOPIES)

String formed by concatenating NCOPIES copies of STRING.

RESHAPE(SOURCE, SHAPE, <u>PAD</u>, <u>ORDER</u>)

Returns the array having shape specified by one-dimensional array SHAPE and constructed by placing the elements of SOURCE into the array using the subscript order given by ORDER (or in the usual array-element order if ORDER is omitted), filling any extra values with elements of PAD; ORDER is a one-dimensional array whose elements are a permutation of $(1, 2, \ldots, \text{SIZE(SHAPE)})$.

RRSPACING(X)

Reciprocal of the relative spacing of the model numbers near real X (see DIGITS(X)); this value is ABS(FRACTION(X)) * FLOAT(RADIX(X))$^{\text{DIGITS(X)}}$.

SCALE(X, I)

The scaled value $\text{X} \times b^{\text{I}}$, where $b = \text{RADIX(X)}$; X is real; I is integer.

SCAN(STRING, SET, <u>BACK</u>)

Location of leftmost character of STRING that is in string SET, if BACK is .FALSE. or is omitted; the rightmost such character if BACK is .TRUE.; 0 if no such character is found.

SELECTED_INT_KIND(R)

The kind type parameter for an integer type with values between -10^{R} to 10^{R}, -1 if no such type is available. If there is more than one such kind, the value returned is for the smallest decimal exponent range.

SELECTED_REAL_KIND(<u>P</u>, <u>R</u>)

The kind type parameter for a real type whose values have precision of at least P digits (see PRECISION(X)) and a decimal exponent range of at least R (see RANGE(X)), -1 if the precision is not available, -2 if the exponent range is not available, and -3 if the neither is available. If there is more than one such kind, the value returned is the smallest kind number for the smallest decimal precision.

SET_EXPONENT(X, I)

A real number that, in the real data model (see DIGITS(X)), has the same fractional part as the fractional part of X but whose exponent part is $\perp$.

SHAPE(SOURCE)

A one-dimensional integer array whose elements are the extents of the dimensions of SOURCE.

SIGN(A, B) {ISIGN (I → I), SIGN (R → R), DSIGN (DP → DP)}

Absolute value of A times the sign of B; A and B are integer or real.

SIN(X) {SIN (R → R), CSIN (C → C), DSIN (DP → DP)}

Sine of X (radians); X is real or complex.

SINH(X) {SINH (R → R), DSINH (DP → DP)}

Hyperbolic sine of real X.

SIZE(ARRAY, DIM)

The extent of ARRAY along dimension DIM or the number of elements in ARRAY if DIM is omitted.

SPACING(X)

The absolute spacing of the model numbers near X (see DIGITS(X)); this value is (RADIX(X))$^{\text{EXPONENT(X) - DIGITS(X)}}$ for nonzero X, and TINY(X) if X is 0.

SPREAD(SOURCE, DIM, NCOPIES)

Returns an array with rank-rank(SOURCE) + 1 constructed by copying SOURCE NCOPIES times.

SQRT(X) {SQRT (R → R), CSQRT (C → C), DSQRT (DP → DP)}

Square root of X; for X complex, result has the form $x + yi$ with $x \geq 0$ or $0 + yi$ with $y \geq 0$; X is real and nonnegative or complex and nonzero with imaginary part in $(-\pi, \pi]$.

SUM(ARRAY, DIM, MASK)

Like PRODUCT(ARRAY, DIM, MASK), but sums elements of ARRAY; returns 0 if all elements of MASK are false or ARRAY has size 0.

SYSTEM_CLOCK(COUNT, COUNT_RATE, COUNT_MAX)

Subroutine that returns data from a real-time clock. COUNT is set to some processor-dependent value based on the current value of the system clock; this value is incremented by 1 for each clock count until COUNT_MAX is reached and will then be reset to 0; it is HUGE(0) if there is no clock. COUNT_RATE is set to the number of clock counts per second, or 0 if there is no clock; COUNT_MAX is set to the maximum value that COUNT may have.

TAN(X) {TAN (R → R), DTAN (DP → DP)}

Tangent of X (radians); X is real or complex.

TANH(X) {TANH (R → R), DTANH (DP → DP)}

Hyperbolic tangent of X, which is real.

TINY(X)

The smallest possible positive value for numbers of the same type and kind as X, which may be a real array or scalar.

TRANSFER(SOURCE, MOLD, SIZE)

Returns a value with physical representation identical to that of array or scalar SOURCE but interpreted with the type and kind of scalar or array MOLD; SIZE is the number of elements in the result.

TRIM(STRING)

The string obtained from STRING by removing all trailing blanks.

UBOUND(ARRAY, DIM)

Like LBOUND(ARRAY, DIM), but returns upper bounds.

UNPACK(VECTOR, MASK, FIELD)

Returns an array obtained by unpacking the elements of one-dimensional array VECTOR, using logical array MASK to determine where to place these elements. The result contains an element of VECTOR in each position for which the corresponding element of MASK is true and an element of FIELD otherwise.

VERIFY(STRING, SET, BACK)

Checks if SET contains all the characters in STRING; returns location of leftmost character of STRING that is not in SET, if BACK is .FALSE. or is omitted; the rightmost such character if BACK is .TRUE.; 0 if each character in STRING is in SET or STRING is empty.

B

Sample Data Files

This appendix contains descriptions of sample data files that are referred to in some of the exercises in the text: INVENTOR.DAT, STUDENT.DAT, USERS.DAT, INUPDATE.DAT, STUPDATE.DAT, USUPDATE.DAT, and LSQUARES.DAT. Descriptions of these files and the first few lines from each file follow. The complete files can be downloaded from the ftp site given in the preface.

AN INVENTORY FILE

INVENTOR.DAT

COLUMNS	CONTENTS
1–4	Item number
5–28	Item name
29–33	Unit price (no decimal point, but three digits before and two after the decimal point are assumed)
34–36	Reorder point
37–39	Number currently in stock
40–42	Desired inventory level

The file is sorted so that the item numbers of the records are in increasing order.

INVENTOR.DAT

```
1011TELEPHOTO POCKET CAMERA 5495 15 20 25
1012MINI POCKET CAMERA      2495 15 12 20
1021POL. ONE-STEP CAMERA    4995 10 20 20
                ⋮
```

AN INVENTORY-UPDATE FILE

INUPDATE.DAT

COLUMNS	CONTENTS
1–7	Order number (three letters followed by four digits)
8–11	Item number (same as those used in INVENTOR.DAT)
12	Transaction code (S = sold, R = returned)
13–15	Number of items sold or returned

The file is sorted so that item numbers are in increasing order. (Some items in INVENTOR.DAT may not have update records; others may have more than one.)

INUPDATE.DAT

```
CCI75431012S 2
LTB34291012S 7
DJS67621021S 9
    ⋮
```

A STUDENT FILE

STUDENT.DAT

COLUMNS	CONTENTS
1–5	Student number
6–20	Student's last name
21–35	Student's first name
36	Student's middle initial
37–59	Address
60–66	Phone number
67	Gender (M or F)
68	Class level (1, 2, 3, 4, or 5 for special)
69–72	Major (four-letter abbreviation)
73–75	Total credits earned to date (an integer)
76–78	Cumulative GPA (no decimal point, but one digit before and two after the decimal point are assumed)

The file is sorted so that the student numbers are in increasing order.

STUDENT.DAT

```
10103Johnson     James     LWaupun, Wisconsin      7345229M1ENGR 15315
10104Andrews     Peter     JGrand Rapids, Michigan 9493301M2CPSC 42278
10110Peters      Andrew    JLynden, Washington      3239550M5ART  63205
                    ⋮
```

A STUDENT-UPDATE FILE

STUPDATE.DAT

COLUMNS	CONTENTS
1–5	Student number (Same as those used in STUDENT.DAT)
6–12	Name of course #1 (e.g., CPSC141)
13–14	Letter grade received for course #1 (e.g., A–, B+, C♭)
15	Credits received for course #1
16–22	Name of course #2
23–24	Letter grade received for course #2
25	Credits received for course #2
26–32	Name of course #3
33–34	Letter grade received for course #3
35	Credits received for course #3
36–42	Name of course #4
43–44	Letter grade received for course #4
45	Credits received for course #4
46–52	Name of course #5
53–54	Letter grade received for course #5
55	Credits received for course #5

The file is sorted so that the student numbers are in increasing order. There is one update record for each student in STUDENT.DAT.

STUPDATE.DAT

```
10103ENGL176C 4EDUC268B 4EDUC330B+3P E 281C 3ENGR317D 4
10104CPSC271D+4E SC208D-3PHIL340B+2CPSC146D+4ENGL432D+4
10110ART 520D 3E SC259F 1ENGL151D+4MUSC257B 4PSYC486C 4
                        ⋮
```

A USERS FILE

USERS.DAT

COLUMNS	CONTENTS
1–15	User's last name
16–30	User's first name
31–35	Identification number
36–43	Password
44–47	Resource limit (in dollars)
48–52	Resources used to date (no decimal point, but three digits before and two after the decimal point are assumed)

The file is sorted so that the identification numbers of the records are in increasing order.

```
USERS.DAT
```

```
Babbage      Charles        10101ADA'S#1  75038081
Newton       Isaac          10102apple4u  65059884
Leibniz      Gottfried      10103Calculus 25019374
                .
```

A USER-UPDATE FILE

```
USUPDATE.DAT
```

COLUMNS	CONTENTS
1–5	Account number
6	Blank
7–10	Resources used (no decimal point, but three digits before and two after the decimal point are assumed)

The file is sorted so that the account numbers are in increasing order.

```
USUPDATE.DAT
```

```
10101   732
10101  2133
11003  3502
         .
```

A LEAST-SQUARES FILE

```
LSQUARES.DAT
```

This is a text file in which each line contains a pair of real numbers representing the x-coordinate and the y-coordinate of a point.

```
LSQUARES.DAT
```

```
2.18   1.06
7.46   12.04
5.75   8.68
        .
```

C

Answers to Selected Practices

1. Problem analysis and specification
   Data organization and algorithm design
   Program coding
   Execution and testing
   Program maintenance
2. Input and output
3. False
4. flowchart
5. syntax
6. Syntax errors
   Run-time errors
   Logical errors
7. Input: temperature on Celsius scale
   Output: corresponding temperature on Fahrenheit scale

This algorithm converts a *Celsius* temperature to the corresponding *Fahrenheit* temperature.

1. Enter *Celsius*.
2. Calculate *Fahrenheit* = 1.8 * *Celsius* + 32.
3. Display *Fahrenheit*.

12.

```fortran
PROGRAM Temperature
!------------------------------------------------------------
! Program to convert a temperature of Celsius degrees to
! corresponding temperature on the Fahrenheit scale.
! Variables used are:
!   Celsius     : temperature on the Celsius scale
!   Fahrenheit : temperature on the Fahrenheit scale
!
! Input:  Celsius
! Output: Fahrenheit
!------------------------------------------------------------

  REAL :: Celsius, Fahrenheit

  ! Get the Celsius temperature
  PRINT *, "Enter the temperature in degrees Celsius:"
  READ *, Celsius

  ! Compute the corresponding Fahrenheit temperature
  Fahrenheit = 1.8 * Celsius + 32.0

  ! Display Fahrenheit
  PRINT *, Fahrenheit temperature is: ', Fahrenheit

END PROGRAM Temperature
```

SECTION 2.1

1. Integer, real, complex, logical, character
2. apostrophes ('), double quotes (")
3. a letter
4. 31
5. Not legal: a blank is not legal in an identifier.
7. Legal
9. Legal
11. Not legal: the character / is not legal in an identifier.
13. Not legal: the character $ is not legal in an identifier.
15. None: Commas are not allowed in numeric constants.
17. Character
19. Real
21. Real
23. None: Doesn't begin with a digit or a sign and is not enclosed in quotes.
25. None: Doesn't begin with a digit or a sign and is not enclosed in quotes.
27. Integer
29. Character
31. REAL :: Temperature, Pressure, Volume
35. REAL, PARAMETER :: Celsius_Boiling_Point = 100.0, &
                       Fahrenheit_Boiling_Point = 212.0

```
39.  CHARACTER(4) :: Department = "CPSC"
     INTEGER :: Course1 = 141, Course2 = 142
```

SECTION 2.2

1. 1	3. 2	5. 11	7. 12.25
9. 2	11. 2	13. −9.0	15. 4
17. 6.0	19. "abcde"	21. 1	23. 5.1
25. 6.25	27. "Fortran-90"	29. "Fort"	

```
31.  10 + 5 * B - 4 * A * C
```

SECTION 2.3

1. Valid
3. Valid
5. Valid, but not recommended because it is a mixed-mode assignment.
7. Valid
9. 12.25
11. 6
13. 5.0
15. 1.0
17. `Distance = Rate * Time`
19. `Count = Count + 1`
25. `"1"`
27. `"12ƀƀƀƀƀƀƀƀ"`
29. `"1,000"`
31. `"Fortran-90"`
33. `"footlbsƀƀƀ"`
35. `"foot-lbsƀƀ"`
37. `"randomƀƀƀƀ"`
39. `"anan"`

SECTION 2.5

1. Heading, specification part, execution part, subprogram part, END PROGRAM statement
2. Any characters following an exclamation mark (!)—except within a string constant—and running to the end of the line form a comment.
3. True
4. False
5. False
6. False
7. True
8. A blank line
9.
```
37.0   7
X =   1.74  I =   29
4.23
15
```

SECTION 3.1

1. `.TRUE. .FALSE.`
2. `<, <=, >, >=, ==, /=`
3. `.NOT., .AND., .OR., .EQV., .NEQV.`
5. `.FALSE.`
7. `.TRUE.`
9. `.FALSE.`

11. .FALSE.
13. .TRUE.
15. 2 < Y .AND. Y < 5
17. (Alpha > 0 .AND. Beta > 0) .OR. (Alpha < 0 .AND.
     Beta < 0) or simply, Alpha * Beta > 0
21. (P == Q) .AND. (Q == R)
23. A .AND. B .AND..NOT. C

SECTION 3.3

1. Legal
5. Not legal: logical expression is not correct.
9. 6
13. Excellent
17. Bad
19. IF (X <= 1.5) THEN
         N = 1
      ELSE IF (X < 2.5) THEN
         N = 2
      ELSE
         N = 3
      END IF

3. Legal
7. 6
11. 10
15. Good

SECTION 3.4

1. 198
5. 456

3. default
7. Not a legal CASE construct—selector may not be real.

SECTION 3.6

1. False
2. False
11. .FALSE.
17. Okay = (X > 0) .AND. (X < 10)
19. Okay = (X > 0) .AND. (Y > 10) .OR. (X < 0) .AND.
     (Y < 0) or simply, Okay = X * Y > 0
21. Okay = .NOT. X < 0 .AND..NOT. X > 100

2. False
6. True
13. .FALSE.

3. False
7. True
15. .FALSE.

4. False
9. .TRUE.

SECTION 4.2

1. (a) *Repetition controlled by a counter,* in which the body of the loop is exe-
        cuted once for each value of some control variable in a specified range of
        values.

    (b) *Repetition controlled by a logical expression,* in which the decision to con-
        tinue or to terminate repetition is determined by the value of some logical
        expression.

3. ```
   Hello
   Hello
   Hello
   ```
5. ```
   6

   36
   5

   25
   4

   16
   3

   9
   2

   4
   1

   1
   ```
7. No output is produced.
13. Control variable may not be modified within the loop.
15. ```
    Values
    1   1
    2   1
    2   2
    The end
    ```

CHAPTER 4 APPLICATION

1. In a pretest loop, the logical expression that controls the repetition is evaluated *before* the body of the loop is executed. In a posttest loop, the termination test is made *after* the body of the loop is executed.

2. False

3. True

5. (a) 0   (b) No output is produced.
       1
       2
       3
       4

7. ```
   DO
       IF (X <= 0) EXIT
       PRINT *, X
       X = X - 0.5
   END DO
   ```

9. ```
   Number = 0
   Square = 0
   DO
   ```
   ```

```
              PRINT *, Square
              PreviousSquare = Square
              Number = Number + 1
              Square = Number**2
              IF (Square - PreviousSquare > 50) EXIT
         END DO
```

13. Input: A table of noise levels for 10 different models of cars with 5 different engines

    Output: The average (over all possible engines) for each model and the average overall noise level

    Algorithm to determine average noise level over all possible (5) engines for each of 10 different models of cars, and to determine the overall noise level over all models. *ModelSum* is the sum of all noise levels for a given *Model*, *Total* is the sum over all models and all engines.

    1. Initialize *Total* (the sum of all noise levels) to 0.
    2. Do the following for each *Model* number from 1 through 10:
       a. Set *ModelSum* (the sum of noise levels for *Model*) to 0.
       b. Do the following for each *Engine* type from 1 through 5:
          i. Read the next *NoiseLevel* for this *Model* number and *Engine* type.
          ii. Add *NoiseLevel* to *ModelSum*.
          iii. Add *NoiseLevel* to *Total*.
       c. Calculate and display the average noise level *ModelSum*/10 for this model.
    3. Calculate and display the overall average noise level *Total* /50.

SECTION 5.2

```
1.   Computer science -- Exercise 5.2
     ------------------------------------------------

3.   Computer science -- Exercise 5.2
     ------------------------------------------------

5.   Computer science -- Ex5.2
     ------------------------------------------------

7.   1234587.6543
     ------------------------------------------------
     12346 0.88654E+02
     ------------------------------------------------

9.   12345 = 12345
     ------------------------------------------------

     ============
     ------------------------------------------------

11.  12345 87.65 12345 87.7
     ------------------------------------------------
     12345 87.7
     ------------------------------------------------

13.  ------------------------------------------------
       12345   12346   87.65430      88.654       89.
     ------------------------------------------------

15.  77, 550, 123.77, 6.0
```

17. ƀƀƀ77123.77
     ƀƀ550ƀƀƀ6.0
19. 123.77   (or ƀ12377)
     ƀƀƀ77

     ƀƀƀ6.0ƀƀƀ550
     Fortran
21. Fortranƀƀƀƀƀƀƀƀƀƀƀƀ77ƀƀƀƀ123.77

SECTION 6.2

1. Functions and subroutines
2. Heading, specification part, execution part, and END PROGRAM statement
3. Formal arguments
4. REAL
5. As an internal subprogram, a module subprogram, or an external subprogram
6. scope
7. True
8. actual
9. 6
10. True
11. False
13.
```
FUNCTION Range(Number_1, Number_2)

    INTEGER :: Range
    INTEGER, INTENT(IN) :: Number_1, Number_2

    Range = ABS(Number_1 - Number_2)

END FUNCTION Range
```
15.
```
xFUNCTION Number_of_Bacteria(N, K, T)

    REAL :: Number_of_Bacteria
    REAL, INTENT(IN) :: K, T
    INTEGER, INTENT(IN) :: N

    Number_of_Bacteria = N * EXP(K * T)

END FUNCTION Number_of_Bacteria
```

CHAPTER 6 APPLICATION

1. Trapezoidal approximation with $n = 50$:
    $v(1) = 0.0662044$
    $v(2) = 0.4983123$
    $v(3) = 1.518813$
    $v(4) = 3.119597$
    $v(5) = 5.065156$

3. Trapezoidal approximation with $n = 40$:

E*:	0.5	1	1.5	2	2.5	3
	0.8678827	0.6922752	0.5318199	0.3990791	0.2946982	0.2152221

5. Trapezoidal approximation with $n = 100$: 4.277981

SECTION 6.4

1. Recursion
2. Its definition consists of two parts:
   1. An *anchor* or *base case*, in which the value of the function is specified for one or more values of the argument(s).
   2. An *inductive* or *recursive step*, in which the function's value for the current value of the argument(s) is defined in terms of previously defined function values and/or argument values.
3. RECURSIVE
4. RESULT
5. True
6. 15
7. 0
8. 0
9. N * X
11. Sum of the digits of N
13.
```
RECURSIVE FUNCTION Number_of_Digits(N) RESULT
NumDigits

   INTEGER, INTENT(IN) :: N
   INTEGER :: NumDigits

   IF (N < 10) THEN
      NumDigits = 1
   ELSE
      NumDigits = 1 + Number_of_Digits(N/10)
   END IF

END FUNCTION Number_of_Digits
```

SECTION 7.1

1. Functions and subroutines
2. Heading, specification part, execution part, and END SUBROUTINE statement
3. Formal arguments
4. 1. Functions are designed to return a single value to the program unit that references them. Subroutines often return more than one value, or they may return no value at all but simply perform some task such as displaying a list of instructions to the user.

2. Functions return values via function names; subroutines return values via arguments.

3. A function is referenced by using its name in an expression, whereas a subroutine is referenced by a CALL statement.

5. Cannot be used. Calculate must be referenced with a CALL statement.

7. Cannot be used. Incorrect number of arguments.

9. Cannot be used. Incorrect number of arguments.

13.
```
!-Convert_Length-----------------------------------------------
! Subroutine to convert a measurement in Centimeters to the
! corresponding measurement in Yards, Feet, and Inches.
!
! Accepts: Centimeters (real)
! Returns: Yards (integer), Feet (integer), and Inches (real)
!
!-------------------------------------------------------------

SUBROUTINE Convert_Length(Centimeters, Yards, Feet, Inches)

  REAL, INTENT(IN) :: Centimeters
  INTEGER, INTENT(OUT) :: Yards, Feet
  REAL, INTENT(OUT) :: Inches

  Inches = 0.3937 * Centimeters
  Feet = INT(Inches / 12.0)
  Inches = MOD(Inches , 12.0)
  Yards = Feet / 3
  Feet = MOD(Feet, 3)

END SUBROUTINE Convert_Length
```

SECTION 7.2

1. True
2. False
3. EXTERNAL
4. The number of arguments, the type of each argument, and the type of the value returned by the function
5.
```
INTERFACE
  FUNCTION F(X, Y, N)
    REAL :: F
    REAL, INTENT(IN) :: X, Y
    INTEGER, INTENT(IN) :: N
  END FUNCTION F
END INTERFACE
```

CHAPTER 7 APPLICATION

1. (a)   ←blank line
       123

2. (a)   ←blank line
     876543

3. (a) 321
4. (a) 321
       123

SECTION 8.2

1. subscripted   2. subscript or index   3. False
4. True   5. True   6. False
7. False
9. `INTEGER, DIMENSION(-5:5) :: IntArray`
11. `LOGICAL, DIMENSION(100) :: LogicArray`
13.
```
LOGICAL, DIMENSION(20) :: LogicArray
INTEGER :: I

DO I = 1, 20
   LogicArray(I) = MOD(I, 2) == 0
END DO
```
15. 0, 1, 1, 2, 2, 3, 3, 4, 4, 5
17. 1, 2, 0, 4, 5, 0, 7, 8, 0; Number(10) is undefined.
19. ␢1␢2␢3␢4␢5
    ␢6␢7␢8␢9␢0
21. ␢␢1.␢␢2.␢␢3.␢␢4.␢␢5.
    ␢␢6.␢␢7.␢␢8.␢␢9.␢␢0.
23. ␢A␢1␢B␢2␢C

SECTION 8.3

1. False
3. 32.0, 16.0, 8.0, 4.0, 2.0, 1.0, 0.5, 0.25, 0.125, 0.0625
5. 2.2, 3.3, 4.4, 5.5, 6.6
7. 8, 1, 4
9. 4.4, 5.5, 6.6, 7.7, 8.8, 9.9, 0.0, 1.1, 2.2, 3.3
11. 64.0, 33.1, 18.2, 11.3, 8.4, 7.5, 7.7, 8.2, 9.05, 10.025
13. 10.0, 11.0, 12.0, 13.0, 14.0, 15.0, 6.0, 7.0, 8.0, 9.0
15. 32.0, 14.9, 5.8, 0.7, 2.4, 4.5, 6.1, 7.45, 8.675, 9.8375
17.
```
SUBROUTINE Powers_of_Two(N, Powers)

  INTEGER, INTENT(IN) :: N
  INTEGER, INTENT(OUT), DIMENSION(:) :: Powers
 INTEGER :: I

  DO I = 1, N
     Powers(I) = 2**I
  END DO

END SUBROUTINE Powers_of_Two
```

SECTION 8.5

1. `REAL, DIMENSION(5, 10) :: Array1`
3. `INTEGER :: I, J`

```
DO I = 1, 5
   DO J = 1, 10
      Array1(I, J) = I + J
   END DO
END DO
```

5. $\text{Array} = \begin{bmatrix} 2 & 3 & 4 \\ 3 & 4 & 5 \\ 4 & 5 & 6 \end{bmatrix}$

7. $\text{Array} = \begin{bmatrix} 0 & -1 & -1 \\ 1 & 0 & -1 \\ 1 & 1 & 0 \end{bmatrix}$

9. $\text{Array} = \begin{bmatrix} 1 & ? & ? \\ ? & ? & ? \\ ? & ? & ? \end{bmatrix}$? = undefined

11. $\text{Array} = \begin{bmatrix} 1 & 2 & 3 \\ 4 & 5 & 6 \\ 7 & 8 & 9 \end{bmatrix}$

13. $\text{Array} = \begin{bmatrix} 1 & 4 & 7 \\ 2 & 5 & 8 \\ 3 & 6 & 9 \end{bmatrix}$

15. `Number = [1 2 3 4 5 6 ]`

$\text{Array} = \begin{bmatrix} 2 & 3 & 4 \\ 3 & 4 & 5 \\ 4 & 5 & 6 \end{bmatrix}$

CHAPTER 9 APPLICATION

1. False
2. `SELECTED_INT_KIND(15)`
3. True
4. `SELECTED_REAL_KIND(12, 40)`
5. False
6. True
7. False
8. $(-10.0, 11.0)$
9. False
10. True
11. False
13. $(-28.0, 96.0)$
15. 6.0
17. $(-8.0, 6.0)$
19. 10.0
21. $(2.0, 0.5)$
23. $(1.0, 0.0)$
24. `REAL(KIND = SELECTED_REAL_KIND(12)) :: Alpha`

SECTION 9.3

1. derived, structure
2. False
3. the component selector %
4. True
5. `MyPC%Manufacturer = "IBM"`
7. `PRINT *, MyPC%DiskSpace`

9. ```
   PRINT *, PCArray(3)%Manufacturer
   PRINT *, PCArray(3)%DiskSpace
   PRINT *, PCArray(3)%RAM
   PRINT *, PCArray(3)%ClockSpeed
   PRINT *, PCArray(3)%CDROM
   ```

11. ```
    Item%StockNumber = 11782
    ```

13. ```
    IF(Item%PC%Manufacturer == "Apple") PRINT *, &
        "Made by Apple"
    ```

15. ```
    DO I = 1, 6
        PRINT *, Item%ListPrice(I)
    END DO
    ```

17. ```
    Day = Date("July", 4, 1776)
    ```

19. ```
    TYPE InventoryInfo
        CHARACTER(20) :: Name
        INTEGER :: StockNumber
        TYPE(Date) :: Received
    END TYPE InventoryInfo
    ```

21. ```
    READ *, Item%Name, Item%StockNumber, &
            Item%Received%Month, Item%Received%Day, &
            Item%Received%Year
    ```

SECTION 10.1

1. ```
   INTEGER, POINTER :: P1
   ```

3. ```
   ALLOCATE(P1)
   P1 = -1234
   ```

5. Undefined, associated, diassociated

7. ```
   123
   456
   ```

9. ```
   34
   34
   ```

11. Error—P3 does not point to a value of type NumberNode.

13. ```
    34
    34
    34
    34
    ```

SECTION 10.2

1.

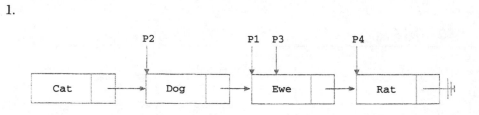

3.

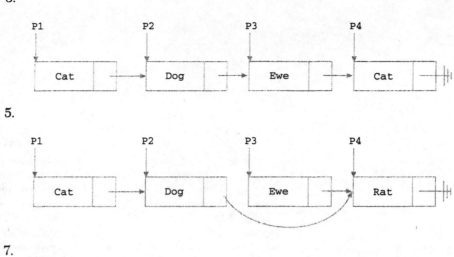

5.

7.

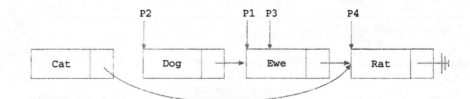

9.

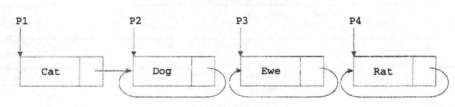

Index